I believe that music surpasses even language in its power to mirror the innermost recesses of the human soul.

George Crumb

George Crumb: Profile of a Composer

With an Introduction by Gilbert Chase

Compiled and Edited by Don Gillespie

C. F. PETERS CORPORATION

NEW YORK LONDON FRANKFURT

Library of Congress Cataloging in Publication Data
Main entry under title:

George Crumb, Profile of a Composer.
(Composer profiles ; 2)
Bibliography: p.
Discography: p.
1. Crumb, George. 2. Composers—United States—Biography. 3. Composers—United States—Addresses, essays, lectures. I. Gillespie, Don C. II. Title.
ML410.C944G4 1985 780'.92'4 [B] 84-26507
ISBN 0-938856-02-2

373 Park Avenue South, New York, N.Y. 10016

Earlier volumes in the series: Roger Reynolds

Front Cover Photo by Harry Zeitlin
Front Cover Music from *Makrokosmos I ("Spiral Galaxy")*
Back Cover Music from *Ancient Voices of Children*

Design by Pamela Tucker
Typesetting by Sans Serif
Printing by Edwards Brothers, Inc.

Contents

2 **George Crumb: Portraits and Patterns**
Gilbert Chase

6 **George Crumb**
David Burge

8 **Biography**
David Cope

16 **Music: Does It Have a Future?**
George Crumb

20 **George Crumb, American Composer and Visionary**
Suzanne Mac Lean

26 **George Crumb: Two Personal Views**
27 **Reflections on Twenty Years** Jan DeGaetani
28 **Recording *Ancient Voices of Children*** Teresa Sterne

30 **Quotes from Reviews**

34 **Interview: George Crumb/Robert Shuffett**

38 **Crumb's Music: Excerpts**

57 ***Makrokosmos I* and *II*:**
A Case Study of George Crumb's Compositional Process
Christopher Wilkinson

62 **The Element of Sound in *Night of the Four Moons***
Stephen Chatman

66 **George Crumb: Friend and Musical Colleague**
Richard Wernick

70 **Photographs**

74 **De Oraculo Crumbi**
Eugene Narmour

76 **Contributors**

78 **Bibliography**

85 **Discography**

87 **Reviews of Recordings**

89 **Reviews of Printed Music**

90 **Selected Reviews of Performances**

102 **Selected Choreography to Crumb's Music**

104 **Annotated Chronological List of Works**

George Crumb: Portraits and Patterns

Gilbert Chase

It is always fascinating to attempt to assess a composer's impact as refracted through the medium of contemporary music criticism. In the case of George Crumb, however, the prolific documentary data presents such a range of multifaceted interpretations that one wonders if there are not indeed many George Crumbs masquerading under one name. By merely scanning the headlines of a number of articles selected almost at random from the plethora of journalistic excerpts spread out over my writing table, I find:

□ In the whimsical vein: "Who Is George Crumb and Why Is He Telling All Those Stories?—Of Drones and Whales and Strings That Go 'Bump' in the Night" (an interview by Stuart Liebman that appeared in *The Boston Phoenix* of November 12, 1974).

□ In the sober and serious manner: "A Modern Composer Finds Fame, and Fortune Are Hard to Obtain" (*Wall Street Journal* of August 15, 1974).

□ In the mystical mode: "The Star-Child's Song Defeats the Apocalypse" (*Village Voice*, May 23, 1977).

□ In a coldly analytical style: "Symmetrical Structures in George Crumb's *Five Pieces for Piano*" (*Journal of the Graduate Music Students at The Ohio State University*, Fall 1984).

□ In a deprecating tone: "After Grab for the Stars, Crumb Must Settle for Gazing" (*New York Post*, May 6, 1977).

□ And even from an ecological viewpoint! (re *Vox Balaenae*): "A Special Homage to Leviathan" (*Washington Star*, March 23, 1975).

To be sure, every writer's own personality becomes necessarily involved in the critical process; nonetheless, Crumb's music seems to evoke the most disparate, contradictory, and inconsistent responses.

It was in the 1970s that Crumb's career came to be widely publicized, with music critics for newspapers and periodicals eager to write about him, especially when they had the opportunity to talk with him personally. As they soon found out, George Crumb is articulate, his West Virginian reticence notwithstanding, but his personality (as expressed in his words and in his music) presents certain paradoxes. John Rockwell noted this in his lengthy article about Crumb in the *Los Angeles Times* of March 5, 1972: "Looking at George Crumb's picture, and armed with the knowledge that he teaches at the University of Pennsylvania, one would hardly suspect the hot-tempered, coolly controlled Romanticism which lurks within his compositional soul." And then this personal touch:

> Yes, the hair is suspiciously tousled, and yes, there is a drooping moustache, however conventionally fashionable it may be. But this looks still like the face of an academician. In fact, it *is* the face of an academician, and one who by all reports fits the stereotype further by being a reticent and quiet man.

What are precisely those elements in Crumb's music which seem to obsess the critics? First, of course, George Crumb's very personal *world of sound*. Donal Henahan described this world in his review of the world premiere of *Ancient Voices of Children*: "Working out of what can only be poetic need, and never for the sake of making novel noises, Crumb in effect invents his own orchestra, one with his own highly imaginative sonorities and timbres . . . The instrumentalists do not only man multitudes of chimes and bells and cymbals, drums great and small, harp, toy piano, mandolin, oboe and musical saw, but also join in the vocalizing, humming and shouting and finding a thousand subtle and emotionally potent ways to sustain the score's darkly magical mood." (*New York Times*, November 2, 1970). Writing of the New York premiere, Harold Schonberg, too, found Crumb to be "hypnotized by pure, sheer sensuous sound." (*New York Times*, December 19, 1970).

Coming after a long period of emphasis on the intellectual content of music, the time was indeed ripe for some renewed attention to "sheer sensuous sound." Andrew Porter's "Musical Events" article in *The New Yorker* of January 20, 1975, confirms and further delineates the increasing importance and wide acceptance of Crumb's world of sound as the 70s progressed. This event took place at the Whitney Museum, and we are told that "the line for admissions stretched down to Madison Avenue, and the large room on the second floor was packed to overflowing by an eager audience, some of it on chairs, most of it on the floor." This sitting on the floor was not unusual at the Whitney concerts (as I can verify personally); but the main message on this occasion was that Crumb had truly "arrived," and his image was now irrevocably linked to an unprecedented phase of America's music.

Porter hit the right note, and aptly summarized Crumb's compositional method when he wrote about "Ancient Voices" and its musical "quotations": "By alteration of timbre and tempos, and because of the different lights thrown by the new contexts, Crumb makes the images his own." Moreover: "Crumb works by distillation, finding small, precise, quintessential symbols, created by an ear that can distinguish, as it were, between five different qualities of pianissimo on a single note, and make listeners aware of them too. On his scale, an outburst from four players can be as shattering as another man's *ffff* from a thousand."

The now famous "Ancient Voices" brings us to the all-important "Lorca connection," about which so much has been written. On a personal note, it so happened that I became a "Hispanist" in my early years, long before becoming also an "Americanist." It is not surprising that, while I admire all of Crumb's music, I am especially devoted to what is evidently a deep rapport that he had with the ill-fated Spanish poet, Federico García Lorca (1898–1936). This led him to compose such intensely personal works as *Night Music I*, the four books of *Madrigals* the *Songs, Drones and Refrains of Death*, and *Night of the Four Moons*, in addition to "Ancient Voices." As Brian Fennelly observes (*Notes* of the Music Library Association, March,1973), "At the core of Crumb's success is his ability to mirror and reflect upon the rich poetry of the chosen García Lorca excerpts, with particular sensitivity to mood and special timbral possibilities." Crumb's empathy with the stark and direct imagery of Lorca's poetry was immediate and long-lasting.

The widespread journalistic attention to Crumb was not confined to our shores, and, in fact, European attention to his music also grew progressively throughout the 1970s. When Crumb was scheduled to visit England in October of 1978, *The Musical Times* of London carried an article by Richard Steinitz which began as follows:

> The music of George Crumb compels interest on several accounts. Most of all, there is the extraordinarily haunting and intoxicating magic of its sound. There is often startling imagery, with its many undercurrents of association, and frequent allusion to things animate and inanimate, or to other music. Technically, Crumb's inspired additions to the expressive vocabulary of familiar instruments, combined with his ingenious use of strange and exotic instruments, make a rewarding study. And the superb calligraphy of his scores (published by Peters in facsimile) implies a remarkable harmony between the ear and the eye and, incidentally, assists the composer in pursuing some original forms of symbolism.

We have not the space here to pursue those "original forms of symbolism" that are special to Crumb's music—the numerology of *Black Angels*, the symbolism of the zodiac in the *Makrokosmos* volumes, the theatrical elements of *Vox Balaenae* and *Lux Aeterna* with their masked players, the mystical allusions to his native West Virginia, and so on. But they lie at the heart of what music has meant for him, and are, incidentally, another source of heated critical controversy. Suzanne Mac Lean explores this area in depth in her portrait of George Crumb as Composer and Visionary ("The Phantom Gondolier") found herein.

The present "Profile" is designed to portray many facets of Crumb's music and personality, from personal portraits by performers and composers to analytical essays in musicology and music theory, from David Cope's new biography of the composer to Crumb's own writings and observations about music. Don Gillespie's exhaustive listings of published writings, interviews, reviews, and recordings which conclude the volume should make it indispensable for future Crumb research.

When asked to formulate his "Credo," George Crumb replied: "Music might be defined as a system of proportions in the service of a spiritual impulse." This indicates that technical and structural matters are every bit as important to the composer as the purely expressive and sonorous features that first captured the critics' attention, a fact that is too often overlooked.

Crumb's influence on the music of our time has been penetrating and pervasive. From the toy piano of *Ancient Voices of Children* to the cosmic canvas of *Star-Child*, we (and George Crumb's critics) have heard a unique musical voice.

Who could ask for anything more?

I am often haunted by the thought that all of the many musics of the world are coming together to form one music. "Lux Aeterna" was conceived in the spirit of this idea.

George Crumb

George Crumb

CHARLES ABBOTT

David Burge

For each of us there is that series of events that creates major seismic upheavals on our lifelines, displacing our previously hard-earned (or unthinking) prejudices, rendering askew our self-assurance, setting us off in a rush in new, untried directions. These revelatory happenings can take place any time, but are probably most deeply telling in our younger days. I recall with deafening clarity, as if it happened yesterday, being raised out of my seat by a single scintillating turn of phrase in a Mozart sonata played by William Kapell a third of a century ago, a musical gesture that, in a single second, married the arts of singing, piano playing, dancing and, for all I know, love-making, and changed my life as it relates to all of those wondrous pastimes. And, in those postwar college days when the newly invented long-playing record first brought magically unbroken performances to our tiny student quarters, I remember the vertiginous sense of a spiraling, plunging otherworldliness that consumed me as I listened, dry-mouthed and unbreathing, to the first recording of one of the Bartók string quartets (I could not tear my eyes away from that thick, translucent, *red* disc), after which I staggered outside onto the busy street, mainlined by this unprecedented sonic experience, knowing that if any number of cars hit me they would pass right through, unfelt.

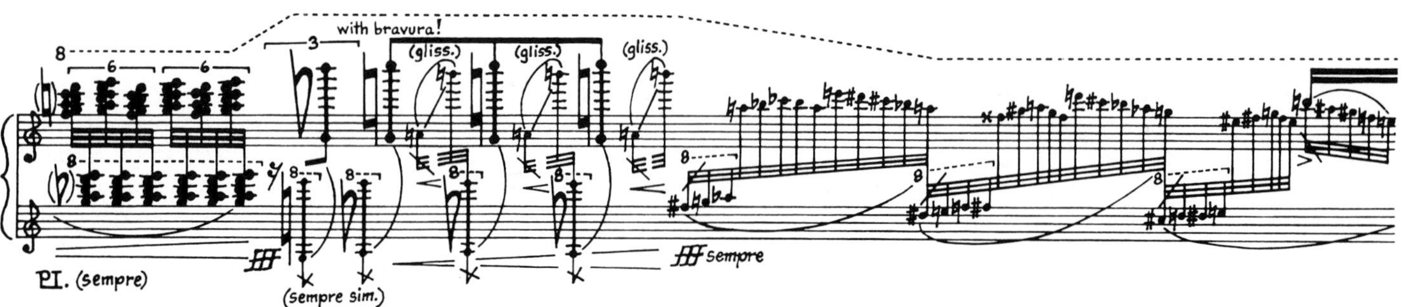

Getting to know George Crumb was not so instantaneous a matter, but the effect on me of our early acquaintanceship was as revelatory as any I have had before or since. We were, by coincidence (when is it *not* coincidence?), thrown together in 1962 when I joined the piano faculty of the University of Colorado where he was already teaching. A slight, quiet man with dark, thinning hair and intense eyes (the latter trait recognizably shared with Bartók and Lutoslawski), he had been hired several years earlier to teach Group Piano, an occupation for which his shy, retiring temperament suited him miserably. By the time I met him he was no longer allowed to cope with these groups but was lodged, not very happily, at the bottom of the so-called "secondary piano" ladder of the school. He was thirty-two years old at that time, and if he were going anywhere as a musician there was little evidence of it.

We hit it off from the start. I had, for a number of years, been playing increasing amounts of twentieth-century music, an activity that was, in the fifties and early sixties, even more esoteric than it is today. George knew most of the music I was doing and, in his quiet and unforceful way, began to reform my thinking about what was happening in the world of composition, introducing me to new scores as they mysteriously found their way into his possession, explaining (in a questioning, gentle, somewhat ambiguous way) things I would never have thought about, even in pieces I was until then under the impression I already knew well, and talking, talking, talking. It seemed as though he never *did* anything, just talked a lot, and I, still a young and wretchedly compulsive *doer*, listened and talked back when I could and wondered only slightly if he would ever accomplish anything other than to talk slowly in his drawling West Virginia way.

Well, we did do *some* things. Throwing stones, for example. At that time Pat and I were just beginning to raise jumping and cross-country horses and so we lived on a big ranch in the Colorado foothills. There was a large reservoir near our little cabin, and often in the fall of '62 Liz and George would come out and then he and I would see who could still hit the water with a stone from furthest away. George was naturally lazy and, at the same time, a wonderfully coordinated natural athlete, and his relaxed windup and throw was Olympic in grace and effectiveness. Mine was less pretty, but I had longer arms and, besides, I practiced. We could both throw more than twice as far as anyone we knew, and though our competition was never verbalized beyond—"Yep, that one hit, George," or "Didn't see any splash that time, Dave"—it was fierce, and I went to bed with a badly aching right shoulder many nights.

Of course I soon learned that George was trying to finish his doctorate in composition, and he eventually showed me what was completed of the *Variazioni for Large Orchestra*, the work that was to be his dissertation. He turned the large, carefully copied pages and chuckled under his breath as he told me that he had been told that the work was "unplayable" by a number of eminent composers and conductors. I laughed and said nothing, but wondered to myself why anyone would write an "unplayable" piece, even for a doctoral dissertation.

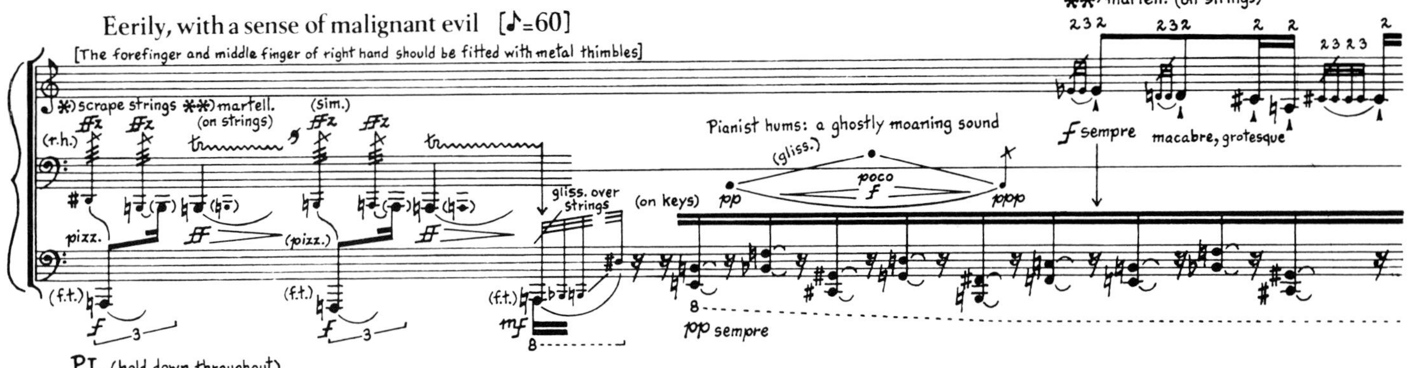

On another occasion he took out the score of a string quartet he had written earlier and produced a tape recording of it in which the fact that the players were never together was mercifully masked by the additional fact that the tape had been overloaded to the point of non-recognition. It was hard to know how he felt about such things; he was so quiet and non-committal.

Then there were the days when I found him sitting in the foyer of the student union building, holding a cup of coffee in his hand and staring into space, oblivious of the people moving around him and the noise they were making. When I would walk up to him he would come out of it and greet me quietly and pleasantly as always, shrugging off my question and allowing as how he was "just thinkin'." Then he would finish his coffee and we would slowly walk across the campus, talking, and go back to our duties.

One day, idly, I said he ought to write some piano music for me. He didn't say anything, just nodded, and I didn't push it further, deciding he wasn't really interested. So I was surprised in November to receive a call from him saying he had been thinking about that piano piece I had requested and—hesitantly—how did I feel about playing *inside* the piano? Well, I thought that was a terrible idea, though I didn't say so, and I also thought the very idea was rather insulting, but I didn't say that either. It occurred to me that, at the rate he moved, the piece would never get done anyway, so why worry? So I replied that, yes, it would be quite unusual to play inside the piano, that I had never done it, and that if he thought it necessary, I guessed I would learn how. I tried not to be overly encouraging.

A few weeks later, in December, he presented me with the completed score of the *Five Pieces for Piano*, a work now recognized as his first mature composition. I would never forget that first examination. I had never seen anything like that score. For that matter, neither had anyone else. I buried myself in the music, and in the piano's insides, and gave the first performance the next month. The following month Karlheinz Stockhausen visited our campus and listened to the pieces repeatedly, shaking his head and exclaiming over and over about all the things in the score that *he* wished *he* had done.

That year, 1963, I played the *Five Pieces for Piano* dozens of times in concerts across the country. The pieces provoked amusement, puzzlement, sarcasm, and—among a few—astonishment and deep admiration. Unfortunately what was too often heard was the surface of the music—the extraordinary and unprecedented combinations of sounds made on the keys and inside the instrument—rather than the even more extraordinary sense of musical shape and the exquisite craftsmanship that informs every note of each of the five movements. It was a problem that was to plague George for years, a problem then seen only in microcosm in one relatively short work by a then completely unknown composer who, as a novice, could be patronized for his supposed shortcomings or eccentricities by people who did not bother to look beyond the novelty into the fresh new musical vision which he had discovered.

Working with George after the advent of the piano pieces, I was to become more and more impressed with the vast knowledge of and curiosity about music—*all* music—which he now displayed and, more important, the creative fire and determination that burned deep inside this shy, soft-spoken man. Once he had started, the ideas came quickly, and I was soon pressed into service as a percussion player in the initial performance of his first Lorca setting, *Night Music I*. Here the arresting nature of the vocal writing as well as the (for 1963) fiercely demanding requirements of the instrumental parts made one wonder just how far a composer could go—but all of this paled when, in actual performance, the absolutely hair-raising emotional impact of the work's climaxes swirled around the stage and through the audience in paroxysms of madness, fury, and untempered passion.

It is a rare human experience, thinking one is reaching down to help someone out, to be suddenly leap-frogged by that person, to find out not only that one's own mild conceptions are being completely out-distanced but to realize that *this person has probably always been far, far ahead of one, only requiring the right time and place to let it be known*. And George leaped! Or, rather, his music did, for he remained as quiet and, apparently, unassuming as ever as he moved rapidly from being an unknown secondary piano teacher to one of his generation's best known and most often played composers.

Later, long after George had left Colorado, and when I was able to conduct the "unplayable" *Variazioni*, the *Echoes of Time and the River* that won him the Pulitzer Prize, *Ancient Voices of Children*, *Night of the Four Moons*, and many other works, I would think of him sitting in the student union with his coffee during that autumn of 1962, staring wide-eyed, solemn, and unseeing. I would try to think of clues that he might have given me as to the demonic fury that erupts in *Black Angels* or the poignant, immovable calm that closes the now famous "Spiral Galaxy" of the volume of *Makrokosmos* he so kindly wrote for me a decade after the *Five Pieces*. He was always so quiet and pleasant! Where did it come from?

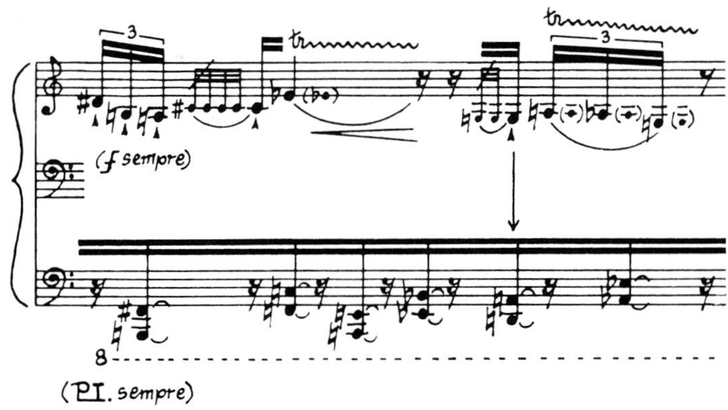

We met again briefly a month ago on the occasion of the New York premiere of his *Gnomic Variations* for solo piano. He spoke, gently, of his departure for South America the very next day, of a trip to Australia in the summer, of Liz and the kids. The black fringe of hair was gray, and the stoop of his shoulders made me think his stones wouldn't fly so far as they once did. If the fires were burning inside, I still couldn't see them in his smile or hear them in his gentle, West Virginia voice. I hope they are still there, waiting to flare up anew in the next work and again in the one after that. I really hope so.

(April 25, 1984)

Biography

David Cope

Both of George Crumb's parents (George Henry Crumb, Sr. and Vivian Crumb [formerly Reed] of Chehalis, Washington) had an intense interest in music-making. His father (born 1894) came from the Cincinnati area where he had studied the clarinet privately (he never earned a college degree). As a youngster, around the turn of the century, he was enlisted in the "Crumb Family Orchestra," a chamber group organized by his parents which performed summers at various resort hotels. After moving to Charleston, West Virginia, he became principal clarinet in the local symphony and, for a period, conducted an area Shriners' band. He also worked as a professional music copyist and arranger. The latter occupation often required that he copy out and harmonize melodies from radio broadcasts or records, thereby demonstrating genuine analytical skills and an "educated" ear. He performed a great deal of commercial dance music in the Charleston area and during the "silent film era" conducted a pit orchestra which provided the incidental music for the movies of the day. A local chamber music society provided him opportunities to perform the music he most loved: the classics. He died quite suddenly and unexpectedly on August 8, 1950 of a pulmonary thrombosis at the age of 56.

Crumb's mother, Vivian (born 1903; the middle of three sisters), played cello in the family chamber music sessions and performed as cellist (eventually as principal) with the Charleston Symphony for 25 years (1939–64), not missing a single concert during her tenure. She credits her husband in part with inspiring her tenacity: "I don't know how much longer I would have kept my music up if I hadn't married a musician."[1] She finally retired from performing in the mid-1960s due to arthritis.

The Crumbs' first child (George Henry, Jr.) was born on October 24, 1929 (the "Black Thursday" of the great stock market crash) in Charleston. A second son, William (Bill) Reed was born on February 26, 1932 and became an accomplished flutist and singer (though he never performed professionally). During young George's formative years the family lived on Greenbrier Street in a rather nondescript Victorian house (distinguished only by an impressive octagonal room which became the family "music room"). Not far from the house was the Kanawha River, where young George often engaged in stone throwing contests. Renowned pianist David Burge, who later played a decisive role in Crumb's career by commissioning and premiering two of his major piano works, recalls his early acquaintance with the composer: "He had a way of catapulting stones immense distances with an effortless kind of roundhouse underarm whipping motion that was astonishing and intimidating."[2] Crumb fondly recalls his childhood years as "idyllic," despite the privations of the ongoing depression.

During these early years Crumb heard a great deal of "country music" and church music in a "revival" (gospel) style, though neither bears significant influence in his scores except in the use of certain folk instruments such as the harmonica, the musical saw, and the banjo. When quite young he attended band concerts (conducted by his father), and he vividly recalls the powerful impressions evoked by the brass instruments in the Sousa marches. Still more impressive was the sound of a symphony orchestra when he and his brother were taken in tow by their parents to rehearsals and concerts.

Since music was the focal point in Crumb's life from a very early age on, all else seemed peripheral. He found school unexciting and recalls that he was "barely average" in scholastic attainment. He much preferred books found in his father's library (Thayer's *Life of Beethoven* and Einstein's *Mozart* were especial favorites) to the onerous reading assignments of his high school years. He attended a Presbyterian Church Sunday School but holds little interest in organized religion today (although his music abounds in Biblical references).

Crumb's early musical training was somewhat unsystematic but his musical experience was extremely varied. When he was seven years old he received his first clarinet lessons from his father, using the little E-flat instrument (he humorously explains that this experience gave him a certain bias toward the treble register later in life). Two years later he had his first piano lessons, and in time piano became his preferred instrument. Probably the most significant influence of his early musical life was the family tradition of chamber music in the home. He often played flute and clarinet duos with his brother and clarinet duos with his father. Later on, as pianist, he played the Beethoven and Brahms clarinet trios with his parents. His father would occasionally make arrangements of works by Mozart and Haydn for the entire family. Crumb's mother gives most of the credit for his early interest and musical education to George Sr., who encouraged his early efforts in composition and was especially helpful with suggestions regarding proper notation and idiomatic writing for instruments.

Crumb's aunt (father's side) had studied violin in Berlin during the years between the wars and, with scores being so inexpensive in Germany during the depression, purchased nearly the entire Eulenburg catalog for her brother. Thus, Crumb had access to several hundred scores in his father's collection. Early on he would sit and listen to music on the radio or on records while following the score. They often received the Sunday New York Philharmonic broadcasts and, under favorable atmospheric conditions, could even bring in New York City's WQXR. Later, as his keyboard sightreading skills improved, he began playing orchestral scores at the piano, reading principal parts while filling in the missing voices by ear. He frequently took scores to school and read them during class, trying to approximate the live sound in his head. All this self-teaching was an immensely valuable tool for the young composer.

Crumb started to compose "Mozart-like" pieces at the age of 10 or 11 (his mother recalls being surprised to discover manuscripts in his room at age 11). He wrote rapidly and prolifically during these precollege years and often composed "forgeries" in the styles of Beethoven, Chopin, and Debussy. A piano trio in Brahms' style still exists, though most of the other works were lost or destroyed. The rural nature of the West Virginia hill country provided a kind of insulation from cosmopolitan life, a provincial feeling of being separated from the mainstream of musical developments. Thus, it seemed natural to model his works after the master composers of the past.

He is described by those who knew him then as shy and retiring, but an innate exuberance, normally repressed, would surface when he was with people he knew very well. His mother recalls never

1)

2)

1) The "Crumb Family Orchestra," ca. 1904 (Cincinnati?). (George's father is the drummer.)

2) George Crumb's parents – George, Sr. (clarinet) and Vivian (cello), Charleston, West Virginia, ca. 1925.

3)

4)

seeing him really angry or aggressive; when annoyed or frustrated, "Bun" (George's nickname) would go to the music room and begin improvising at the piano.

During his Charleston High School years (1944–47) Crumb played clarinet in the school orchestra and increasingly occupied his time with composition and piano study. Diversions included hiking through the nearby hills and his track team performances in the running broad jump and high jump. During this period he also developed a curious interest in pyrotechnics and, up to recent years, no Fourth of July was "traditional" without an array of his homemade Roman candles and giant firecrackers.

During these high school years, Crumb composed his first two orchestral essays: *Poem* (1946) and *Gethsemane* (1947). Both were performed by the Charleston Symphony, providing extraordinary lessons for the young composer's "ear" and testing his ability to hear sounds from the score during composition. Several songs and small choral pieces also received occasional readings or performances.

It was also during these same years that he met his wife-to-be, Elizabeth May Brown, who, in remembering that period, recalls: ". . . teachers used to yell at George because he wore his hair long, was a terrible dresser, and composed music in English class."[3] Elizabeth was studying the piano during this period (she continues to teach piano to this day). Crumb married "Liz," his first and only "girlfriend," on May 21, 1949 (he was 19; she: 20); at this time they were both students at Mason College in Charleston (a conservatory of music subsequently absorbed by Morris Harvey College, which gave Crumb an honorary doctorate in 1969). He graduated in 1950 with a Bachelor of Music degree after 3 years of study. During all these years he seriously pursued his piano studies. Charles Graybill provided early private instruction and Arthur McHoul fostered his keyboard proficiency while at Mason (where Crumb had actually a double major: piano and composition). Later teachers included Stanley Fletcher and Benning Dexter.

During his years at Mason College he earned extra money as pianist for a local ballet studio and also served as organist/choir director for a small Baptist church in Marmet, West Virginia, just outside of Charleston (he recalls that his organ playing was "atrocious," particularly his pedal technique). Occasionally, too, he helped his father with copying jobs and, although his own calligraphic techniques developed quite differently, he admired the flowing quality and stylized beauty of his father's work.

Crumb had heard good reports about the music program at the University of Illinois, and in 1951 he and his wife moved to Champaign-Urbana for the continuation of his studies. This was the year after his father died and their first child was born: Elizabeth Ann Crumb (now working as an actress in New York City). He studied composition with Eugene Weigel and produced several works, of which the most substantial were *Trio* (1952) for strings and *Sonata* (1953) for viola and piano (both strongly influenced by Hindemith and Bartók).

While in Urbana Crumb also began studying the viola. Although he later discontinued practicing this instrument, as he had earlier the clarinet, he has often stated how important he feels the need for young composers to acquire firsthand knowledge of instruments and

5)

3) **George Crumb in Charleston, West Virginia, 1948.**
4) **Elizabeth, Ann and George Crumb on the Rhine River, 1955.**
5) **Louise Toth, David Burge, Thomas MacCluskey, Paul Parmelee and George Crumb, rehearsing *Night Music I*, Boulder, Colorado, February, 1964.**

to actively perform. At about this time, too, Crumb developed an obsessive interest in foreign languages and eventually acquired, through self-teaching, some reading knowledge in Spanish, German, French, and Italian.[4] (He remains frustrated, however, with his inability to speak any foreign tongue with fluency and explains, somewhat defensively, that the "musical ear" differs from the "language ear.")

He completed his Master of Music degree in 1952 and in 1953 moved to Ann Arbor for doctoral studies at the University of Michigan with Ross Lee Finney as his composition teacher. Finney's attention to meticulous notation had a great impact on Crumb's own score writing. Finney never restricted his students to any particular style, though analysis in his seminars dealt with mainstream composers such as Bartók, Schoenberg, Webern, and Stravinsky. Concomitantly Crumb continued to study the music of the past and to this day considers that resource the most valuable in a composer's life.

At the University of Michigan he continually held Teaching Fellowships and gained important instructional skills which would prove invaluable in his later teaching career. It was also here that he heard a work by a fellow graduate student (Edward Chudacoff) set to a text of Federico García Lorca ("Casida of the Boy Wounded by the Water") which subsequently led not only to his own setting (in *Songs, Drones, and Refrains of Death*) of the same text but his immersion in Lorca's poetry and the famed "Lorca cycle."

While completing his degree requirements, he won the Elizabeth Croft Scholarship in 1955, which enabled him to attend the Berkshire Music Festival in Tanglewood. Here he had composition lessons with Boris Blacher which were to continue during the following academic year in Germany (he had been awarded a Fulbright Fellowship for study at the Hochschule für Musik in Berlin). However, once in Berlin, he spent most of his time attending concerts and studying piano with Erich Riebensahm; the composition lessons with Blacher were infrequent and somewhat less than satisfying.

At the conclusion of his year abroad Crumb returned to Ann Arbor to complete his residency requirements. During his years at the University of Michigan, he completed a number of works, of which only two are still acknowledged by the composer: *Sonata for Solo Violoncello* (1955); and *Variazioni* (1959) for large orchestra. The *Sonata*, a derivative work, was eventually published and recorded, though Crumb had once expressed a desire to withdraw it from circulation. Dedicated to the composer's mother and cast in a Bartókian classic-romantic style, its three movements (Fantasia, Tema pastorale con variazioni, and Toccata) contain virtually no contemporary techniques of the time. *Diptych* for orchestra, also composed in 1955, was withdrawn, the composer feeling its neoclassic roots showed a lack of inventiveness and originality. (He keeps a number of these student works in manuscript form, but apparently more for keepsake value than for eventual publication.) *Variazioni*, his doctoral thesis, includes a 12-tone theme and other Schoenbergian influences, though certainly it could not be termed serial to any degree. In its bolder use of timbral and textural effects it presents a marked contrast to the earlier student works and, though still transitional, represented for Crumb a relatively significant leap into 20th-century idioms.

While Crumb's teaching career had begun at Hollins College in Virginia, where he taught classes in theory and analysis during 1958–59, his pianistic abilities helped him acquire his first substantial teaching position at the University of Colorado at Boulder in 1959, where he remained until 1964. Although the long hours spent teaching secondary piano students afforded only a few occasions to teach composition, he offered classes in contemporary music (with special emphasis on the post-war European composers).

His second child, David Reed Crumb, was born in 1962 (he presently studies cello at the Eastman School of Music). Also in 1962, at the request of David Burge (who had just that year joined the piano faculty in Boulder), Crumb composed *Five Pieces for Piano*, a landmark score for the composer and the first in his mature style. Here the elements of a Webern-like economy, pointillism, and *Klangfarbenmelodie*, fused with a sensitive West Virginia folk heritage, generate an intensely dramatic and coloristic texture known widely as Crumb's trademark. Special timbral effects—produced by pizzicato and glissando techniques, harmonics, and a meticulous use of the damper pedal—are beautifully integrated with conventionally produced sounds to create, in effect, a new instrument. His next two works, *Night Music I* (1963; for soprano, piano/celesta, and percussion), the initial work of the Lorca cycle, and *Four Nocturnes* (1964; subtitled "Night Music II"; for violin and piano) verified the originality and focus of his new style.

In 1964 he received a Rockefeller grant which afforded the opportunity to serve as "Composer-in-Residence" at the Buffalo Center for the Creative and Performing Arts (as a "Creative Associate"). While in Buffalo, Crumb performed (as pianist) in several concerts devoted to the most recent contemporary American and European scores and did some sketching on the first two books of his *Madrigals* (prompted by a commission from the Koussevitzky Foundation). He was invited back to Colorado after the conclusion of his term in Buffalo; however, he had established many warm friendships with East coast performers and composers and, also attracted by the excitement and challenge of the contemporary music scene in the East, determined to establish his permanent residence somewhere in this area.

In late spring of 1965, a position in composition opened at the University of Pennsylvania and Crumb's application was successful. In the summer of this same year, his third child, Peter Stanley Crumb, was born. Crumb's early years at Penn were prolific and his music began to be more widely performed. In the fall of 1965 he completed the final drafts of *Madrigals, Book I* (for soprano, vibraphone, and contrabass), and *Madrigals, Book II* (for soprano, flute/piccolo/alto flute, and percussion). And in 1966 he completed *Eleven Echoes of Autumn, 1965* (for alto flute, clarinet, violin and piano; premiered by the Aeolian Chamber Players in August, 1966). With these works, especially *Eleven Echoes*, Crumb's style expanded to embrace various forms of consonance: whole-tone, modal, and tonal elements (generally avoided since his youth) appear regularly and in more prominent roles. Equally apparent is Crumb's effective use of varying textures as "propellant" for the musical lines, while harmonic motion (the more traditional vehicle) falls subservient to the strikingly diverse vertical densities. One also begins to feel the "improvisational" quality of his often rhapsodic gestures; however, except for an occasional interpolation of ensemble rhythmic flexibility, the music is meticulously determinate.

In 1966 Crumb heard soprano Jan DeGaetani premiere his *Madrigals, Books I* and *II* in Washington, D.C., and a critical and long-lasting relationship developed between the two. DeGaetani's enormous range of pitch and timbre, mastery of avant-garde performing techniques, and extraordinary precision made her the ideal medium for Crumb's unique and delicate sonic palette. She eventually performed and recorded virtually all of his chamber works for the soprano voice. Two important later works, *Ancient Voices of Children* and *Apparition* (like the earlier books of *Madrigals*) were written expressly for her.

Crumb received a number of significant awards and honors during these early years at Penn: a Guggenheim Fellowship (1967), a National Institute of Arts and Letters Award (1967), and the Pulitzer Prize in Music (1968) for his *Echoes of Time and the River* ("Echoes II; Four Processionals for Orchestra"). *Time and the River* received initial notoriety due to its requirement that certain players move slowly and ritualistically about the stage during performance (the work was premiered by the Chicago Symphony Orchestra in May, 1967; Irwin Hoffman, conductor). More lasting, however, are the work's measured intensity and convincing musical gestures. The eerie whispers of a phrase from Lorca—"los arcos rotos donde sufre el tiempo" ("the broken arches where time suffers"), the lowering of a struck gong into a tub of water (to produce a "bending" of the pitch), and the use of a choir of whistlers[5] for the final *morendo* passage all add that mysterious touch of suppressed tension which is so characteristic and charismatic in Crumb's music.

Crumb's next work, *Songs, Drones, and Refrains of Death* (for baritone, percussion, and electric: guitar, contrabass, and piano/harpsichord), was completed in 1968. The earliest sketches for this work date back to 1962, but the original conception and formal plan were subjected to numerous revisions as the work evolved. *Songs, Drones, and Refrains* was the first work of Crumb to require electronics for dynamic enhancement and remains one of his personal favorites.

During the following year, 1969, Crumb added three new works to his ongoing Lorca cycle: *Madrigals, Book III* (for soprano, harp, and percussion), *Madrigals, Book IV* (for soprano, flute/piccolo/alto flute, harp, contrabass, and percussion), and *Night of the Four Moons* (for alto, alto flute/piccolo, banjo, electric cello, and percussion), composed during the nine-day Apollo 11 flight. Each of these works further explores the coloristic possibilities of voice and instruments. The conclusion of *Night of the Four Moons*, undoubtedly one of the most beautiful passages in Crumb's music, contains extended phrases of tonal music in a quasi-Mahlerian style (and might be seen as a premonition of the "neo-romantic" aesthetic of the 1980s!).

In 1970 (aptly on Friday, March 13), Crumb completed *Black Angels* (subtitled "Images I: Thirteen Images from the Dark Land" for electric string quartet [with performers doubling on maracas, tamtam, and tuned crystal goblets]). The rigorously applied references to numerology (the use of prime numbers 7 and 13 for determining intervals, rhythms, and formal structures) and the extramusical images embodied in the movement titles (e.g. "Night of the Electric Insects") suggest a preoccupation with the occult.[6] The composer, however, would disclaim any personal obsession with the "supernatural" and sees such symbolism simply as part of our cultural heritage. *Black Angels* shows an especially strong predilection for symmetry, often expressed in palindromic forms. The work quotes from a number of classical sources including the *Dies Irae* and the slow movement of Schubert's "Death and the Maiden" Quartet (in section #6: "Pavana Lacrymae," a hauntingly macabre music somewhat reminiscent of Ives).

In this same year, on commission from the Coolidge Foundation, Crumb completed *Ancient Voices of Children* (for soprano, boy soprano, oboe, mandolin, harp, electric piano, and percussion) while a visiting composer at Tanglewood. *Ancient Voices*, premiered in October, 1970, at The Library of Congress in Washington, received immediate critical acclaim and remains one of Crumb's most widely-known compositions. The recording, with Arthur Weisberg conducting the Contemporary Chamber Players, is regarded as a benchmark in technical and musical excellence, winning the Koussevitzky International Recording Award in 1971 (the work also won the International Rostrum of Composers [UNESCO] Award in this same year). The extraordinary variety of timbral and textural configurations in *Ancient Voices* derives in part from the composer's inclusion of a number of unusual instruments in the score: toy piano (in a quotation from the *Notebook of Anna Magdalena Bach*), Tibetan prayer stones, Japanese temple bells, musical saw, and harmonica. The vocal writing, which ranges from an intensely lyrical expression to passages of extreme virtuosity, synthesizes and brings to fruition many concepts introduced in the earlier Lorca works. *Ancient Voices* also shows the composer's fascination with non-Western music (e.g. the Moorish character of "Dances of the Ancient Earth") and his fondness for oblique reference to earlier composers (e.g. Ravel's *Bolero* or Mahler's *Das Lied von der Erde*).

In 1971 Crumb completed two chamber works for "masked" performers: *Vox Balaenae* ("Voice of the Whale") (for electric: flute, cello, and piano), inspired by the singing of the humpback whale, and *Lux Aeterna* (for soprano, bass flute/soprano recorder, sitar, and percussion), a setting of the traditional Latin text from the Requiem. The extraordinary opening passage of *Vox*—a "Vocalise" for the flutist, who is required to play and sing simultaneously—exemplifies the composer's literacy in innovative instrumental techniques. The concluding movement ("Sea-Nocturne") reaffirms Crumb's interest in tonality. Crumb conceived both *Vox Balaenae* and *Lux Aeterna* as "theater" works and has suggested an appropriate stage-lighting and, in the case of *Lux*, the optional inclusion of a solo dancer. The year 1971 also marked the first publication of a mature Crumb work by C. F. Peters Corporation (Peters had published his early *Sonata for Solo Violoncello* in the late 1950s).

In 1972 Crumb was invited to participate in the Warsaw Autumn Festival and this trip to Poland (with Elizabeth: Crumb has a superstitious fear of travelling alone on trips abroad) marked the beginning of a series of journeys to far places for performances of, and lectures on, his music. Subsequent "professional" travels included

6) With Paul Zukofsky, Buffalo, May, 1965.

7) With David Burge at the premiere of *Makrokosmos I*, Colorado Springs, February, 1972.

8) Richard Dufallo, Jan DeGaetani and George Crumb, Aspen, 1974.

6)

7)

CHARLES ABBOTT

8)

9)

10)

9) With the Penn Contemporary Players, 1975.
10) At work on *A Little Suite for Christmas*, Media, 1980.

several journeys to the Far East, Australia, and New Zealand, numerous trips to Europe, and memorable stays in Iceland, Israel, Brazil, Colombia, and Mexico. (Crumb finds travel "intoxicating and obsessive" and meticulously documents each trip with photographs and memoranda.)

During the years 1971–74 Crumb worked intensively on his *Makrokosmos* series of piano works. *Makrokosmos, Volumes I* and *II* for solo amplified[7] piano were completed in 1972 and 1973, respectively; *Music for a Summer Evening* (*Makrokosmos III*) for two amplified pianos and percussion was completed in 1974 (Crumb had been awarded a second Guggenheim grant in 1973). Each of the solo volumes consists of "Twelve Fantasy-Pieces after the Zodiac" and each piece is inscribed with the initials of a person whose astrological sign corresponds to that associated with the piece (e.g. E.M.C.: Elizabeth May Crumb [Aquarius]; D.R.B.: David Russell Burge [Aries]; R.M.: Robert Miller [Sagittarius]). The solo volumes of *Makrokosmos* use all the timbral devices first found in *Five Pieces*, but in a much more elaborate manner. These works are also distinguished by an enormous range of expression and a sure instinct for form. Several of Crumb's most striking "symbolic notations" (reminiscent of certain Medieval and Renaissance practices, in which the staves are bent into various configurations) occur in *Makrokosmos*; especially beautiful are the "Spiral Galaxy" of Volume I and the "Twin Suns" of Volume II. Throughout these works one finds the influence of two of Crumb's favorite composers: Chopin and Debussy, particularly the stylistic synthesis so characteristic of their late piano works.

Music for a Summer Evening, although to some degree conceptually and even thematically related to the solo *Makrokosmos* volumes, is on a much larger scale. The combination of two pianos and percussion was suggested by Bartók's similarly scored *Sonata*; Crumb, however, uses a much greater variety of percussion instruments (including such unusual items as an African log drum, a metal "thunder" sheet, and a quijada [jawbone of an ass]). Interesting references to earlier music are to be found in the isorhythmic construction of the "Myth" movement and quoted excerpts from Crumb's "favorite" Bach fugue (the d-sharp minor from *The Well-Tempered Clavier*, Book II) in the concluding "Music of the Starry Night." *Summer Evening* contains extraordinary examples of the composer's use of "time suspension," particularly in the final phrases of the work, where time perceptibly slows and seems to stand still.

In 1976, Crumb was awarded a grant from the National Endowment for the Arts and completed *Dream Sequence* (for violin, cello, piano, percussion, and offstage "glass-harmonica"), the second of his works to be premiered by the Aeolian Chamber Players (October, 1976). The work is a study in stasis and fragility and its subtitle "Images II" recalls the delicate and evocative timbral shadings of certain passages in *Black Angels* ("Images I").

Crumb's second major orchestral work, *Star-Child*, commissioned by the Ford Foundation, was completed in 1977. In addition to a very large orchestra (woodwinds in fours, eight percussionists, etc.), the work calls for solo soprano, childrens' choirs (used antiphonally), a male speaking chorus (doubling as bell ringers), and several offstage trumpets. The work's Latin texts were drawn primarily from anonymous Medieval sources ("Dies Irae" and "Massacre of the Innocents"). *Star-Child*'s multi-layered texture, which derives from a counterpoint of independent musics, occasions the necessity for four conductors. In contrast to the quasi chamber music scoring of *Time and the River*, *Star-Child* projects a sense of monumentality and epic scale. The work was premiered in May, 1977 (with Irene Gubrud, soprano, and the New York Philharmonic under the general direction of Pierre Boulez).

In 1979, Crumb completed the fourth work in his *Makrokosmos* series: *Celestial Mechanics* (for amplified piano, four hands). The work shows his usual fecundity in idiomatic and coloristic invention, but also contains interesting examples of counterpoint (a rarity in Crumb's music). *Celestial Mechanics* was premiered in New York City in November, 1979 by Gilbert Kalish and Paul Jacobs. Later in this same year, on request from Jan DeGaetani, Crumb composed *Apparition* (a cycle of elegiac songs for soprano and amplified piano on texts extracted from Walt Whitman's "When Lilacs Last in the Dooryard Bloom'd"). This work, his first setting in English since the days of his youth, explores new realms of lyric expression and shows an altogether unconventional treatment of the traditional voice-piano medium. The most haunting of the songs, "Come Lovely and Soothing Death," evokes echoes of Berg in its chromatically inflected tonality.

Over the next few years, Crumb completed a series of four works for solo performer: *A Little Suite for Christmas, A.D. 1979* (1980; for solo piano), *Gnomic Variations* (1981; for solo piano), *Pastoral Drone* (1982; for solo organ [his first work in this genre]), and *Processional* (1983; for solo piano). However, his orchestral work, *A Haunted Landscape* (completed in 1984 for the New York Philharmonic), indicates a renewed interest in the potentialities inherent in larger forces. These later works show a progressively more inclusive use of tonality and interesting new approaches to formal organization. Although Crumb's stylistic "fingerprints" are indelibly impressed on every page, one also perceives an ongoing tendency toward new modes of expression.

The Crumbs' home in Media (a small town west of Philadelphia) is typical of other dwellings in this predominantly suburban area. His small composing room is cluttered with various sketch pages of the work-in-progress (he also keeps sketchbooks to which he frequently refers). Scattered stacks of manuscript surround an old piano. Curiously, the rather disheveled interior (with his often spectacular score notations pinned to the wall) creates a unique impression of quiet energy and almost monastic seclusion. Various unusual instruments (banjo, sitar, mandolin, African thumb pianos, gongs and bells of all descriptions) sit or hang in several locations in the house.

Crumb continues to work very slowly, often completing but one work a year. He believes in strong initial conceptions which propel him into an obsession to develop and complete a new work. David Burge has described these early stages of composition: ". . .when starting a new piece he gives the outward impression of having all the time in the world. . .He wanders distractedly to his study and tries a single sound on the incredibly decrepit hulk of a piano that inhabits the room—an untunable, unplayable piano. He tries the sound, varies it, a dozen times, a hundred times. Then to the desk to write himself a note. . .and leave it in the chaos of letters and manuscript."[8]

The fatigue of completing a work inevitably leaves Crumb uncertain and self-critical. He claims that once a work is finished, he loses the sense of it, and only repeated hearings over a period of time can restore his perspective. He rarely writes about his music, though examples (such as the program notes for *Black Angels* and *Ancient Voices of Children*) demonstrate an uncanny aptitude for articulating and clarifying his musical intentions. However, composing with words comes even more slowly than with notes; this, combined with his belief that music itself is more meaningful than verbal interpretations of it, creates little incentive for further narrative expositions.

As a teacher, Crumb appears "low-key," allowing his love of music to dominate the classroom (he believes that the really essential elements of composition can not be taught). Richard Wernick, a colleague in composition at the University of Pennsylvania, notes that his methods are so subtle that students end the semester knowing "an incredible amount about music without realizing how it happened."[9] Typically Crumb works with only a few graduate students, both privately and in class. Inevitably some students attempt to imitate his style and especially his unique approach to notation. He doesn't promote or seek such mimicries; on the contrary, he gently encourages his students to develop their own modes of expression. Most recently he has taught analysis courses in the piano music of Chopin and Debussy, composers he has idolized since his youth.

Aside from teaching, composing, editing music, and assuming family responsibilities, Crumb spends his days reading (especially books on astronomy, archeology, and history, as well as Sherlock Holmes and various novels of intrigue) and playing chamber music or four-hand piano music with friends. He remains completely unaffected by the many honors presented to him over the years (including membership in the National Institute of Arts and Letters and the American Academy of Arts and Sciences, six honorary doctorates, a Brandeis University Creative Arts Award, honorary membership in the Deutsche Akademie der Künste and the International Cultural Society of Korea, and his appointment in 1983 to the Annenberg Chair at the University of Pennsylvania). Inevitably, a certain quality of ambivalence and caution (perhaps typical of the West Virginian mountaineer) comes to the fore: "Of course I am delighted when my music is played and understood. However, I feel that I have not yet made my definitive statement. Then, too, the acid test comes with time."

---

[1]Pat Poliskey, "Cellist's Final Concert with Symphony Set; Completes 25 Years," *Charleston Daily Mail*, March 31, 1964.

[2]David Burge, "George Crumb and I," *Contemporary Keyboard* (August, 1976), 42.

[3]R. G. Freeman, "A Modern Composer Finds Fame, Fortune Are Hard to Attain," *Wall Street Journal*, August 15, 1974.

[4]This fascination with language would be later reflected in Crumb's use of purely phonetic sounds in several works composed between 1965 and 1974. Also, *Black Angels* contains shouted or whispered passages in six different languages (including Hungarian and Swahili).

[5]Crumb attributes his fondness for the peculiar timbre of the whistled tone (used in several of his works) to the influence of his brother, whom he regards as a virtuoso whistler.

[6]It is of interest that "Night of the Electric Insects" from *Black Angels* would later appear in the soundtrack of the movie "The Exorcist" (1974).

[7]Although Crumb uses the terms "amplified piano" and "electric piano" interchangeably, it should be stated that in all cases he desires simple amplification of a conventional instrument.

[8]Donal Henahan, "Crumb, The Tone Poet," *New York Times Magazine*, May 11, 1975, p. 54.

[9]*Ibid.*

Music: Does It Have a Future?

George Crumb

The question "What will the music of the future be like?" frequently arises in discussions with composers and with audiences. I suspect that some ulterior meaning is usually implied—either a sense of doubt that music will ever again be as vigorous and impressive as it was in some past "golden age," or conversely, the hope that the undeniably frenetic activity of the present presages some future "golden age," as glorious and as rich in achievement as any of the past! Even the most timid attempt at prophecy must be based on a close appraisal of earlier developments and present trends. The future will be the child of the past and the present, even if a rebellious child.

The retrospective glance is a relatively easy gesture for us to make. If we look at music history closely, it is not difficult to isolate certain elements of great potency which were to nourish the art of music for decades, if not centuries. The dynamic concept of sonata-structure is a striking example of an idea that bewitched composers for two centuries, at least through Béla Bartók. Sonata-structure was, of course, intimately connected with the evolution of functional tonality, and tonality itself, independently, represents another germinal concept of great potency.

What, then, are the significant and characteristic tendencies and impulses in contemporary music which might conceivably project into the future? I am certain that most composers today would consider today's music to be rich, not to say confusing, in its enormous diversity of styles, technical procedures, and systems of esthetics. Perhaps an attempt to isolate the unique aspects of our music will give us some perspective on our future prospects.

One very important aspect of our contemporary musical culture—some might say the supremely important aspect—is its extension in the historical and geographical senses to a degree unknown in the past. To consider firstly the extension through time: in a real sense, virtually all music history and literature is now at our fingertips through both live performances and excellent recordings, whereas earlier composers knew the musics of only one or two generations before their own time. The consequences of this enlarged awareness of our own heritage are readily evident in many of our recent composers. For example, the influence of medieval music on the British composer Peter Maxwell Davies comes to mind. For many such composers, the sound of medieval music—at times harsh and raw, at times fragile and hauntingly sweet—would more closely approximate the contemporary ideal than would, say, the sound of a Brahms or of a Richard Strauss. I have observed, too, that the people of the many countries that I have visited are showing an ever increasing interest in the classical and traditional music of their own cultures. Perhaps we have come to think of ourselves as philosophically contemporaneous with all earlier cultures. And it is probable that today there are more people who see culture evolving spirally rather than linearly. Within the concentric circles of the spiral, the points of contact and the points of departure in music can be more readily found.

The geographical extension means, of course, that the total musical culture of Planet Earth is "coming together," as it were. An American or European composer, for example, now has access to the music of various Asian, African, and South American cultures.

Numerous recordings of non-Western music are readily available, and live performances by touring groups can be heard even in our smaller cities. Such influences would, of course, be felt on different levels: only a few Western composers would have a sophisticated technical knowledge of the Indian *Raga*, for example; but, in general, the sounds, textures, and gestures of this music would be well known. This awareness of music in its largest sense—as a world-wide phenomenon—will inevitably have enormous consequences for the music of the future.

Unquestionably, our contemporary world of music is far richer, in a sense, than earlier periods, due to the historical and geographical extensions of culture to which I have referred. As a standard for comparison, it is revealing to take a representative European composer of the nineteenth century and define his "cultural horizons." I think a good choice is the French composer Hector Berlioz, since his music was regarded as avant-garde by his contemporaries. If we first consider the historical dimension, I think we should have to agree that Berlioz's contact with any music written before the Viennese Classical period was minimal, although Beethoven was avowedly a very powerful influence on his development. I doubt that Berlioz had any real understanding of Baroque style or technique, judging from the curiously inept handling of the *fugato* style in several of his works. Berlioz spoke of Palestrina in disparaging terms. In regard to his contact with non-Western music, we know that he visited London in 1851 in connection with the Great Exhibition held there. While in London, Berlioz heard some Chinese and Indian music in authentic performance, and this most progressive and modernistic composer of the time could make no sense at all of what he heard. His description of Chinese music:

> I shall not attempt to describe these wildcat howls, these death-rattles, these turkey cluckings, in the midst of which, despite my closest attention, I was able to make out only four distinct notes.[1]

His description of Indian music is even less flattering!

Perhaps the true cross-fertilization process between musical cultures did not begin until after World War II, although one can trace the first premonitions in Mussorgsky and especially in Debussy toward the end of the nineteenth century. This represented a relatively high degree of sophistication, indeed, when compared with Mozart and Beethoven, for whom exotic music meant the cymbal and bass drum borrowed from the Turkish Janissary music!

Apart from these broader cultural influences which contribute to the shaping of our contemporary musical psyche, we also have to take into account the rather bewildering legacy of the earlier twentieth-century composers in the matter of compositional technique and procedure. Although we must be impressed by the enormous accruement of new elements of vocabulary in the areas of pitch, rhythm, timbre, and so forth, I sense at the same time the loss of a majestic unifying principle in much of our recent music. Not only is the question of tonality still unresolved but we have not yet evolved anything comparable to the sure instinct for form which occurs routinely in the best traditional music. Instead, each new work seems to require a special solution, valid only in terms of itself. There is, to be sure, a sense of adventure and challenge in articulating our conceptions, despite the fact that we can take so little for granted; and perhaps we tend to underestimate the struggle-element in the case of the earlier composers. Nonetheless, I sense that it will be the task of the future to somehow synthesize the sheer diversity of our present resources into a more organic and well-ordered procedure.

Perhaps we might now review some of the specific technical accoutrements of our present music and speculate on their potential for future development. The advent of electronically synthesized sound after World War II has unquestionably had enormous influence on music in general. Although I have never been directly involved in electronic music, I am keenly aware that our sense for sound-characteristics, articulation, texture, and dynamics has been radically revised and very much affects the way in which we write for instruments. And since I have always been interested in the extension of the possibilities of instrumental idiom, I can only regard the influence of electronics as beneficial. I recently participated in a discussion with Mario Davidovsky, who, in my opinion, is the most elegant of all the electronic composers whose music I know. Davidovsky's view is that the early electronic composers had a truly messianic feeling concerning the promise of this new medium. In those euphoric days of intense experimentation, some composers felt that electronic music, because of its seemingly unlimited possibilities, would eventually replace conventional music. Davidovsky now regards the medium simply as a unique and important language at the disposal of any composer who wants to make use of it, and as a valuable teaching tool for the ear. In any case, it is obvious that the electronic medium in itself solves none of the composer's major problems, which have to do with creating a viable style, inventing distinguished thematic material, and articulating form.

The development of new instrumental and vocal idioms has been one of the remarkable phenomena of recent music. There undoubtedly have been many contributing factors: the influence of folk instrument techniques; the influence of jazz, and, later, rock techniques; the liberation of percussion instruments (a development for which Bartók is especially important); and finally, the advent of an ever-increasing number of young instrumentalists and singers who specialize in the performance of contemporary music, and who themselves are interested in probing the idiomatic resources of their instruments. The development of idiom, of course, has been an ongoing process over the centuries; in fact, it is incumbent upon each age to "reinvent" instruments as styles and modes of expression change.

An example of this process can be seen in the evolution of the piano idiom. In the hands of Beethoven the expressive range of the instrument was progressively enlarged. The gradual expansion of the piano in terms of range, sustaining power, and brilliance and the introduction of the una corda pedal effect were fully exploited in the enormous body of literature which Beethoven conceived for the instrument. It must have seemed to many of Beethoven's contemporaries that nothing more remained to be done. And yet, shortly after Beethoven's death in 1827, Chopin published the *Etudes*, Opus 10. This astonishing new style, based essentially on the simple device of

allowing widely spaced figuration to continue vibrating by means of the depressed damper pedal, opened up a whole new approach to the instrument. Important new breakthroughs in piano idiom were then achieved by Debussy around the turn of the century and by Bartók a few years later. And in our own day, the concept of piano idiom has been enormously enlarged once again by the technique of producing sound through direct contact with the strings. I think it can truly be said that the potential resources of instruments can never be exhausted: the next generation will always find new ways!

The revolutionary treatment of vocal idiom in the new music has been an interesting development. The traditional bel canto ideal has been very much enlarged by the influence of popular styles of singing and also by non-Western types of vocal timbre. In conjunction with this development, the traditional voice-piano medium seems to have given way to a new genre, consisting of voice and a varied instrumental chamber ensemble. A curious phenomenon is that the soprano voice type seems to clearly dominate; the other voice types have been more or less neglected by recent composers, and as a consequence, I suppose, we seem to have very few excellent singers, other than sopranos, who specialize in the new music. Other significant tendencies in the area of vocal composition are the relative neglect of the choral medium and the failure, thus far, to create a new type of large-scale music-theater. In respect to opera, it strikes me that Alban Berg really tied together all the strands of the tradition in his *Wozzeck* and *Lulu*, and I feel that nothing of comparable significance has been done since. In any case, the task of finding fresh approaches to opera and to choral music will be inherited by the future.

Perhaps of all the most basic elements of music, rhythm most directly affects our central nervous system. Although in our analysis of music we have inherited a definite bias in favor of pitch, rather than rhythm, as being primary, I suspect that we are simply unable to cope with rhythmic phenomena in verbal terms. It might be argued that the largest aspect of rhythm is pulse, and it is interesting to observe that, whereas the nineteenth century tended to rank composers on the quality of their slow movements—since it was assumed that slow music was more difficult to write—the situation at the present time has been completely reversed. The problem now seems to be the composition of convincing fast music, or more exactly, how to give our music a sense of propulsion without clinging too slavishly to past procedures, for example the Bartókian type of kinetic rhythm. Complexity in itself, of course, will not provide rhythmic thrust; and it is true that harmonic rhythm has to operate in conjunction with actual rhythm in order to effect a sense of propulsion.

Three composers—two traditional and one contemporary—especially interest me with regard to their imaginative handling of rhythm and might possibly have some bearing on our current approach to rhythmic structure. The first is Beethoven, whose sense of rhythmic control was absolutely uncanny. Of all composers, he was the master of the widest possible range of tempos, from prestissimo to molto adagio. The Beethoven adagio, particularly of the third style period, offers a format which might be further explored in contemporary terms: within the context of an extremely slow pulse, a sense of much faster movement is achieved by tiny subdivisions of the beat. Such a device offers contrast and yet gives a sense of organic unity. Another composer whose rhythmic sensitivity impresses me is Chopin. I am thinking primarily of certain of the nocturnes, in which he achieves a sense of "suspended time" (as in much new music), but also provides a feeling of growth and progression through time. And lastly, I would mention Messiaen with regard to his use of the "additive rhythmic principle," which, in his *Technique of My Musical Language*, he associates with Hindu music. I feel that this principle could become increasingly important in the further development of our rhythmical language.

When we come to a discussion of the role of pitch in new music, we enter an arena of widely conflicting opinions. In general, I feel that the more rationalistic approaches to pitch-organization, including specifically serial technique, have given way, largely, to a more intuitive approach. There seems to be a growing feeling that we must somehow evolve a new kind of tonality. Probably the ideal solution, anticipated, it seems to me, by Bartók, is to combine the possibilities of our chromatic language—which is so rich and expressive in its own right—with a sense of strong tonal focus.

An interesting practice in music since the atonal period of the Viennese composers has been the widespread use of a few tiny pitch cells. One such cell, which pervades the music of Anton Webern and Bartók, is the combined major-minor third: C—E—E-flat; another such universally used cell is the perfect fourth flanked by tritones: C—F-sharp—B—F; another is the chromatic cluster: C—C-sharp—D. These three cells, in various permutations, together with a few other basic types, are astonishingly prevalent in contemporary music of whatever style.

There has been considerable experimentation in the field of microtones in recent years, but to Western ears at least, a *structural* use of microtones is frustratingly difficult to hear. Microtones seem to be most frequently used in a *coloristic* manner, for example in "bending" pitches. It would be very difficult to predict what role any microtonal system might play in a work composed in the twenty-fifth century, but since music must somehow relate to our central nervous system, which has evolved over countless eons, a widespread use would seem problematical.

I have already alluded to the problem of form in new music, arising primarily from the erosion of so many traditional forms which depended on functional tonality. Of course the simpler, more primitive forms remain to us, and the variation principle is always available. Two basic types of form, both of which were known to earlier music, seem to have a peculiar attraction for recent composers. These two types are diametric opposites. One is the "non-repetitive" principle, which implies a progression along a straight line without ever referring back to itself. The other could be called the "minimal" type, which usually consists of a repetition ad infinitum of one idea, whether it be a rhythmic motif, a chord, or a melodic succession of pitches. Curiously, both types are represented in Arnold Schoenberg's music: the "non-repetitive" in several works, and the "minimal" in the "Sommermorgen an einem See (Farben)" from the *Five Pieces for Orchestra*. Of course, both types could more correctly be termed formal procedures rather than conventionally articulated formal structures like the sonata-structure or the rondo-structure. In any case, these aforementioned two types do not easily lend themselves to large-scale structure; their overextension would most likely produce fatigue and monotony. And so, perhaps we must again reevaluate the more traditional principle of repetition-with-contrast, which served the earlier composers so well.

Perhaps many of the perplexing problems of the new music could be put into a new light if we were to reintroduce the ancient idea of music being a reflection of nature. Although technical discussions are interesting to composers, I suspect that the truly magical and spiritual powers of music arise from deeper levels of our psyche. I am certain that every composer, from his formative years as a child, has acquired a "natural acoustic" which remains in his ear for life. The fact that I was born and grew up in an Appalachian river valley meant that my ear was attuned to a peculiar echoing acoustic; I feel that this acoustic was "structured into" my hearing, so to speak, and thus became the basic acoustic of my music. I should imagine that the ocean shore or endless plains would produce an altogether different "inherited" acoustic. In a broader sense, the rhythms of nature, large and small—the sounds of wind and water, the sounds of birds and insects—must inevitably find their analogues in music. After all, the singing of the humpback whale is already a highly developed "artistic" product: one hears phrase-structure, climax and anticlimax, and even a sense of large-scale musical form!

I am optimistic about the future of music. I frequently hear our present period described as uncertain, confused, chaotic. The two decades from 1950 to 1970 have been described as "the rise and fall of the musical avant-garde," the implication being that nothing at all worthwhile was accomplished during those years. I have even heard the extremely pessimistic idea expressed by some composers that "*Comœdia finita est*"—all possible combinations have by now been exhausted and music has finally reached a dead end. My own feeling is that music can never cease evolving; it will continually reinvent the world in its own terms. Perhaps two million years ago the creatures of a planet in some remote galaxy faced a musical crisis similar to that which we earthly composers face today. Is it possible that those creatures have existed for two million years without *new* music? I doubt it.

---

[1]Hector Berlioz, *Evenings with the Orchestra*, trans and ed Jacques Barzun (New York: Alfred A. Knopf, 1956), pp 249–50.

(This article, here slightly revised, originally appeared in *The Kenyon Review*, summer, 1980.)

George Crumb, American Composer and Visionary

("The Phantom Gondolier")

Suzanne Mac Lean

I have always considered music to be a very strange substance, a substance endowed with magical properties. Music is tangible, almost palpable, and yet unreal, illusive. Music is analyzable only on the most mechanistic level; the important elements—the spiritual impulse, the psychological curve, the metaphysical implications—are understandable only in terms of the music itself. I feel intuitively that music must have been the primeval cell from which language, science, and religion originated.[1]

These are the words of George Crumb. Crumb is more than a composer. He is a visionary who expresses himself musically in a neo-Romantic, almost mystical style. His presence is somewhat anachronistic in this mechanistic and materialistic age, but George Crumb doesn't mind. While many contemporary composers obsessively explore and electronically manipulate all the parameters of sound, many admitting they don't care what the music is trying to "say," George Crumb quietly dedicates himself to another task, that of fulfilling what he feels is the primary purpose of music—that "substance endowed with magical properties"—the communication of a transcendental message about life.

Crumb's musical works evoke and explore the deeper and darker meanings of life, subjects like the many dimensions of time, the presence and purpose of evil, rebirth and self-renewal, and the cyclical nature of life. His means of communication include not only some of the most exquisite and innovative sounds yet realized by musicians, but elements of poetry, visual art and theater as well. Audiences listen, and respond to his message.

It is unlikely that George Crumb intentionally sets out to provide a spiritual awakening for his listeners. He just composes, intuitively. But his acute awareness of life's polarities and ironies and his idealism become a subtly interwoven, natural part of his sensitive musical fabric. In his words:

> When I look around at the world today I couldn't prove that things are necessarily taking a turn for the better. But I have always been fascinated by the idea of children somehow giving new meaning or regenerating the earth, not only in the physical sense, but in the spiritual sense. That is our hope, and in sharing it I guess I am basically an optimist.[2]

A transcendental view of the world pervades Crumb's music, and the nature of his creativity is such that it can move and transform others. His music touches emotional depths in his listeners, and leaves them with the feeling that serious music, which for so long seemingly abandoned them, is once again succeeding in communicating.

The philosophical framework of the musical compositions of George Crumb is in itself a superstructure which forms an important part of his communicative power. The extra-musical aspects of his work are at least as important to his popular reception as the musical sounds he creates.

Crumb arrived gradually at his unique form of personal musical expression. His earlier works—a *String Quartet* (1954), *Sonata for Solo Violoncello* (1955) and *Variazioni* for large orchestra (1959)—

THE NEW YORK TIMES

1)

1) At the Brontë Parsonage, Haworth, England, 1978.
2) "The Phantom Gondolier."
3) At the Cathedral of Freiburg, summer, 1983.

2)

THE NEW YORK TIMES

3)

ANN CRUMB

were composed in standard classical forms. In 1963 with the composition of *Night Music I*, George Crumb began to use the haunting and elemental images of Spanish poet, Federico García Lorca (1898–1936) to help express his own personal vision. Lorca's preoccupation with the subjects of life and death, earth, moon, sea, rain, love, and children, and his powerful word pictures found a responsive chord in Crumb, who has written several works around poems or fragments of poems by Lorca.

From *Night Music I* come the words "y los arcos rotos donde sufre el tiempo" (and the broken arches where time suffers) which stimulated Crumb's explorations in several works of the various psychological, metaphysical and musical meanings of time. The words reappeared first in *Eleven Echoes of Autumn, 1965* (1966) where they are whispered by the performers, who play from a staff in the form of broken circles or arches. Notational circles, spirals and even a cross symbolize both the musical and philosophical intentions of the composer in given works, and have become hallmarks of Crumb scores.

In *Echoes of Time and the River* (1967), Crumb's Pulitzer Prize winning orchestral work, the line of poetry reappears and an exploration of time is continued with movements entitled "Frozen Time," "Remembrance of Time," "Collapse of Time," and "Last Echoes of Time." As the titles imply, the work attempts to deal with new ways to perceive the concept of time, giving to time dimensions often ascribed to physical objects, such as "frozen" and "collapse of." Crumb manipulates the emotional effects of time on the listener by using such musical devices as long pauses, echoes which add the dimension of distance to time, motives of repeated notes with changing dynamics, and long passages at extremely soft dynamic levels which lull the listener into an almost meditative state. Crumb's experiments with time in these works foreshadow his later preoccupation with man's relationship to the cosmos, to the past and to the future.

In the several compositions based on the poetry of García Lorca which follow,[3] Crumb selected random lines of poetry for musical setting because of specific imagery which attracted him. However, in many of the pieces, the chosen fragments of poetry revolve around given themes which focus on aspects of the relationship between man and his universe. The *Madrigals, Books I–IV*, composed from 1965–69, have a common thread of the impermanence of earthly life and a sense of time past. A recurring reference to death pervades the fragments.[4] Likewise, the poems of *Songs, Drones, and Refrains of Death* on which Crumb worked intermittently from 1962 to 1968, are filled with a provocative imagery of grief, sorrow and death.[5] All of the lines of poetry chosen by Crumb for these musical works evoke penetrating questions about the nature and meaning of life, without any answers. It is as though the composer, in his selection of these fragmentary thoughts and feelings of García Lorca, was intentionally posing certain metaphysical dilemmas for himself and his listeners concerning the nature of reality, which in later works he would try to illuminate.

George Crumb composed *Night of the Four Moons* during the July 1969 Apollo 11 flight, and appropriately chose four poems of Lorca, each dealing with the moon. He said himself that this composition was intended to communicate his own ambivalent feelings about the Apollo flight. Crumb has made similar direct social comments with other works: *Black Angels*, his comment on the Vietnam War, which was (in his words) "finished on Friday the Thirteenth, March, 1970 (in tempore belli)," (in time of war), and *Vox Balaenae* (*Voice of the Whale*), an ecological piece inspired by the singing of the humpback whale.

In the *Night of the Four Moons* cycle, the first poem and third poem suggest the idea of rebirth.[6] The climax of the cycle occurs with the fourth poem ("Run away moon, moon, moon!"), which has certain parallels with Goethe's narrative poem *Erlkönig*, set to music by Franz Schubert. In the poem a dialogue takes place between a threatening moon and a teasing child, which is resolved in the final lines: "Through the sky goes the moon holding a child by the hand." The relationship between man and the heavenly body is depicted musically by Crumb as "a simultaneity of two musics: Musica Mundana (Music of the Spheres) and Musica Humana (Music of Mankind)," in his words. This specific distinction is one which the composer also uses in other works (*Star-Child*, for example) as a means of calling the attention of the listener to the larger context of human life. The listener, however, must really see the score where the distinction between the two musics is appropriately marked, to be fully apprised of the composer's meaning.

Important written allusions of this sort occur in many of Crumb's scores. It is therefore particularly important that at all performances of his music, full program notes and descriptions of references in the score be given to the listener, so that he may receive the total experience which the composer intends. It is typical of Crumb's complex creative nature that his thoughts are expressed through various artistic means simultaneously: the musical (through sounds), the visual (his calligraphic scores), and the poetic (his allusions and written comments to the performer).

After 1970 Crumb abandoned the Lorca poetry as a means of evoking the metaphysical/philosophical atmosphere he wished to create. Later works either have no particular text, or contain textual fragments from many varied sources. The organizational device which most of these works share is a use of allusion to structures or constructs in one or more of the following systems of thought: metaphysics, religion, evolution, archaeology, astrology, numerology, and astronomy. These thought systems are all attempts to systematize information about life and its meaning. The allusions, which appear as titles or performance instructions, reflect Crumb's broad intellectual interests as well as his deep concern for a system of principles for life. There is no purist attempt on the part of the composer to organize these references within individual works with internal coherence. Poetic, astrological and evolutionary allusions occur side by side. The allusions and suggestive titles serve the purpose of evoking powerful stimuli for Crumb, both for his musical composition and for his less overt objective of awakening his audience to an awareness of larger cosmic forces.

Vox Balaenae (Voice of the Whale) (1971) is an example. The work opens with a "Vocalise (. . . for the beginning of time)," followed by "Variations on Sea Time," a theme and five variations. The theme is called "Sea-theme," and the variations are named after the eras of geological time: Archeozoic, Proterozoic, Paleozoic, Mesozoic, and Cenozoic. The work closes with a "Sea-Nocturne (. . . for the end of time)," thus organizing the phenomena of physical life from the beginning to the end of time around the main divisions of geology, the science which deals with the physical nature and history of the earth. The Latin title gives an ancient and scholarly perspective to the work.

Further philosophical implications are added to *Vox Balaenae* by the use of two musical references to Richard Strauss' *Also sprach Zarathustra*. Crumb frequently utilizes direct or altered quotations from well-known musical works in his pieces to suggest a continuity with the past or to arouse certain symbolic associations. According to Crumb, the parodied Strauss excerpt, which makes its initial appearance in "Vocalise (. . . for the Beginning of Time)," is partially restated later in the work to symbolize the emergence of man in the Cenozoic era. *Also sprach Zarathustra*, which Strauss wrote in 1896, was described by its composer as follows: "I meant to convey by means of music an idea of the development of the human race from its origin, through the various phases of evolution, religious as well as scientific, up to Nietzsche's idea of the Superman." Crumb's use of the quotation may be intended to point ironically to the achievements of man thus far in the Cenozoic age.

Black Angels (Images I: Thirteen Images from the Dark Land) (1970), from the same period, utilizes numerology, another construct for interpreting the cosmos, for one level of conveying its message. The work is consistently organized around the numbers seven and thirteen. The number seven is thought to have special esoteric significance relating to the condition of man's physical existence. It is of considerable importance in the Scriptures (the seven days of Creation, for example), as is thirteen, the number which symbolically depicted Jesus and his twelve disciples.

Of the thirteen movements of *Black Angels*, movement one—"Threnody I: Night of the Electric Insects"; movement seven—"Threnody II: Black Angels"; and movement thirteen—"Threnody III: Night of the Electric Insects," are key points in a symmetrical arch form. In a second superimposed framework, Crumb divides the work into three major sections labeled "Departure," "Absence" and "Return," again overt references to ideas of rebirth and redemption.

Crumb conceives of the work as

> a kind of parable on our troubled contemporary world. The numerous quasi-programmatic allusions in the work are therefore symbolic, although the essential polarity—God versus Devil—implies more than a purely metaphysical reality. The image of the "black angel" was a conventional device used by early painters to symbolize the fallen angel. . . The work portrays a voyage of the soul. The three stages of this voyage are Departure (fall from grace), Absence (spiritual annihilation) and Return (redemption). [7]

References within the work to the "Dies Irae" chant from the *Mass for the Dead*, and Schubert's "Death and the Maiden" Quartet, plus titles of specific movements such as "Devil-Music" and "God-Music" add to the symbolic apparatus of the piece. As previously mentioned, Crumb inscribed the work as completed on Friday the thirteenth, in time of war.

In the *Makrokosmos* cycle, four works written between 1972 and 1979, the composer becomes more ardent in his use of symbolic references from different systems of thought as organizational and communicative devices. The very title with its tribute to Bela Bartók implies the largest possible cosmic context.

Volumes I and II are written for solo piano, and each is subtitled "Twelve Fantasy-Pieces After the Zodiac." Each of the twelve pieces of each set is associated with an astrological sign and dedicated to a person born under that sign. To pose a pleasant enigma, only initials are given. Each of the twenty-four pieces likewise has an evocative title, such as "Ghost-Nocturne: for the Druids of Stonehenge (Night-Spell II)"; or "A Prophecy of Nostradamus."

A typical movement has a fanciful title—"Dream Images (Love-Death Music)"; its Zodiacal sign—Gemini; and a set of initials—F.G.L., which in this case is a dedication to the poet Federico García Lorca. The composer himself is depicted in a movement called "The Phantom Gondolier (Scorpio) (G.H.C.)," silently, almost subconsciously leading us down the river between life and death. The process is painful for Crumb who indicates in this particular movement instructions to the performer: "Eerily, with a sense of malignant evil" and has the pianist hum "a ghostly moaning sound" throughout.

The various references and allusions in the first two volumes of *Makrokosmos*, most appearing as titles or subtitles of movements, come from the multiple thought systems previously mentioned. They can be construed in a number of ways, but viewed in the context of Crumb's total work to date, the ultimate intentions of the composer seem clear. Despite the lack of continuity in the symbolism, there is a continuous suggested progression from darkness to light, from pagan ritualism to Western theology, from temptation and threats of damnation to ultimate salvation and transcendence. In Volume I, the ultimate goal is the "Spiral Galaxy." In Volume II, the final movement is a large "Prayer-wheel," notated as a circle with the designation, "Agnus Dei."[8]

Makrokosmos III for two amplified pianos and percussion, whose real title is *Music for a Summer Evening*, follows a similar pattern. The work proceeds from a state of beginning with its first movement, "Nocturnal Sounds (The Awakening)," to a sense of exploration in movement two, "Wanderer-Fantasy." A revelation is suggested in "The Advent," movement three, which contains "Hymn for the Nativity of the Star-Child." This section foreshadows Crumb's later orchestral work, *Star-Child* (1977). A slight relapse to primitivism occurs with "Myth," movement four, but final enlightenment is forthcoming in movement five with "Music of the Starry Night" and subsections, "Fivefold Galactic Bells" and "Song of Reconciliation." The progression of the first three volumes of *Makrokosmos* has been described as "primal chaos to cosmic union."[9]

Star-Child, Crumb's largest work to date, is also the most consciously metaphysical. A parable for soprano, antiphonal children's voices, male speaking choir (and bell ringers), and large orchestra,

CARL CRUMB

4)

4) **With cousin Virginia Crumb, Seattle, 1971.**

the work opens with "Vox clamans in deserto," a voice crying in the wilderness, represented by a human-sounding trombone. Strings provide an obbligato background to this in the form of "Musica Mundana" (Music of the Spheres), notated in a circle. A soprano voice soon interjects a mixture of vocalise and the text, "Libera me, Domine" (Deliver me, O Lord), symbolically chosen from the *Mass for the Dead*. This is followed by what Crumb calls "Musica apocalyptica" (confirming the referential source of the work) and shouting of textual fragments from the "Dies Irae."

The dynamic level and intensity of the music increases with the arrival of the "Four Horsemen of the Apocalypse," represented by sixteen tomtoms playing in complex counter-rhythms. The symbolism continues with "fateful, oracular" passages by the "Seven Trumpets of the Apocalypse," and thundering timpani announce "Adventus puerorum luminis" (the arrival of the children of light), the children's choir. The soprano sings "Domine, dona eis lucem" (O Lord, grant them light!); and further, in translation, "The ancient law is no more. . . And the bonds of death are broken!"

Children, solo soprano, woodwinds and percussion celebrate "Hymnus pro novo tempore," Hymn for the new age (text extracted from "Massacre of the Innocents," an anonymous 13th-century poem). With circle notation, instruments of "Musica Humana" (Music of Mankind) join them. An echo of "Musica Mundana" closes the piece with three solo violins playing "A Distant Music," "misterioso" from afar. The integration of the earthly and the ethereal is complete. From a starting point of desolation, the listener has been guided to joyous rebirth, expressed in the voices of children, the positive message to be derived from the *Book of Revelations*.

It seems clear that the compositional process is for George Crumb not only an involvement in the symbols and sounds of music but a spiritual quest as well. He invites listeners to share his prophetic vision through his fanciful instructions to the performers, the elaborate constructs of his titles, and his copious program notes. Much in the manner of a Wagner *Gesamtkunstwerk*, but on a smaller scale, Crumb controls all aspects of the aesthetic experience: the visual and auditory, and the intellectual and philosophical. It is impossible to listen to the music of George Crumb without total commitment. The unusual and compelling sonorities envelop the listener, and the fantasy framework stimulates the imagination. Perhaps today's audiences yearn for just such a romantic musical experience, and for the profound message of hope which composer Crumb brings.

[1]Oliver Daniel, "George Crumb," Brochure of Broadcast Music, Inc. (1975).

[2]William Bender, "Star-Child: Innocence and Evil," *Time Magazine* (May 16, 1977).

[3]All of the following compositions utilize poetry of Federico García Lorca:

Night Music I (1963)
Madrigals, Books I-IV (1965-1969)
Eleven Echoes of Autumn, 1965 (1966)
Echoes of Time and the River (1967)
Songs, Drones, and Refrains of Death (1962-1968)
Night of the Four Moons (1969)
Ancient Voices of Children (1970)

[4]Some lines from *Madrigals* follow:

Verte desnuda es recordar la tierra
(To see you naked is to remember the earth)

Los muertos llevan alas de musgo
(The dead wear mossy wings)

Caballito negro. ¿Dónde llevas tu jinete muerto?
(Little black horse, where are you taking your dead rider?)

[5]Some lines from *Songs, Drones, and Refrains of Death*:

Quiero bajar al pozo,
quiero morir mi muerte a bocanadas,
quiero llenar mi corazón de musgo,
para ver al herido por el agua.
(I want to go down to the well.
I want to die my own death, by mouthfuls,
I want to stuff my heart with moss,
to watch the boy wounded by the water.)

[6]Some lines from *Night of the Four Moons*:

La luna está muerta, muerta;
pero resucita en la primavera.
(The moon is dead, dead;
but it is reborn in the springtime.)

Otro Adán oscuro está soñando
neutra luna de piedra sin semilla
donde el niño de luz se irá quemando.
(Another obscure Adam
dreams neuter seedless stone moon
where the child of light will be kindling.)

[7]George Crumb, Notes to *Black Angels*. Edition Peters No. 66304.

[8]For a complete listing of the contents of *Makrokosmos, Volumes I* and *II*, see the Annotated Chronological List of Works, pp. 108 and 109.

[9]Robert Moevs, "Reviews of Records: George Crumb," *Musical Quarterly* (April, 1976).

George Crumb: Two Personal Views

Teresa Sterne, Arthur Weisberg, Jan DeGaetani, George Crumb, with the just-released *Nonesuch* album of *Ancient Voices of Children*, New York City, May, 1971.

Reflections on Twenty Years

Jan DeGaetani

Memories:

Drinking champagne in the lobby of a hotel in Adelaide, Australia to celebrate an evening of George Crumb's music and its momentous reception.

Singing Madrigals *for the first time in Washington, D.C., and being aware during the performance that players for the other works on the concert were literally hanging out of the wings to hear this beautiful music.*

Riding on the Aspen chair-lift, exchanging kai-o-ko-ko*'s with all the Crumb family in front, and echoes all around.*

Recording Ancient Voices of Children *in a fiendishly cold hall all night long, sharing some Remy Martin to keep warm, going home to my apartment early in the morning for breakfast with George, happy and exhausted. Being greeted by my children (both of whom eventually sang the child's part in* Voices*), who loved to call George: Mr. Crumbun.*

Playing ping-pong (at which I am moderately good) and piano four-hands (at which I am totally inept) with George in his big music room in Media. Finding that under his good-natured and gentle prodding, I could, more or less, with no talent, get through the Siegfried Idyll.

Becoming aware during the week before the Ancient Voices *premiere that a great work lay before me, was in my keeping. The fear and exhilaration and the sense of oneness with my colleagues. The tears flowing from every face backstage, and hands reaching out to sustain and reward between every bow before an audience that was on its feet and openly cheering. George as always, shy and somewhat rumpled, shuffling on and off to be hailed.*

I am writing these thoughts of George Crumb in Germany where my colleague Gilbert Kalish and I recently gave a *Liederabend* which included the European premiere of *Apparition*. So many memories flood in, of other places and concerts, particularly concerts that took place specifically because Crumb's music was wanted so much: Australia, Finland, Japan, England, Switzerland, France, Spain.

Everywhere the response is the same: this music touches the heart. It seems not to matter if the audience is young or old, has experience with twentieth-century music, or understands the language of the songs. There is always an immediate and clear sense of communication and reward.

During the German trip, I have had ample opportunity to speak with members of the audience who have been eager to describe their responses to me. For the most part they are cultured, knowledgeable, willing listeners and the words I hear are: "overwhelming," "heart-breaking," "astonishing." Only a week ago my daughter, a college student, played *Ancient Voices* for some new friends who have no classical music background, but have instead grown up with the rock and folk idioms. She reported words like "fantastic," "wonderful," and the same sense of immediate connection to the music.

It has been my privilege for some years now to be involved in sharing and passing on these works, both to audiences and to students, and most especially, to learn to be a good, open channel through which the music can present itself. It is a fascinating process. George is a study in contradictions and opposites. Personally he presents himself rather gently, with wit and introspection. Musically, the George one encounters is often unabashedly lyrical and poetic, or, just as often, savage and demanding.

Performers are often tempted to think that knowing a composer will make performing his music in some way easier. Not so, I find. Knowing the composer brings all kinds of rewards and satisfactions, but not necessarily that one. You must still absorb the message and gesture of the page in some private (often obscure) fashion, with intuition as your best guide and your technical skills to serve as tools when you finally decipher what the music wants from you. Quite often you must take time to learn a new skill.

Certainly this has been true for me with Crumb's music. I feel certain that he was not concerned with that, but rather, with what was possible and needed in the context of his own musical thought. The assumption was made that I would find a way to realize those needs vocally.

In the case of George's works, the page is always glorious to look at. It is intended to excite and stimulate. One *wants* to learn this music, to ask questions, to understand the gestures. It makes the whole process of learning and practicing such a pleasure.

One of the deep satisfactions in working with a great composer is the gift he gives you of knowing yourself more fully. He invents things that you've never done before and presents you with the need to leap into that unknown space and find a way to do them.

For the most part, the pitches are not difficult to learn, and the patterns emerge quickly: tritones, uses of 5 and 7 rhythmically, chromatic intervals, displaced octaves. Most of this is not new and has been part of the modern vocabulary for many years. The newness, the freshness comes in other ways—in the variety of articulations one must use, the sense of exact rhythmic proportion, the eloquent use of silence, the passing from singing to speech or vocal percussion sounds. These are the things that bring the music in such a new fashion to the audience. They are also the things that make the music seem hard for many singers looking at it for the first time, since they are among the things singers do not practice. Very often they lack even a coherent vocabulary for discussing them.

One of the facets of George's work that *does* lend itself beautifully to a good singer's kind of awareness is his use of words and images to describe the mood of a piece. One finds: "gently floating" or "wild, demonic." Since our instruments are hidden from view, singers are often forced to learn through the use of images, and part of technique is an attempt to define the proper sensations that come with good singing. Each vocabulary is personal and often has to do with the inner feeling of the music as well. George's great color sense brings about a use of language that most good singers would understand readily and be at home with artistically.

It is impossible to know what place history will award to Crumb or his music. My personal belief is that it will last and continue to touch and inspire. Because what he wants to say is full of deep human understanding, both gentle and wild, this music deserves to be heard.

Recording *Ancient Voices of Children*

Teresa Sterne

The recording of a musical composition is not, nor should it seek to be, an electronic replica of a concert-hall performance. Few would argue this point today, but a direct participation is almost essential in order to perceive the disparity of climate between a recorded performance and a stage presentation. The history of one particular Nonesuch recording—now more than a dozen years past—provides a dramatic illustration.

George Crumb's *Ancient Voices of Children* was composed in 1970 to a commission from the Elizabeth Sprague Coolidge Foundation in The Library of Congress, and it was first performed on October 31, 1970, in Washington, D.C., at the Library's Coolidge Auditorium. The performers were the Contemporary Chamber Ensemble conducted by founder-director Arthur Weisberg, with vocal soloists Jan DeGaetani, mezzo-soprano, and Michael Dash, boy soprano. Miss DeGaetani, already noted at that time for her phenomenal renditions of the most difficult contemporary scores, was a regular performer with the Ensemble; Michael, then a 13-year-old student at the Washington Community School of Music, had made several appearances in the title role of *Amahl and the Night Visitors*. The occasion was the 14th Festival of Chamber Music sponsored by the Coolidge Foundation and The Library of Congress, in collaboration with the Koussevitzky Music Foundation, the Gertrude Clarke Whittall Foundation, and the McKim Fund.

It was a wonderful season: Washington's splendid tree-lined avenues were molten gold in autumn foliage, and Congress was out of town on the election trail. But all was jumping at The Library of Congress, with three cram-packed concert programs to be presented within 24 hours—at least ten hours' worth of brand-new music, more than half of it played by the Contemporary Chamber Ensemble. Towards the middle of the second concert—an afternoon affair lasting over three hours—one noticed the quiet disappearance of a number of distinguished audience members: the program was running longer than expected and several official receptions were scheduled at that hour. It was at this point that the performance of *Ancient Voices of Children* was to commence, with its first fantastic vocalise based on purely phonetic sounds. For a half-hour of what seemed to be suspended time, the audience sat literally spellbound by this "*music filled with a strange new magic*," as *The Washington Post* was to report. A shaken group of America's most sophisticated musical *cognoscenti* rose in a body at the piece's end; "*Mr. Crumb and the performers were awarded the kind of standing, cheering ovation that modern-music audiences rarely are aroused to*," wrote the *New York Times* critic. I had been timing the performance—we must record this music, was my immediate reaction. I had not met George Crumb before, and in the press of after-concert introductions and excited babble, one had the impression of a terribly shy, quiet man.

Ancient Voices of Children is a cycle of songs to texts by Federico García Lorca for mezzo-soprano, boy soprano, oboe, mandolin, harp, electric piano and percussion. About the piece, Mr. Crumb would later write, for our Nonesuch album:

> In *Ancient Voices of Children*, as in my earlier Lorca settings, I have sought musical images that enhance and reinforce the powerful yet strangely haunting imagery of Lorca's poetry. I

> feel that the essential meaning of this poetry is concerned with the most primary things: life, death, love, the smell of the earth, the sounds of the wind and the sea. These "*ur*-concepts" are embodied in a language which is primitive and stark, but which is capable of infinitely subtle nuance.
>
> . . . The texts of *Ancient Voices* are fragments of longer poems which I have grouped together into a sequence that seemed to suggest a "larger rhythm" in terms of musical continuity.

Back in New York the following week, Arthur Weisberg and I began moving towards a recording schedule. (This was when I first made the personal acquaintance of the remarkable "C. F. Peters family"; just that year, Peters had become Crumb's publisher.) Our sessions were set for January—now 1971. All of the artists had a fully booked season, and only two days could be found on which all were able to assemble. There was still a hitch: two of the percussion players had an immovable commitment to play at the Metropolitan Opera that first night. Could we plan a daytime session? Very dangerous, I advised Weisberg. The hotel ballroom in which we were to record, on West 73rd Street in Manhattan, had windows facing the street and traffic noise would be unavoidable. However, the options were severely limited—an added pressure was the fact that Michael Dash's voice was on the verge of changing!—and we agreed apprehensively to try for a noontime start. (The "we" consisted of myself and Elite Recordings engineering-producers Joanna Nickrenz and Marc Aubort.)

Snow had fallen that week, and, although the weather was bright, temperatures were dropping steadily that day. Moreover, a "job action" involving New York's police force, plus the icy condition of the streets, was exacerbating the city's nervous, noisy traffic patterns. After careful balance-settings, we were ready to record at 3 p.m. The first "takes" were wonderful, but every one of Crumb's long sustained melismas was punctuated by a car horn, skidding wheels, racing motors. Meantime, we had begun to notice that the heat was diminishing rapidly; sweaters and jackets were gradually topped by overcoats, scarves, hats, even gloves. The hotel was not one in which we had worked before and the manager was noncommittal about the problem. After tiptoeing down to the basement to verify that the heating system had indeed broken down, I called a halt to the proceedings. The Ensemble was performing spectacularly, but against impossible odds: street-noise intrusion had reached a crescendo of absurdity, the cold was numbing, nerves were frayed. "Dear friends," I addressed the shivering little band, "You see what's happening, and there's nothing we can do about it. The traffic noise will increase for a couple of hours, the heat's gone off, and you percussion players will have to leave for the Opera by 7:30. We've been at it for hours and we don't have a single usable take. And tomorrow will very likely be the same. Here are the alternatives. One—we wipe the slate clean and find the next available dates for everyone, even if it's in the spring. The other—and I do not recommend it—is to try for a late-night session. That means starting around 10:30 or 11 o'clock. Now, Michael's been up since dawn to get here from Washington. I know you're heroic people but how can you work under these circumstances? It's inhuman." There was silence for about five seconds. Then Jan DeGaetani said, "George, Michael, you can come to our apartment and catch a few hours of sleep and have some good hot soup I made last night." Percussionist Raymond DesRoches pushed his fur *shapka* further down on his head and harpist Susan Jolles pulled a shawl tighter around her neck as a blast of cold air cut across the room. Gilbert Kalish, pianist of the Ensemble, spoke up, "We'd like to try. If we're lucky, maybe we can finish the whole piece during the night." I groaned, "You're all crazy. But okay, see you at 10:30."

One could predict it. Reassembling, the musicians were imbued with do-or-die energy. They had gone home to soak in hot tubs, drink hot coffee—I doubt that many had napped. The hotel's heating system had struggled faintly to emit some tepid warmth for about one hour, but an automatic "off" switch followed its usual routine at 10 p.m. Now a piercing wind had come up, and along with the sharp gusts blowing through cracks, there was added the rattling of loose shutters and swaying of ancient elevator shafts. No matter, the music-making proceeded. (At least there were no longer car horns and squealing auto tires to contend with; even New York's night people had pulled the covers over their heads that evening.) *"¿De dónde viene, amor, mi niño?"* cried Jan. *"De la cresta del duro frío,"* came the response from young Michael. His voice was so strong that we decided to have him sing inside a telephone booth located on the mezzanine level; this produced exactly the distant effect the music called for. The sections including boy soprano were recorded first, in order to spare the youngster the all-night marathon.

The tiny room which we had turned into the "control booth" seemed even colder (if that was possible) than the ballroom. George Crumb's overcoat collar was pulled up to his ears. With his quiet good humor, George was a pillar of stamina throughout. Joanna's hands and my feet were completely numb. Percussionist Howard van Hyning had brought along a small electric heater, which became a little island of momentary relief; it was passed from room to room, along with a bottle of cognac. Jacob Glick was playing the musical saw—one of the exotic instrumental sounds in this score—and the freezing temperature began to affect its pitch. "Say, George," Jack wisecracked, "next time you write for saw, could you please make it an electric one?" *"Kai!"* Ray shouted, as indicated in his percussion part. The sound had an especially poignant edge in the frigid air.

Oboist George Haas, whose reed had begun to stick to his lips, was playing with mittens on, in which he had cut holes. The performance became ever more concentrated: these human beings were completely lost in the music. At 6 a.m. the Ghost Dance was recorded— a magical take. The cognac bottle was nearly empty, its contents having been shared gratefully among our 15-member crew. As the last notes were recorded at 7 a.m.—"That was gorgeous . . . a great take . . . you've done it," came Jo Nickrenz's voice over the talkback system—there was the sound of steam radiators beginning to knock. Too late; it didn't matter any more.

The memory of our night of ice is encapsulated forever in the sound of that recording of *Ancient Voices of Children*. And to this day, the amber aroma of Remy Martin cognac remains a comforting one to me—and, I suspect, also to a very special group of musicians. Great people. *Saludos*, George Crumb, *saludos*, García Lorca, *saludos*, ancient voices.

Quotes from Reviews

■ "In my view, George Crumb is the most authentically American composer since Charles Ives, and perhaps the most elemental."

Nat Hentoff
(*Cosmopolitan Magazine*, January, 1975)

■ "The ***Five Pieces*** by George Crumb, which are played as much by plucking the piano strings with fingernails and fingertips as by striking the keys, are even more advanced in organizational conception. To this listener, the work represents the most successful un-self-conscious use of these techniques he has ever heard. The *Five Pieces* are immensely sensitive, and Mr. Burge matched their delicacy with his own."

Lester Trimble
(*Washington Star*, October 21, 1963)

■ "George Crumb's ***Night Music I*** seemed to be the major work of the evening, not only in structural dimensions, but in the richness of rhythmic devices and in the variety of percussive sonorities employed to exploit them. This work . . . shows Mr. Crumb as perhaps one of the most articulate innovators of our time."

Alfredo Rogeri
(*Music Journal*, January, 1965)

■ "The highlight of the evening for the large audience was George Crumb's ***Variazioni*** for orchestra. Crumb proved himself second to none in his mastery of orchestral technique, and the orchestra responded brilliantly."

Lewis Rowell
(*Music Journal Annual*, 1965)

■ [Barraque's *Sequence*] "was overshadowed by Crumb's astonishingly inventive settings of six short extracts from poems by Federico García Lorca . . . The variety of tone color Crumb managed to get from his singer and two instrumentalists was so wide as to be almost beyond belief . . . Crumb's idiom, plainly post-Webernian, actually sounded more impressionistic than serial. To me, it was certainly a wonderfully apt demonstration that there is no necessary conflict between advanced musical thought and immediacy of appeal." [of ***Madrigals I*** and ***II***]

Irving Lowens
(*Washington Evening Star*, March 12, 1966)

■ "The most technically fascinating and, in the writer's experience, the most practically effective piece to emerge from the new school . . . The score impressed one as an extraordinary piece of fantasy. A veritable thesaurus of orchestral novelties, ***Echoes*** [***of Time and the River***] differs from much other new music in that its ideas leap off the page and make themselves perceptible as sonorities . . . Each movement sustained interest by ear alone, too, the delicate sonorities clinging in the memory for days afterward."

Donal Henahan
(*Musical Quarterly*, January, 1968)

■ "The standing ovation given to the Stanley Quartet's superlative premiere performance of George Crumb's ***Black Angels*** came from younger and older listeners together as a spontaneous response to a work of authentic beauty and power. . . Certainly one of the most important events of this (or any) musical season. It is time for the new music to enter the repertoire and not be segregated in special programs; this remarkable quartet could serve well to break the trail."

Edith Borroff
(*Ann Arbor News*, October 29, 1970)

■ "There is always the possibility that one will encounter among the ephemera a full-blown masterpiece such as George Crumb's ***Ancient Voices of Children***, which had its premiere here yesterday at the Library of Congress's 14th Festival of Chamber Music. The piece, conducted with masterly precision and obvious love by Arthur Weisberg, bowled over the musically sophisticated audience that gathered for these concerts . . . This is music that springs to life as a whole and at once, and may just be long-lived."

Donal Henahan
(*New York Times*, November 2, 1970)

■ "I will not follow the common practice of describing what is now common knowledge—how Crumb achieves his colorful sound effects. To do so would be to suggest that the music is of some intellectual interest, which it is not. It is designed to appeal to the senses, and it does this successfully. I would not presume to quarrel with Crumb's direct quotation from Chopin. But the impression I got was of a shallow piece, obvious and dull to the point of monotony but not banality." [of ***Makrokosmos I***]

Robert Evett
(*Washington Star-News*, August 15, 1973)

1)

1) With Pierre Boulez before the premiere of *Star-Child,* May, 1977.
2) Wushan Conservatory of Music, China, May, 1983.
3) Robert Miller, at the time of the premiere of *Makrokosmos II.*

■ [*Lux Aeterna*] "is as fine as any 'sound-piece' I have heard, and I am now quite willing to regard Crumb as one of the most important voices in this genre, right along with his European counterparts, Xenakis, Ligeti, and Penderecki . . . The most remarkable thing about the piece is that every single sound in it seems to be just right."
Tom Johnson
(*Village Voice*, April 20, 1972)

■ "Quiet and subtly enchanting, [*Vox Balaenae*] reveals Crumb's discoveries of new instrumental resources at their most lyrical; this second hearing confirmed that it is not a mere assemblage of sound effects but a sustained and beautiful dream vision of the deep."
Andrew Porter
(*New Yorker*, April 28, 1973)

■ "Let those who would proclaim the demise of 'serious' music in this century confront Crumb and Burge—even singularly, but best together . . . Crumb has an affinity for exploration into sound that seems almost unrivaled by his peers . . . In the ***Makrokosmos [I]***, performer and instrument are nearly one, acting out a huge drama whose 'plot' is so multifaceted that one cannot say what it is really all 'about'—other than that it is metaphysical, even quasi-religious . . . Whatever the structural formulations of the work—and they are enormously complex—for all of that, Crumb's infinitely imaginative music is so very accessible somehow, even if not in any conventional sense. Therein, perhaps, lies his value to us."
Anne M. Culver
(Denver *Rocky Mountain News*, October 25, 1973)

■ "Robert Miller, the lawyer-pianist who has dedicated his career to contemporary music, played the first of three concerts last night in Tully Hall. Last night's premiere was the second volume of George Crumb's *Makrokosmos*. In recent years, Mr. Crumb has forged to the front as one of the most important American composers. He marks, among others, the point where the stranglehold exerted by the post-serialists of the nineteen-fifties and sixties was broken . . . After two decades of the acerbic, academic, intensely organized music we have had . . . ***Makrokosmos II*** actually sounds easygoing, lyric, romantic."
Harold C. Schonberg
(*New York Times*, November 14, 1974)

MARC MUSNICK

3)

DARYL DAYTON

2)

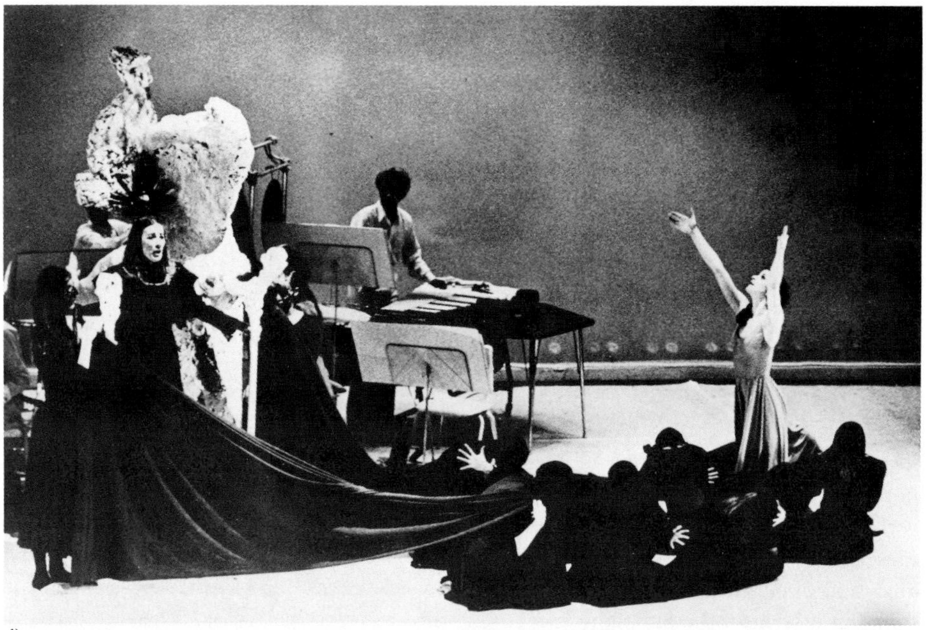

THE WINSTON-SALEM JOURNAL

4)

MARVIN R. A. JOHNSON

5)

■ "George Crumb's imagining of worlds in sound runs as deep as ever in ***Music for a Summer Evening*** . . . Aside from the wider range of timbres, *Music for a Summer Evening* explores fresh paths of instrumental chant, different shapes of harmonic spaces, and new weaves of rhythm. 'The Advent' has a softly-reverberating middle section called 'Hymn for the Nativity of the Star-Child.' The composer said after the performance that the 'star-child' was not Christ or the celestial invader who takes over Planet Earth at the end of '2001', but the concept of a great hope. The music, so richly programmatic in its historically colored allusions to what we still think of as things of the spirit, captures that concept unerringly."

Leighton Kerner
(*Village Voice*, January 20, 1975)

■ [*Makrokosmos III*] "becomes . . . the completion of what must be considered a single large work thirteen years (fatally) in the writing that began with the *Five Pieces for Piano* (1962). Heterogenous borrowings, superimpositions, sometimes rudimentary transcriptions that enter along the way, sounds, motives, phrases, passages, procedures, entire structures, fail to break this persisting unity, but rather point up the sense of constriction produced by the tightly circumscribed use of primary material, an assemblage of spooky effects and symbols chosen to evoke a particular mood, and a compositional method reduced essentially to their simple concatenation. The lack of musical substance, in turn, exposes the emptiness behind the assortment of symbolic-expressionistic titles and descriptions not to be taken seriously (numerological, psychological, mythical, astrological, religious, philosophical, cosmological) that are added throughout and together create the panoply of a *cavaliere inesistente*."

Robert Moevs
(*Musical Quarterly*, April, 1976)

■ "Crumb's ***Night of the Four Moons*** . . . perfectly sums up his unique impact as a composer of new music 'which is already old.' . . .His musical world is filled with electronic drones, whispers, echoes, and a unique and characteristic (often amplified) sound which seems to be recalled, like a

4) *Ancient Voices of Children,* Elizabeth Suderburg, soprano, Winston-Salem, 1975.

5) Left to Right: Carole Morgan, Lambert Orkis and Barbara Haffner perform *Vox Balaenae* (from Robert Mugge's film "George Crumb: Voice of the Whale," 1976).

6) Preparing *Makrokosmos III* in Buffalo, 1976. Left to right: Jan Williams, Morton Feldman, George Crumb, John Newell, John Boulder, Lynn Harbold, Yvar Mikhashoff.

7) Rudolf Nureyev with The Martha Graham Dance Company in *Phaedra* ("Lux Aeterna"), New York City, 1984.

6)

7)

memory play, rather than presently experienced. The spirit of *déjà vu* is so implicit in the music of George Crumb that one feels familiar with it even when it is entirely new. It is modern music which drips with an ineffable antiquity."

Jamake Highwater
(*Soho Weekly News*, April 7, 1977)

■ "Crumb's music is reflective, illustrative, and seldom active in itself as Beethoven's or Berlioz's is: in ***Star-Child*** one finds a vivid picturing but not the musical enactment of the 'struggle.' The composer invites listeners to share his poetic thoughts and visions, to enter a private world of marvels; his method is essentially intimate."

Andrew Porter
(*New Yorker*, May 23, 1977)

■ "When all hell broke loose—during an evocation of the Apocalypse—Supreme Maestro Pierre Boulez could be seen beating with the polyrhythmic fury of a sinner trying to drive off an army of snakes. So it went last week as the New York Philharmonic gave the world premiere of ***Star-Child***, . . . Gimmickry aside, *Star-Child* turned out to be a work of immense power, daring and, at times, even horror."

William Bender
(*Time Magazine*, May 16, 1977)

■ "***Celestial Mechanics*** continues Crumb's exploration of the altogether otherworldly colors and sonorities—in astonishing variety—that can be coaxed out of a piano. The four-movement work is more adamant, assertive, brutal than its predecessors, at least in the first and third movements. But characteristic passages of breath-holding delicacy culminate in a final section in which space seems expanded and time slowed down. The work is carefully shaped around the two extremes."

Shirley Fleming
(*New York Post*, November 19, 1979)

■ ". . . We have been a long time waiting for Crumb's maturity, and the vastly pretentious emptiness of his more recent works have hollowed out even what was appealing in the earlier ones. There remains only husks, remnants of forgotten dreams. Five of those were to be reencountered last night in increasing dismalness." [of *Madrigals, Books I/IV*; *Sonata for Violoncello*]

Paul Griffiths
(*The Times*, June 16, 1981)

■ [The ***Gnomic Variations*** are] "classic in form and restrained and pure in language. The inside of the piano is used, but these sounds are integrated in a seamless way with traditional keyboard writing. In this music Crumb moves beyond theater to create a masterfully unified statement."

Joanne Sheehy Hoover
(*Washington Post*, December 13, 1982)

■ "***A Haunted Landscape*** truly lives up to its title. It is a grandly evocative tone-poem of myriad colors that seems a perfect synthesis of Crumb's entire composing career, executed with individual purpose, imagination and exquisite refinement. . ."

Bill Zakariasen
(*Ovation*, August, 1984)

Interview: Crumb/Shuffett

Robert Shuffett: To begin at the beginning: at what age did you receive your first musical training, and when did you first decide to make music your career?

George Crumb: My first formal training began with the clarinet lessons I received from my father at about age seven. He started me on the little E-flat instrument, since the span of my fingers was too narrow for the B-flat clarinet. I played piano "by ear" at age nine, and also had a few lessons during this period. But it was not until I was fourteen that I buckled down to sustained and methodical study of the piano under an excellent local teacher. I made rapid progress and was soon playing rather difficult pieces by Chopin and Beethoven. Of course, in addition to clarinet and piano study I was teaching myself in other areas. My father had an extensive collection of ancient, dog-eared scores and I spent many pleasurable hours in trying to decipher their meaning. Our record collection probably didn't exceed twenty-five or thirty albums—these were the pre-LP days and the old 78s were relatively expensive—but of course there was also some good music available on radio. I can still vividly recall reading my first score while listening to a recording: it was Beethoven's *Egmont Overture*. In time I worked my way through my father's entire library. As to my choice of career: I never really considered any field other than music—I always simply assumed that this would become my profession.

RS: At what age did you begin composing?

GC: I can't pin that down exactly, because in effect I was "composing" when I improvised at the piano early on. I can remember notating little pieces in a quasi-Mozart style at about age ten or eleven. Only later did I become aware that Mozart at the same age was also writing in the "Mozart style!" [Laughing]

RS: I believe you mentioned that your family was musical?

GC: That's right. My father, as a child shortly after the turn of the century, played with the "Crumb Family Orchestra." This group had been organized by his parents and performed summers at various resort hotels. My father later developed into an excellent clarinettist and, in addition to teaching, played with the local orchestra and with various chamber music groups. My mother was a cellist and my brother a flutist, so that we had ample resources for impromptu chamber music at home. In fact, I wrote many little pieces for our available instrumentation and had that headiest of all experiences for a composer: immediate performance!

RS: I gather, then, that you were a prolific composer in your young years?

GC: Yes, I wrote very rapidly. Only later, during my college years, did my rate of production slow considerably as a result of a more self-critical attitude.

RS: Aside from performances in your own home, were your early pieces otherwise performed?

GC: I was very fortunate as a teenager in hearing my first two orchestral attempts performed by the local symphony orchestra. There were also a few other performances including some little choral pieces and songs. I found the orchestral experience especially exhilarating and was amazed that my imagined sound pretty much corresponded to the actual sound in performance. That is always a very useful thing for a composer to learn.

RS: I know that you consider Ross Lee Finney to have been your principal teacher. Could you comment on how his teaching influenced your own approach to composition?

GC: Ross's approach stressed technique: he insisted on the need for constant rewriting, he emphasized the necessity for logical form and for the "right" notes, and he expected a meticulous notation. He encouraged his students to form their own stylistic viewpoints. Although my personal style did not evolve until after my college years—in fact not until 1962 with my *Five Pieces for Piano*—I am grateful for the sense of discipline he instilled in me.

RS: How was the composition seminar handled during your student years at Michigan?

GC: Primarily it involved close analysis of a range of twentieth-century works. I can remember stimulating sessions on the music of Schoenberg, Webern, Stravinsky, Dallapiccola, and several other more recent composers. And although Ross's viewpoints were expressed with typical verve and enthusiasm and without ambiguity, a strong sense of cameraderie prevailed in the seminars and opposing viewpoints were not discouraged.

RS: Which contemporary composers have influenced your music most strongly?

GC: Of the "classical" twentieth-century composers, probably Bartók and Webern have had the most influence on my music. I also feel a certain stylistic affinity with Ives, Messiaen, and Berio, and there is undoubtedly a degree of influence here, too. But perhaps the most profound influence on my own thinking was Debussy, who of course also has to count as a twentieth-century composer. Incidentally, I knew quite a bit of his later music by the mid-forties, and at that time, in Charleston, West Virginia, this music represented the outer fringes of the avant garde!

RS: Have the collage techniques of Ives influenced the use of collage in your own music?

GC: Yes, especially in several rather recent works. I would mention in particular my *Star-Child*, a work involving many layers of music, including a quiet, ethereal continuum of string music based on an Ivesian stack of fifths. As is frequently the case in Ives, my work is a counterpoint of different musics rather than the traditional counterpoint of lines. *Dream Sequence* is another of my works which shows the influence of Ives' collage technique.

RS: Has any other aspect of Ives' musical language been influential in terms of your own musical thinking?

GC: Well, of course Ives wasn't the first composer to use quotation, but it is a device invariably associated with his music. I have also used quotation to an extent in several of my own pieces, although my psychological motivations for doing so undoubtedly differ from those of Ives.

"A strong initial conception for a piece of music must come from deep within the psyche . . . If a composer remains true to himself, I feel that stylistic consistency would follow naturally."

RS: Eric Salzman, in his *Introduction to Twentieth-Century Music*, terms you a "Stravinskyite turned minimalist."

GC: I've always been very fond of Stravinsky's music. I've noticed in several of my pieces—for example, *Celestial Mechanics* for piano, four-hands—certain characteristics of rhythm which seem to me Stravinskian in their derivation. However, I wouldn't perceive any influence other than the rhythmic.

RS: May I abruptly move on to an area that has always fascinated me: the genesis of a musical work? Why do you think that it is so difficult for most composers to get the flow of ideas started when commencing a new work?

GC: There are a number of factors. One would be the necessity of "getting rid of" the piece you just finished. This is still ringing in your ear, and you may be fairly happy with it, or not. And although it is true that style can only exist when there is a certain degree of continuity from one work to the next, nonetheless there have to be new things that come into the next piece. Maybe inertia is another factor [laughing].

RS: For you, what do the early stages of composition involve?

GC: I usually have to sketch a great deal, as musical ideas never seem to come very easily. I'm always throwing away a lot of material. For me, composition is a very slow and laborious process involving the testing of, and choosing from among, various possibilities.

RS: When you begin a new composition, do you have to wait for inspiration, or can you just begin when you like?

GC: Well, sometimes inspiration comes out of a number of false starts and from sketching in the dark, so to speak. Ideas don't always start flowing right away. A work has to develop momentum. Many ideas have to be evaluated, most of which are ultimately discarded. I envy those composers who can write quickly without sacrificing quality.

RS: Is the basic mood you wish to express the first impulse in beginning a new composition?

GC: That's right. However, "mood" is a somewhat nebulous term. I would prefer "ethos," meaning the essential, innate character of a piece of music. I feel that composers begin a new work with an intuitive sense of the ethos they wish to communicate.

RS: Could you give me a general overview of your schedule when you are into a new project?

GC: For me, the amount of time required to complete a composition can run into many months, and, exceptionally, can even cover a span of years (I am thinking of my *Songs, Drones, and Refrains of Death*, which was first sketched in 1962 and not completed until 1968). My daily work schedule is quite variable: sometimes an hour or two of work will completely exhaust me, while at other times I can sustain my concentration over many hours. Generally, once I fully understand the implications of my materials, the work sessions tend to become longer.

RS: How does a composer writing a piece over a long period of time remain faithful to the original creative impulse as he progresses into the work?

GC: A strong initial conception for a piece of music must come from deep within the psyche. A composer draws on this source according to an urgent need to express. If a composer remains true to himself, I feel that stylistic consistency would follow naturally.

RS: You have been quoted in Vinton's *Dictionary of Contemporary Music* as saying that ". . . music can only exist when the brain is singing." What do you mean?

GC: I must have been in a poetic trance when I wrote that! . . . I do feel that music presents us with a dichotomy of thought and intuition. "Singing" represents the composer's lyrical, intuitive impulses. The role of the brain is to "regulate" such impulses by means of technical discipline. I might add, too, that if either of these basic components is neglected, the result would be unsatisfactory, aesthetically speaking. At one end of the spectrum would be the "irrational" approach, which carries the danger of the music becoming amateurish and dilettantish. The opposite extreme would be the "ultrarational" approach, which could lead to an academic and doctrinaire kind of music. It seems to me that the best music of any period or style shows us an ideal balance between inspiration and thought.

". . . Music presents us with a dichotomy of thought and intuition. 'Singing' represents the composer's lyrical, intuitive impulses. The role of the brain is to 'regulate' such impulses by means of technical discipline."

RS: If we might now proceed from the general to the specific, I should very much like to know what accounted for the abrupt change of style in your *Five Pieces for Piano*?

GC: I can remember quite literally waking up one night in a cold sweat with the realization that I had thus far simply been rewriting the music of other composers. My orchestral *Variazioni* of 1959 was virtually a cross-section of earlier twentieth-century music and contained precious little of my own. Then followed a hiatus of three years which was studded with false starts and aborted attempts. And then one day David Burge informally commissioned me to do a solo work for him, and this resulted in the *Five Pieces*. This work represented for me an entirely new way of handling sonority and timbre (I was at that time totally unfamiliar with Cowell's experiments in "extended piano techniques"). I feel now that this work also embodies certain stylistic "fingerprints" having to do with pitch and rhythmic configurations which persist in my music to this very day.

"I can remember quite literally waking up one night in a cold sweat with the realization that I had thus far simply been rewriting the music of other composers."

RS: Your very next work—*Night Music I*—introduces another element frequently associated with your music: the poetry of Federico García Lorca.

GC: I first encountered Lorca's poetry when I was a student in Ann Arbor. I immediately identified with its stark simplicity and vivid imagery but of course could not imagine that I would one day complete a cycle of eight works based on this poetry.

RS: Technically and stylistically, *Night Music I* represents no significant departure from the *Five Pieces*; the same might be said of *Four Nocturnes* and the first two books of *Madrigals*. I feel, however, that with your *Eleven Echoes of Autumn, 1965*, you have significantly enlarged your musical vocabulary. Whole-tone, tonal, and modal elements are introduced, and from that time on, your music has tended to shift back and forth between various stylistic procedures and materials. In adopting such a stylistic synthesis, it would seem that you did much earlier what so many composers are doing today.

GC: I recall feeling quite restricted by the limitations of an unrelieved chromaticism and felt I had to open up my language. I feel now that virtually any elements can coexist in a musical style, but of course it is nonetheless incumbent upon the composer to make that stylistic synthesis sound cohesive and integrated.

RS: Your *Echoes of Time and the River* for orchestra introduces yet another distinctive element which reappears in several subsequent works. I am referring now to your inclusion of a "theater element"—in this case to the actual processionals which certain groups of players must execute in exact synchronization with the music.

GC: I was thinking of a processional as a metaphor for a journey through time. I wanted not only the visual effect, but also the aural effect of the music actually moving through space. It rarely happens, however, that the work is performed as I envisaged it—orchestral musicians can be very reluctant to go beyond the call of duty!

RS: You seem to be fascinated by what I would call the "spatial dimension" in music. I am thinking now of the offstage oboe and boy soprano in *Ancient Voices of Children*, the offstage crystal goblets in *Dream Sequence*, the offstage "apocalyptic" trumpets in *Star-Child*, and the processionals and offstage "Musica Humana" in *Night of the Four Moons*. Do you feel that electronic music has affected the way in which we hear music?

GC: Yes, it has—in every conceivable way. Not only has our spatial perception been enlarged; we are now much more acutely sensitive to qualities of attack and decay, to timbral subtleties, to dynamic articulations, and to texture generally.

RS: Many of your works—for example, *Black Angels* and the four piano works of the *Makrokosmos* series—require amplified instruments. And yet you have never felt the temptation to work in the electronic medium?

GC: The possibilities of conventional instruments are really limitless, and I have thus far not felt the necessity to explore the electronic field. Then, too, my mode of expression depends so much on the direct, emotional projection of the live performer. I also relish the fact that the tiny nuances are always changing—no two performances are alike.

"I recall feeling quite restricted by the limitations of an unrelieved chromaticism and felt I had to open up my language. I feel now that virtually any elements can coexist in a musical style . . ."

RS: Much new music, and very definitely all of your representative music, seems to be concerned with an ongoing development of new timbral and idiomatic possibilities, both as regards vocal and instrumental music. Therefore the role of the performer is indeed critical. Would you comment on contemporary performance standards in general?

GC: The whole picture has changed dramatically since the early sixties. At that time, really gifted and dedicated performers of the most recent music were rare indeed. People like Jan DeGaetani, David Burge, Gilbert Kalish, Paul Zukofsky, and a few others were the true pioneers. Due to their artistic and pedagogical efforts there now exists a whole new generation of young performers who are technically and musically equipped to deal with contemporary scores. I'm sure that a parallel development has occurred in Europe. Then, too, one mustn't forget the critical role of that new breed of conductor—the virtuoso specialist in new music. I'm thinking of people like Arthur Weisberg and Richard Wernick. Both have set standards for meticulous accuracy in all details and faithfulness to the composer's expressive intentions. Both approach new music in that pragmatic spirit which one associates with Haydn's Esterhazy years.

RS: When you are writing for performers

like Jan DeGaetani or the Aeolian Chamber Players, how close is the collaboration? Are you in close touch throughout the compositional process?

GC: Actually, no. But of course I have an intimate sense of their musical personalities and I am sure that my music is influenced by this in subtle ways. Of course when the work is finally tested in rehearsal, I may make numerous small changes. Sometimes there are awkward passages. I may have miscalculated a timbral effect, or again, there might be a faulty balance in the scoring. I always carefully re-edit my music once I have heard the live sounds. Frequently my performers come up with the ideal solution for a knotty problem. Then, too, as flexible as our notational system is, there are always numerous subtleties which could never be put on paper. It is therefore critically important to have sympathetic performers involved in the premiere performance and recording of a new work, since they are, in fact, establishing a "performance practice" for that work.

RS: How do you manage to invent so many new instrumental effects? Or were some of these suggested by performers?

GC: Indeed they were. For example, the "seagull effect" of multiple glissandos (in my *Vox Balaenae*) was borrowed from the contrabassist Bertram Turetzky and simply transposed to the cello. Harmonics and pitch-bending on the vibraphone (as in my *Madrigals, Book I*) were invented by John Bergamo. And of course I borrow liberally from other composers—or perhaps I should hopefully say "steal," since Stravinsky said something to the effect that good composers steal rather than borrow [laughing].

RS: Since piano is your instrument, I imagine that you explored this territory pretty much on your own.

GC: That's right; I can remember even as a child being fascinated with the inside of our old upright piano.

RS: Do you feel that timbre in music can be as important as the elements of pitch and rhythm?

GC: The virtual explosion of new possibilities in timbre has been a remarkable development in our period and I am sure that it has something to do with our increased knowledge of non-Western and very early Western music. In much music, including my own, the hierarchy of the constituent elements will constantly be shifting, and it can happen that timbre will occasionally be dominant.

". . . My mode of expression depends so much on the direct, emotional projection of the live performer. I also relish the fact that the tiny nuances are always changing—no two performances are alike."

RS: Your calligraphy and careful notation have occasioned much commentary over the years. Would you comment on notation in general?

GC: I endeavor to make my own notation as simple and conventional as possible, since I want to communicate clearly and economically all the necessary information to the performer. If a score is a "book of seven seals," then the composer is working against his own best interests. Of course notation can also be imaginative and provocative—I feel that all good music looks beautiful on the page.

RS: One visually striking aspect of your scores would be your "symbolic notations"—those representations of spirals, circular shapes, and so forth.

GC: Every composer should be permitted an occasional flight of whimsy!

RS: Of the music which you have thus far composed, which is your favorite work?

GC: I feel that *Songs, Drones, and Refrains of Death* most faithfully realized my original conception. But all this is relative, since I have not yet written a piece that totally satisfies me. Perhaps the quest for that elusive "definitive statement" is what drives composers on. My colleague, George Rochberg, once said that to have written only two or three truly superb pages of music would justify one's being a composer. I would one day like to write those two or three pages.

RS: Although you have never written a work expressly for dance—your *Ancient Voices of Children* and *Lux Aeterna* contain only incidental moments where you have suggested an optional use of dance—dancers seem attracted to your music and numerous works have been choreographed both here and abroad. Since your music has the capacity to function in situations other than the concert hall, I wonder if you have ever been attracted to film music?

GC: I was once invited to do the score for the *Exorcist* but declined on the grounds that film music wasn't my métier. I feel that writing good film music requires a specialized talent. Incidentally, a very short excerpt from my *Black Angels* was actually used in that film.

RS: How would you describe the current American activity in the composition field? Do you feel that we have finally reached a degree of maturity?

GC: Recent American music shows enormous vitality. There are so many excellent composers and such a wide range of stylistic approaches. I feel that we have reached maturity in the sense that we certainly no longer function merely as an appendage to European music.

RS: If you were able to return one hundred years from now and sit in a room where someone was listening to your music, what would you like them to say about it?

GC: Well, first of all, I would be astonished if in a hundred years from now anybody would be the least bit concerned about my music [laughing]. We all know that time is merciless and inexorable. And if it is true—as some of our more hostile critics imply—that we are a race of pygmy composers compared to the giants of the early twentieth-century, then perhaps we are condemned to be a "transitional period"—and to be totally forgotten. I would be more than happy if my music can communicate something here and now.

Crumb's Music: Excerpts

for my friend Rolf Gelewski

VARIAZIONI

for large orchestra

GEORGE CRUMB

*) Introduzione: Lento (♪ = ca. 40)

Flauti I. II.
Oboe I.
Clarinetti in Si♭ I. II.
Timpani — ppp ma distinto
Vibrafono
Celesta
Arpa — pp
(lunga)
Violini I.
Violini II.
Viole (div.) — con sord. ppp — (niente)
Violoncelli (div.) — con sord. ppp — (niente)
Contrabassi (div.) — con sord. ppp — (niente)

*) Constructed on two names: (ROL)F GE(L)E(W)S(KI) GE(OR)GE H. C(RUM)B

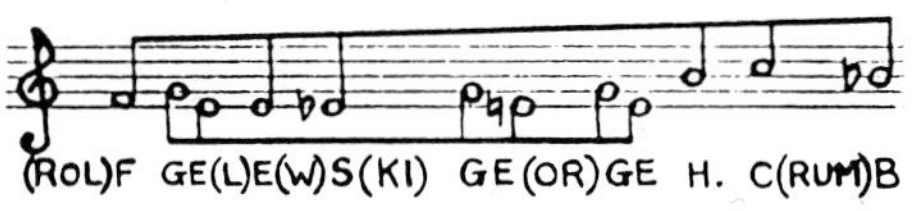

III

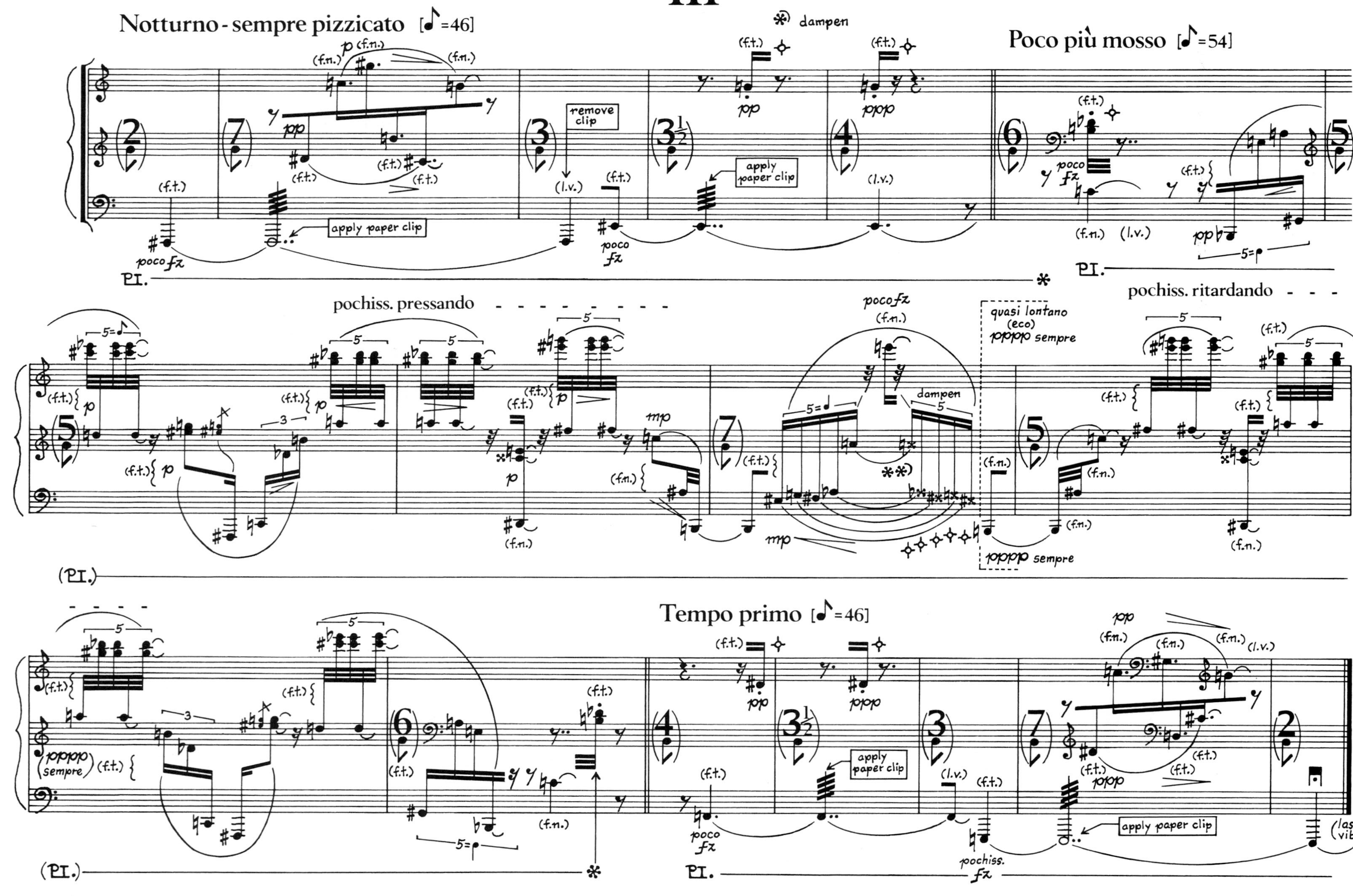

*) Dampen string with fingertip immediately after string is plucked.

**) Dampen vibrating strings with fingertip precisely in rhythm.

(from *Five Pieces for Piano*)

for Ann

FOUR NOCTURNES

(NIGHT MUSIC II)

for Violin and Piano

GEORGE CRUMB

I

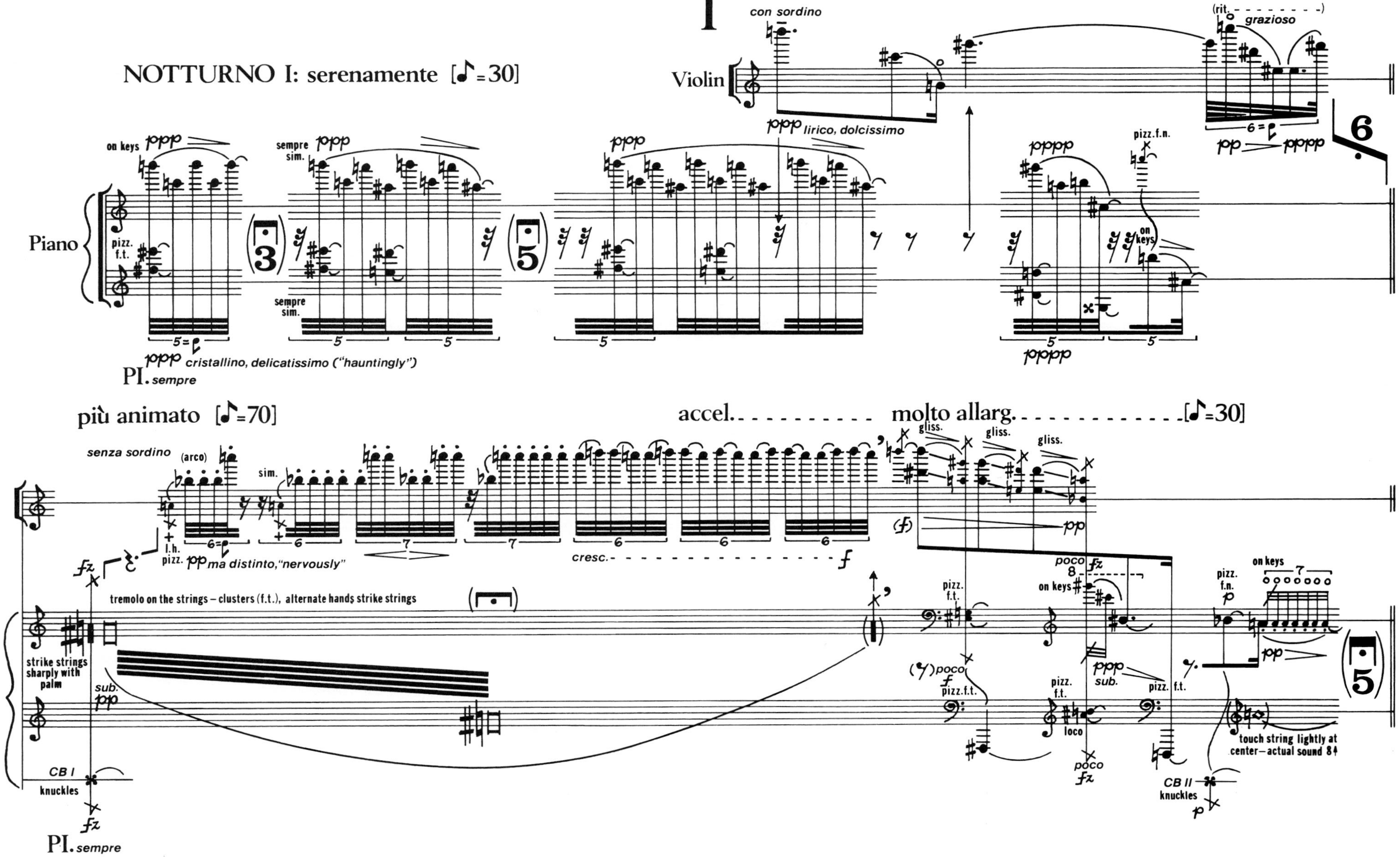

NOTTURNO I: serenamente [♪=30]

con sordino

Violin

ppp lirico, dolcissimo

(rit. - - - - - - -) grazioso

6=♪

pp ⟶ pppp

6

Piano

on keys ppp

pizz. f.t.

sempre sim. ppp

sempre sim.

5=♪

ppp cristallino, delicatissimo ("hauntingly")

PI. sempre

3

5

ppp

pppp

pizz. f.n.

on keys

pppp

più animato [♪=70]

accel. - - - - - - - - - - - molto allarg. - - - - - - - - - - - - - - [♪=30]

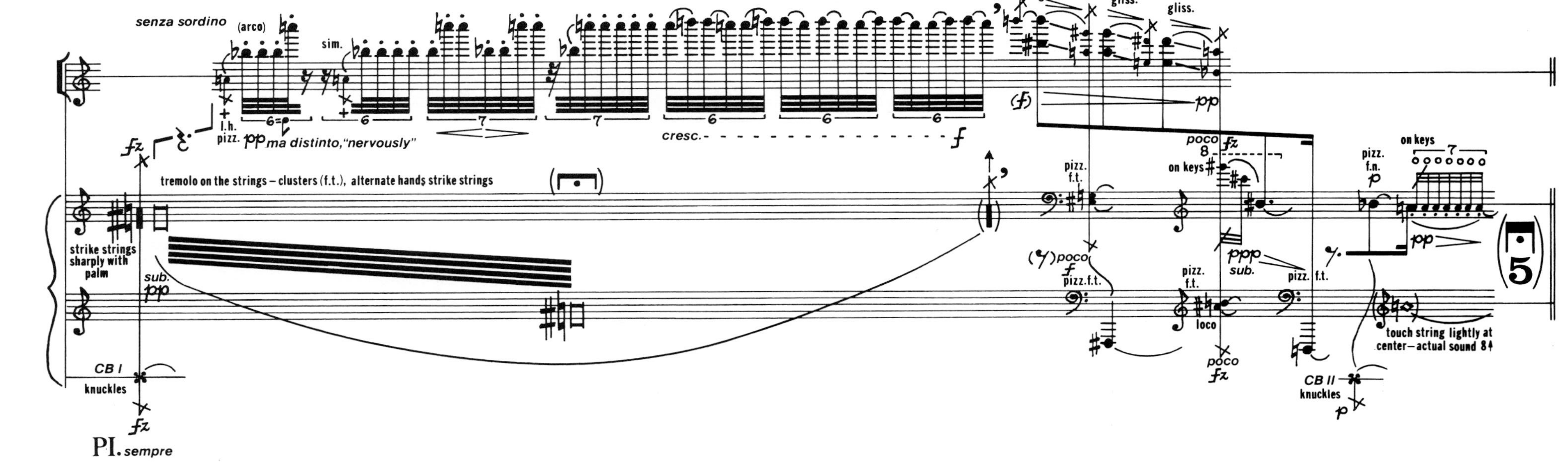

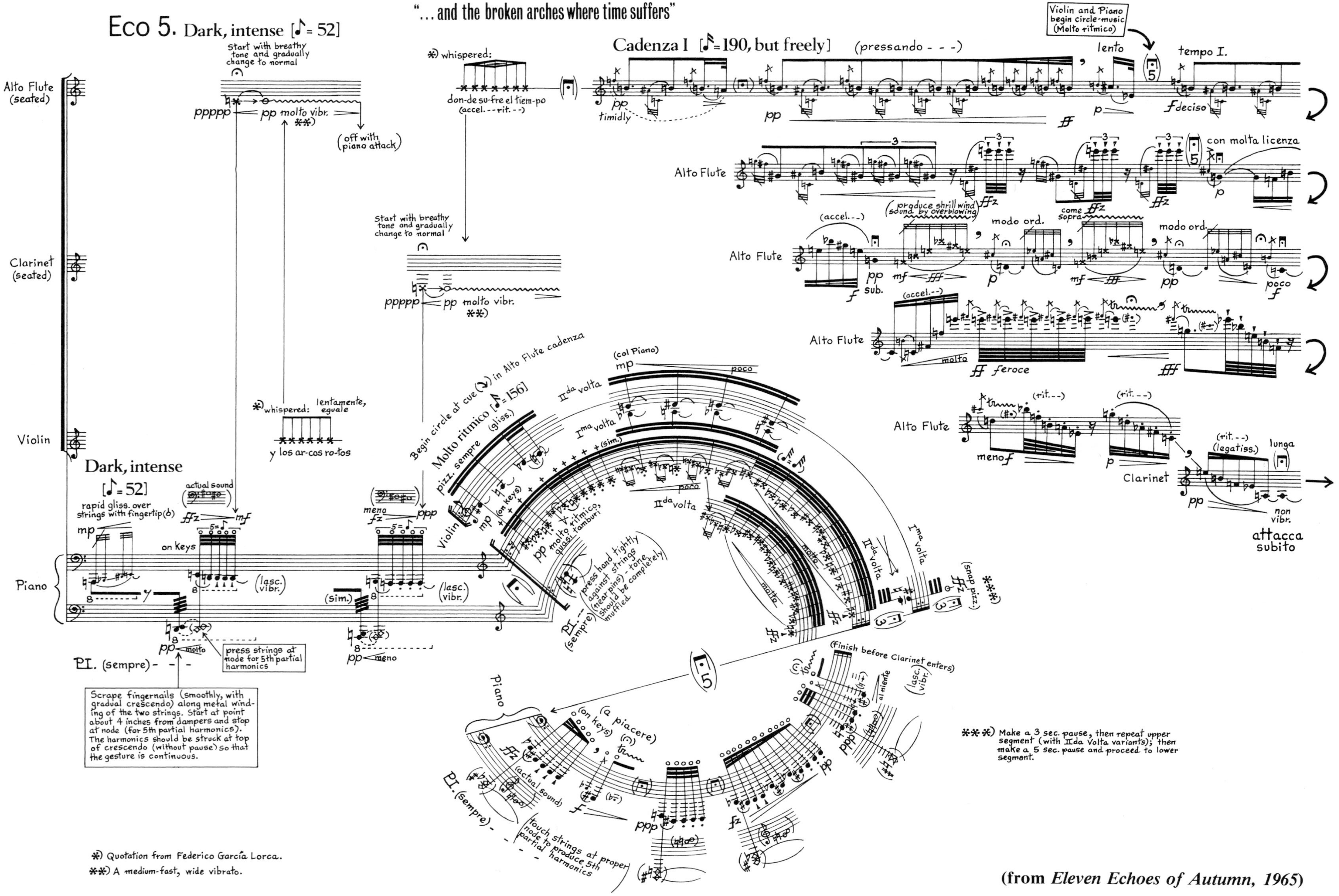

Eco 5. Dark, intense [♪ = 52]

"... and the broken arches where time suffers"

Alto Flute (seated)

Clarinet (seated)

Violin

Piano

Start with breathy tone and gradually change to normal

pppp — pp molto vibr. (**)

(off with piano attack)

*) whispered: don-de su-fre el tiem-po (accel. - - rit. - -)

Start with breathy tone and gradually change to normal

ppppp — pp molto vibr. (**)

*) whispered: lentamente, eguale — y los ar-cos ro-tos

Dark, intense [♪ = 52]

rapid gliss. over strings with fingertip(b)

actual sound

on keys

(lasc. vibr.)

(sim.)

meno

press strings at node for 5th partial harmonics

PI. (sempre) - - -

Scrape fingernails (smoothly, with gradual crescendo) along metal winding of the two strings. Start at point about 4 inches from dampers and stop at node (for 5th partial harmonics). The harmonics should be struck at top of crescendo (without pause) so that the gesture is continuous.

Cadenza I [♪ = 190, but freely] (pressando - - -)

timidly — lento — tempo I. — ƒ deciso

Violin and Piano begin circle-music (Molto ritmico)

Alto Flute — con molta licenza

(produce shrill wind sound by overblowing) — come sopra

Alto Flute — (accel. - -) — modo ord. — modo ord. — pp sub. — poco ƒ

Alto Flute — (accel. - -) — molto — ƒƒ feroce

Alto Flute — (rit. - -) — meno ƒ

Clarinet — (rit. - -) (legatiss.) — lunga — non vibr. — attacca subito

Begin circle at cue in Alto Flute cadenza

Molto ritmico [♪ = 156]

pizz. sempre (gliss.)

Violin — (on keys) — mp — (col Piano) — poco

I^ma volta — II^da volta — (sim.)

molto ritmico, quasi tamburi

press hand tightly against strings (near pins) - tone should be completely muffled

PI. (sempre)

(snap pizz.) (***)

(Finish before Clarinet enters)

al niente — (lasc. vibr.)

Piano — (on keys) — (a piacere)

(actual sound)

PI. (sempre) - - -

touch strings at proper node to produce 5th partial harmonics

***) Make a 3 sec. pause, then repeat upper segment (with II da Volta variants); then make a 5 sec. pause and proceed to lower segment.

*) Quotation from Federico García Lorca.

**) A medium-fast, wide vibrato.

(from *Eleven Echoes of Autumn, 1965*)

III. ¡La muerte me está mirando desde las torres de Córdoba!

[Death is watching me from the towers of Córdoba!]

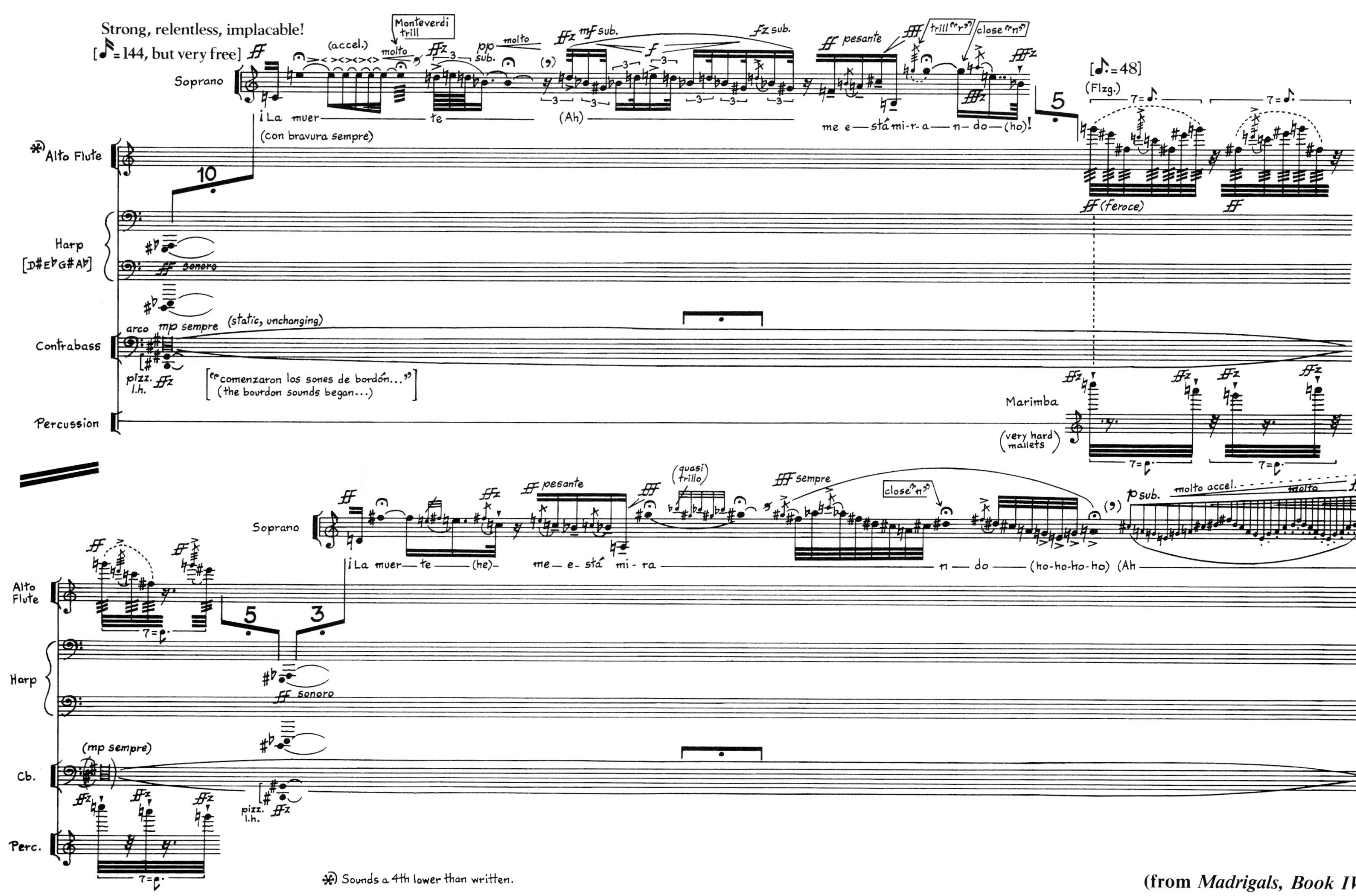

✻ Sounds a 4th lower than written.

(from *Madrigals, Book IV*)

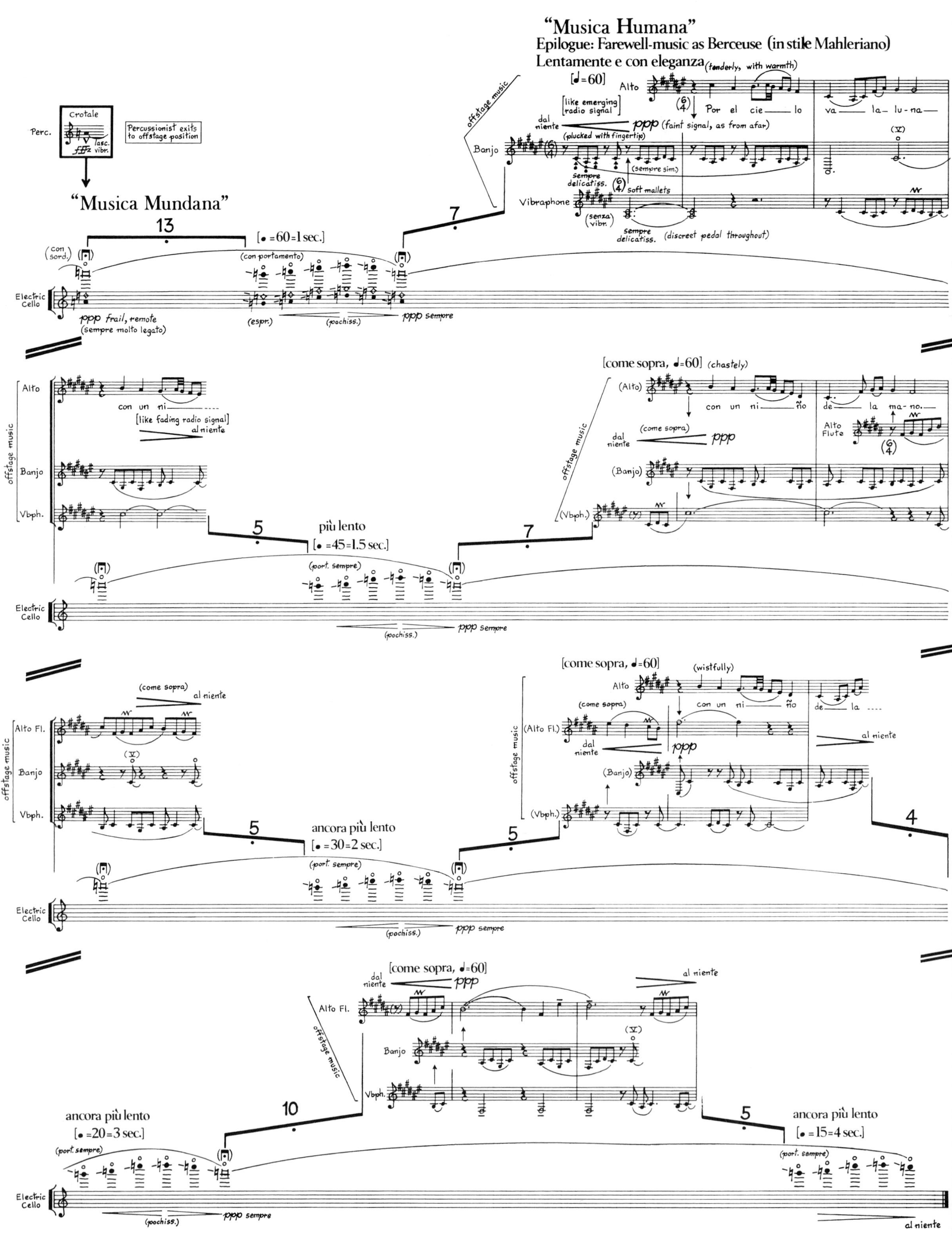

(from *Night of the Four Moons*)

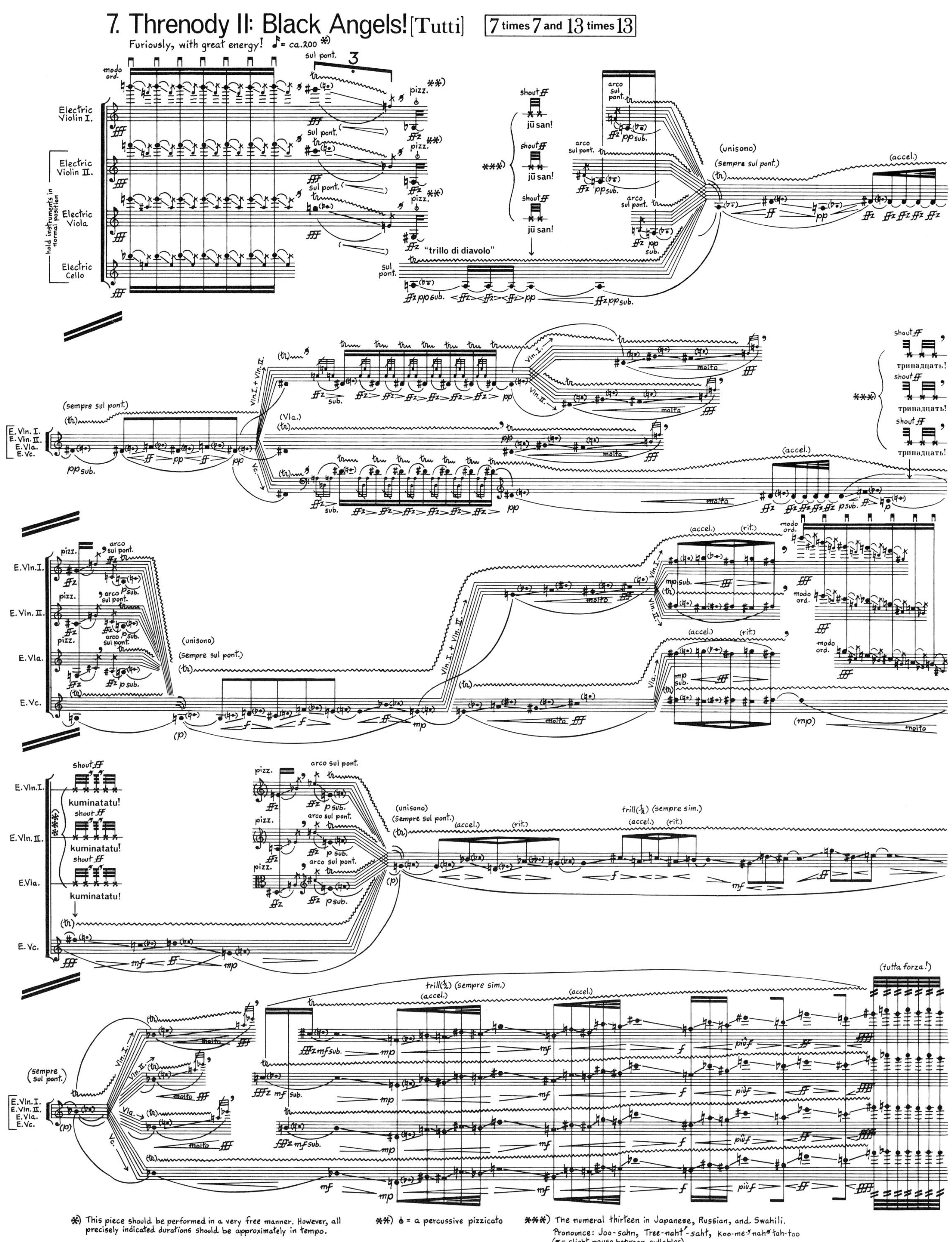

(from *Black Angels*)

(for Jan DeGaetani)

COMMISSIONED BY THE ELIZABETH SPRAGUE COOLIDGE FOUNDATION

Ancient Voices of Children

A CYCLE OF SONGS ON TEXTS BY GARCÍA LORCA

for Soprano, Boy Soprano, Oboe, Mandolin, Harp, Electric Piano and Percussion (Three Players)

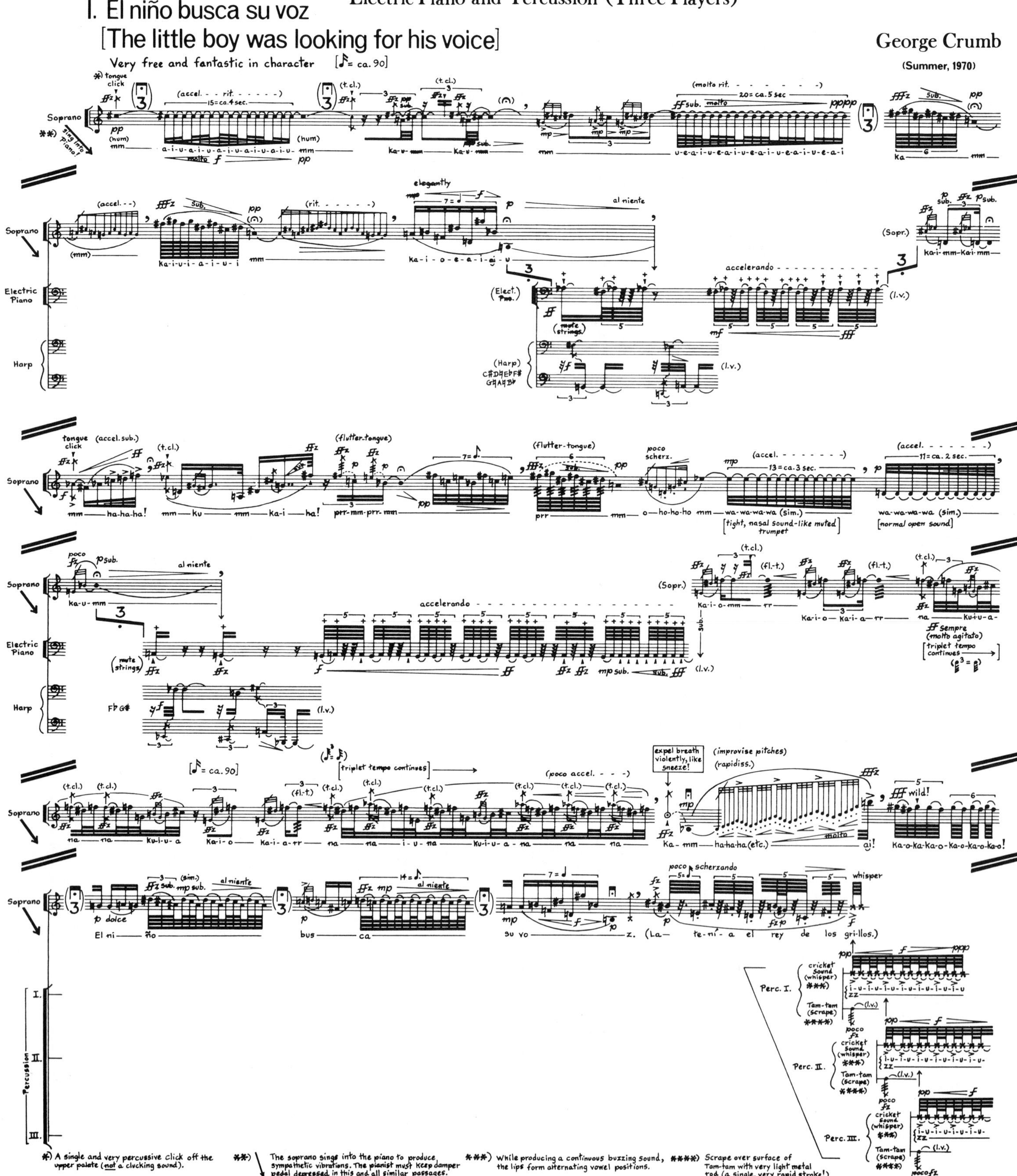

*) A single and very percussive click off the upper palate (not a clucking sound).

**) The soprano sings into the piano to produce sympathetic vibrations. The pianist must keep damper pedal depressed in this and all similar passages.

***) While producing a continuous buzzing sound, the lips form alternating vowel positions.

****) Scrape over surface of Tam-tam with very light metal rod (a single, very rapid stroke!)

for the New York Camerata

VOX BALAENAE

FOR THREE MASKED PLAYERS

(Electric Flute, Electric Cello, and Electric Piano)

George Crumb

Vocalise (..for the beginning of time)

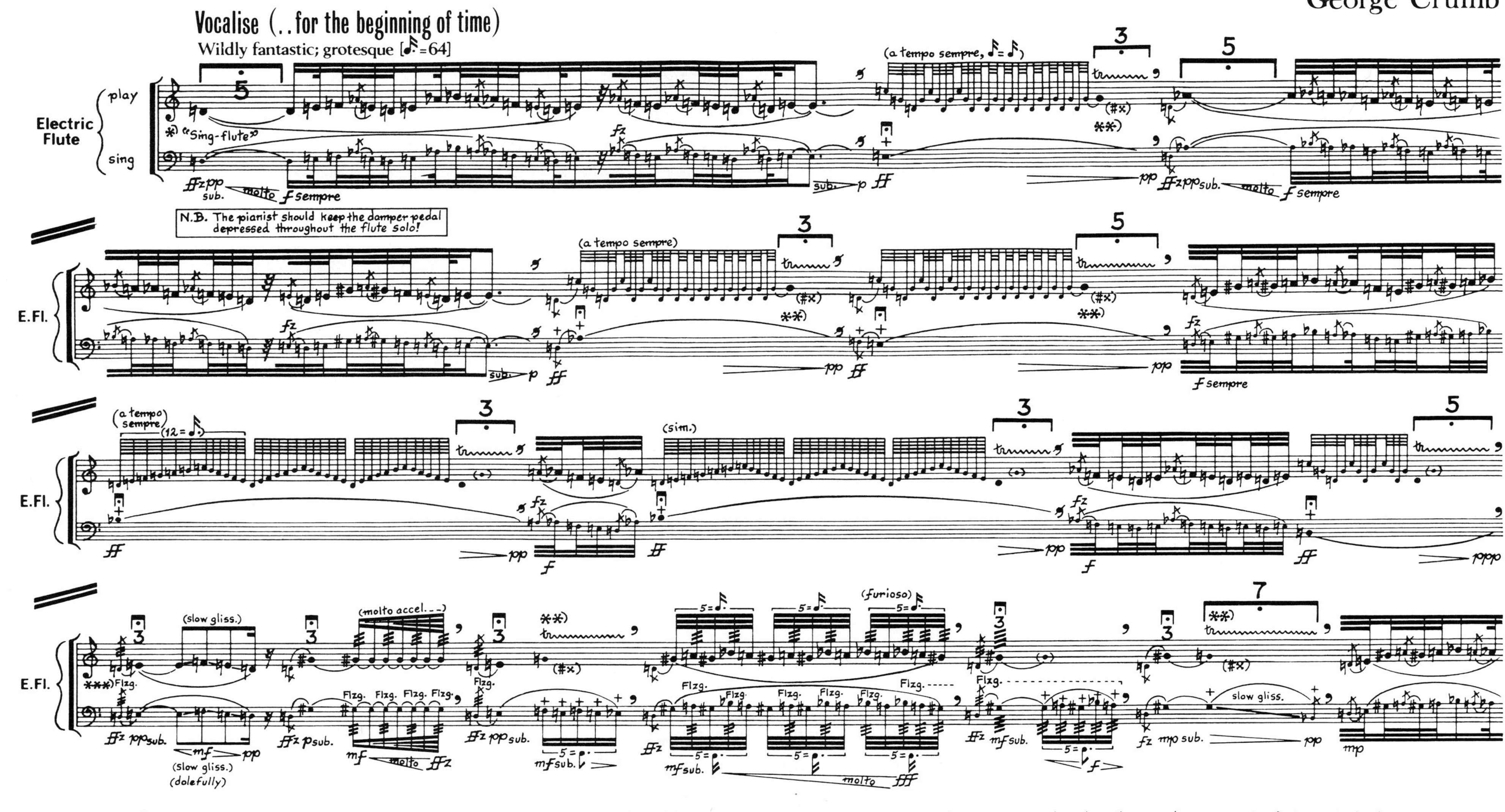

*) The flautist sings while playing! The sung tones and flute tones should be perfectly balanced. Notes marked with the symbol + are to be sung through the flute, i.e. the lips cover mouthpiece so that all tone is projected through the tube. The fingering changes will slightly modify these sung tones, thereby producing a shimmering effect. N.B. If flautist is female the singing should be one octave higher (i.e. in unison with the flute tone).

**) Hold fingering for G♮ while trilling rapidly with the second (lower) D# trill key.

***) Flzg. = flutter-tongue

12. Spiral Galaxy
[SYMBOL]

Aquarius

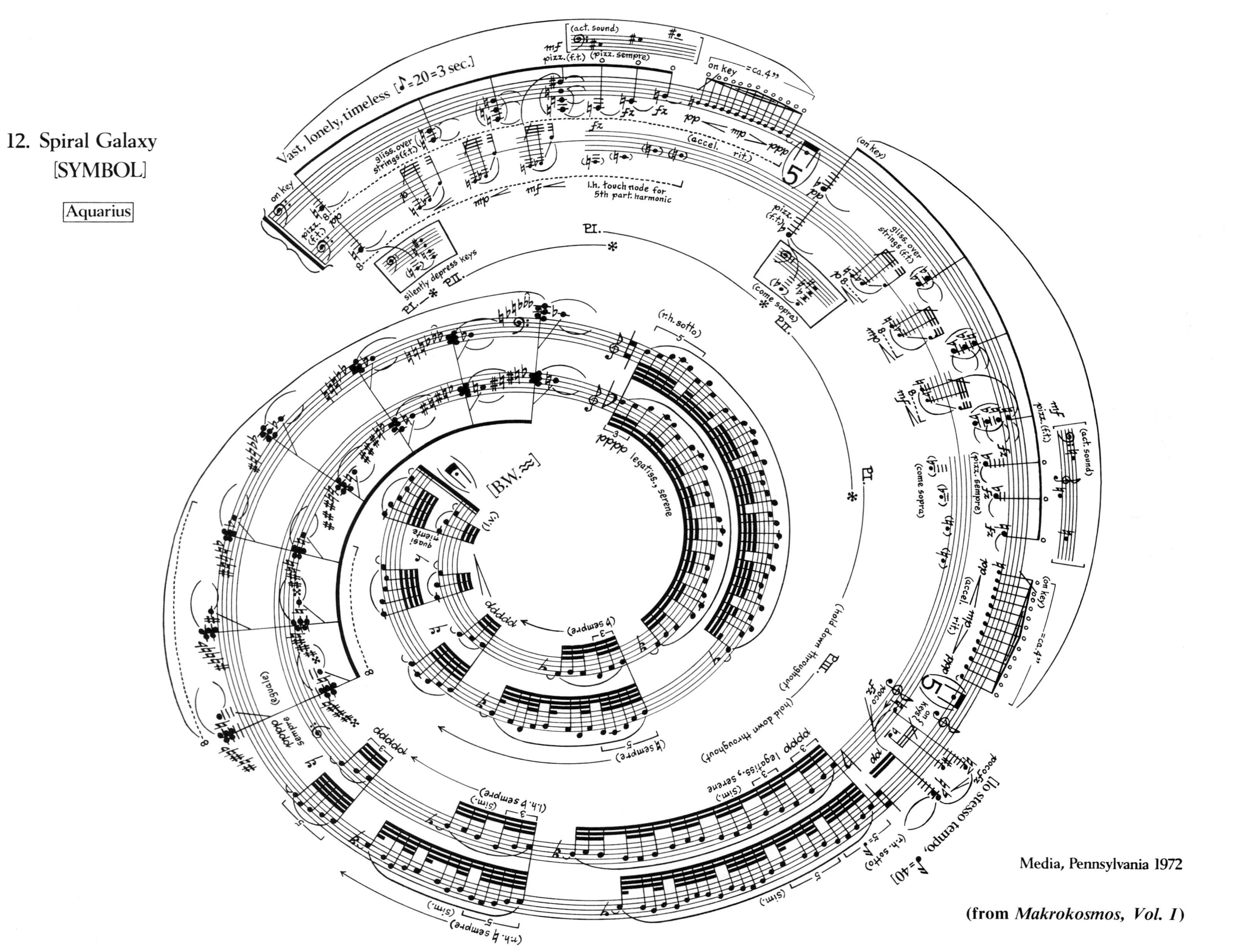

Media, Pennsylvania 1972

(from *Makrokosmos, Vol. I*)

4. Twin Suns (Doppelgänger aus der Ewigkeit)
[SYMBOL]

Gemini

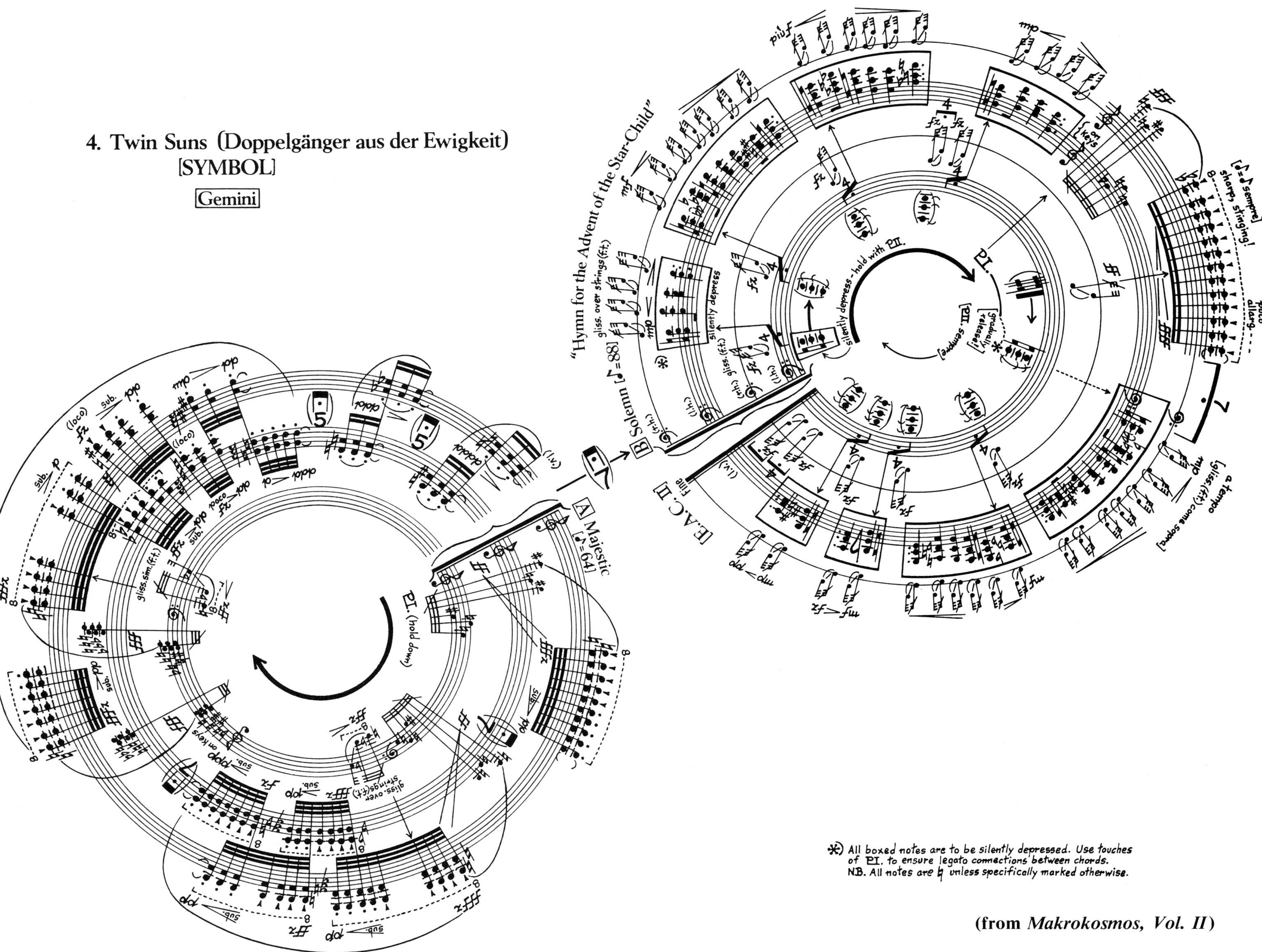

✻ All boxed notes are to be silently depressed. Use touches of PI. to ensure legato connections between chords.
N.B. All notes are ♮ unless specifically marked otherwise.

(from *Makrokosmos, Vol. II*)

Serene, desireless [ancora più lento, ♪=44]

[ancora più lento, ♪=30]

Media, Pennsylvania, 1974

(from *Music for a Summer Evening*)

for David and Peter

STAR-CHILD

A Parable for Soprano, Antiphonal Children's Voices, Male Speaking Choir (& Bell Ringers), and Large Orchestra

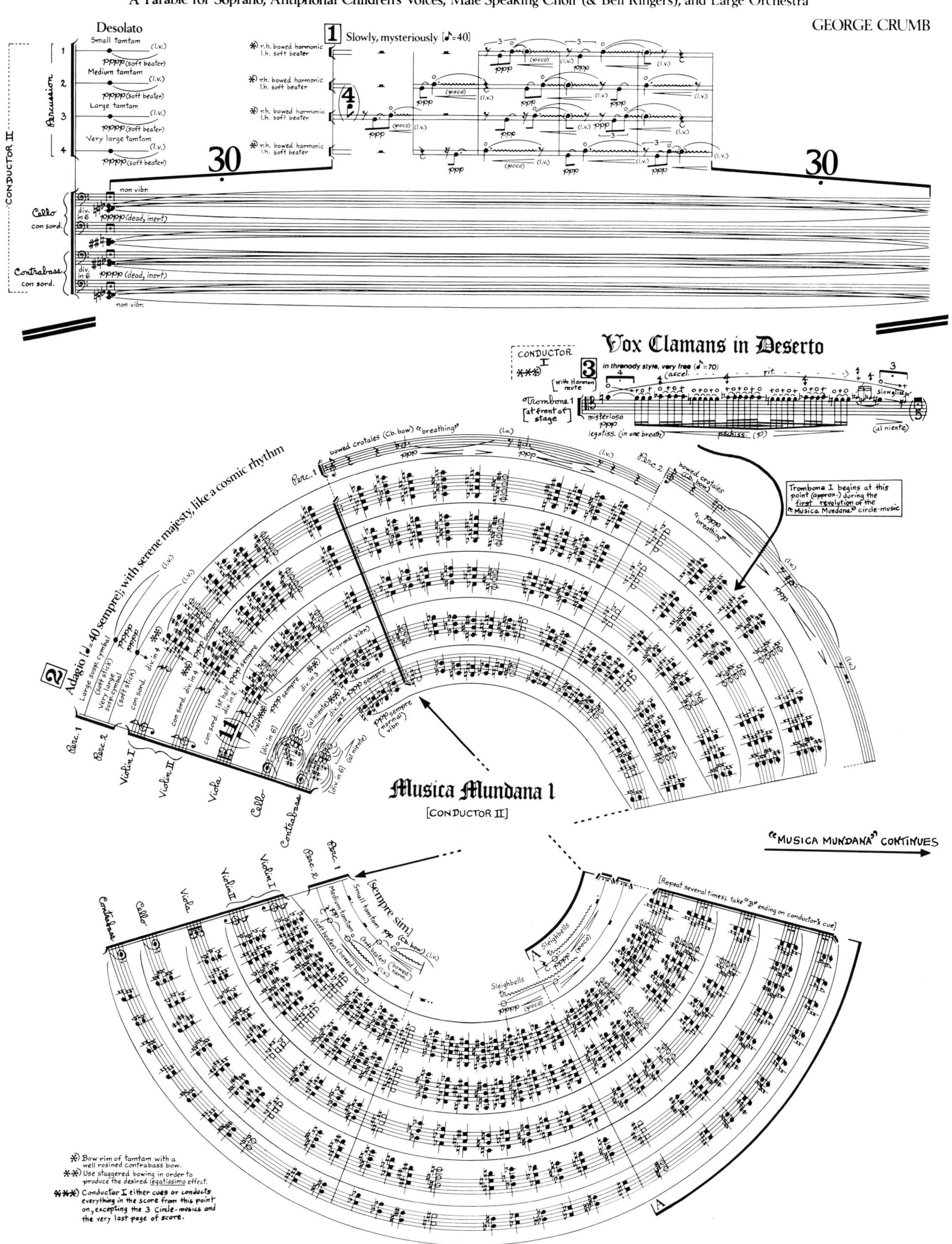

for Jeffrey Jacob

GNOMIC-VARIATIONS

for Piano

GEORGE CRUMB

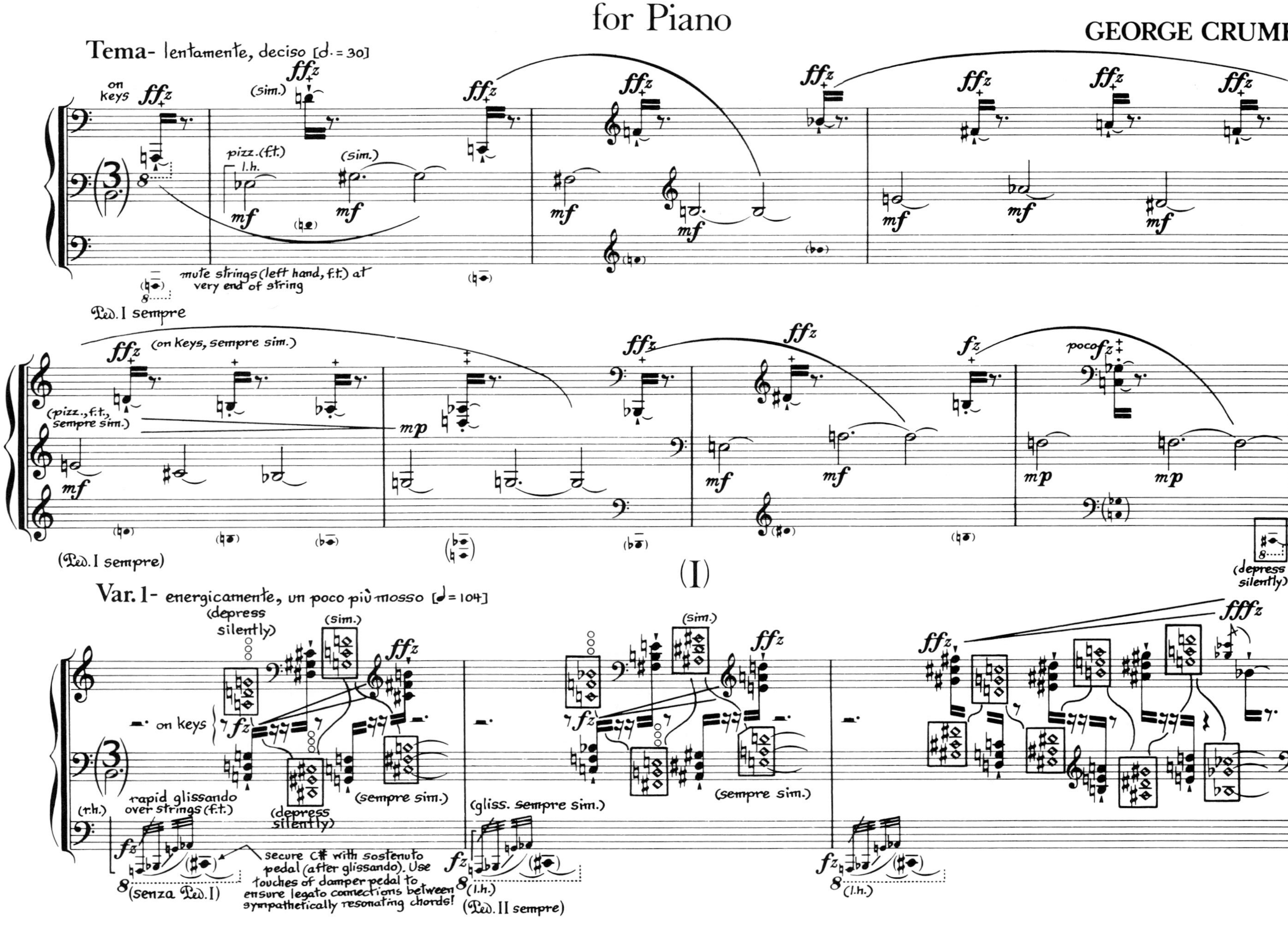

for Gilbert Kalish

PROCESSIONAL

GEORGE CRUMB

Sempre pulsando, estaticamente [♪ = 120]

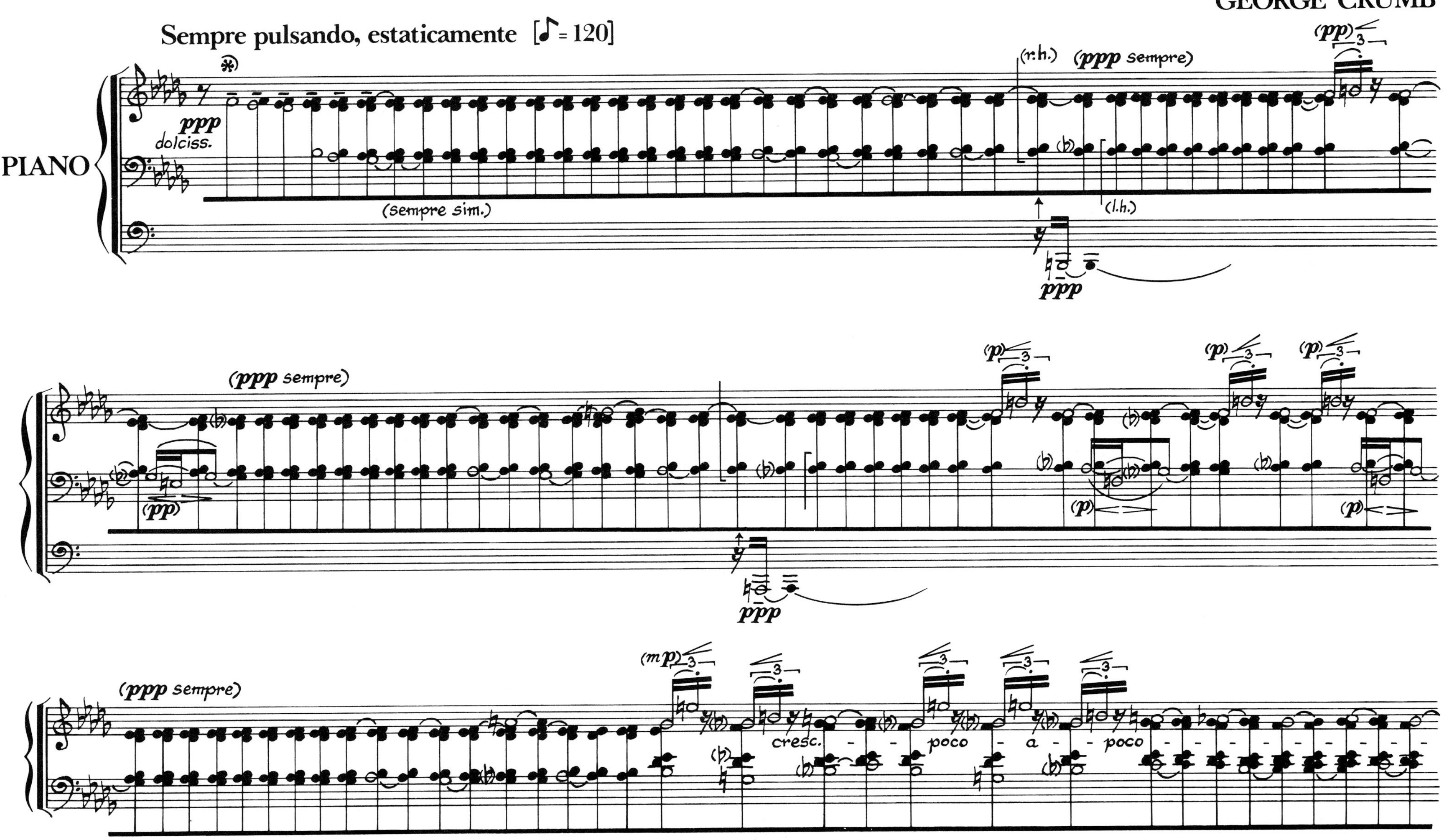

*) White notes should "emerge" from the texture (quasi in rilievo). Motivic groups should always be especially distinct; single notes within the texture should be only very gently emphasized in pianissimo passages, but can come more to the fore in forte passages.

for Arthur Weisberg and the New York Philharmonic Orchestra

A HAUNTED LANDSCAPE

*) The piano should be considerably amplified by means of a conventional microphone positioned over the bass strings. The sound should be projected through 2 speakers positioned at opposite ends of the stage and well forward.

**) The 2 soli contrabassi should alternate throughout by unobtrusively overlapping.

Makrokosmos I and *II*: A Case Study of George Crumb's Compositional Process

Christopher Wilkinson

In 1972, George Crumb completed his *Makrokosmos I*, the first of two volumes of music for amplified piano. *Makrokosmos II*, its companion volume, followed a year later in 1973. Each volume consists of twelve pieces divided into three equal groups, and the two works, taken together, represent Crumb's most substantial contribution to the solo piano genre. These collections originated in the composer's wish to create, in his own words, "an all-inclusive technical work" utilizing "all conceivable techniques."

The *Makrokosmos* volumes are typical of Crumb's music, exhibiting traits that have become virtually synonymous with his style. Not only is the instrument amplified by means of an adjacent microphone (to help project very delicate sounds and also to create a "larger than life" effect in *forte* passages), but in addition, the performer is required to play both at the keyboard and in the piano's interior, plucking, strumming, or drumming on the strings and rapping on the metal crossbeams of the instrument. Additional timbral effects are achieved by the placing of metal chains and sheets of paper on the strings or by having the pianist use a percussionist's wire brush, a paper clip, or metal thimbles to activate the tone. The soloist is even called upon to sing or whistle melodic fragments and to intone a sequence of phonetic syllables, or chant Latin words in an incantatory style.

Although the purely sonic aspects of Crumb's music have evoked much comment (*Makrokosmos I* and *II can* be seen as *compendia* of the "extended piano" techniques of our time), these works also show an exceptionally wide range of compositional approaches and expressive genres. Contemporary chromatic idioms, tonality, modality, and whole-tone elements are magically synthesized to create a multi-dimensional harmonic language. Crumb's inventiveness in rhythm, texture, and melodic structure culminates in this music. *Makrokosmos*, in fact, represents a virtual synopsis of the composer's very original style.

These works are by no means the first examples of a composer's stylistic resumé. Among the best known prototypes are the two volumes of J.S. Bach's *Well-Tempered Clavier*. From Bach's collections of preludes and fugues in all keys, one may trace a line of descent through Chopin's *Preludes*, Opus 28, consisting of 24 pieces, to Debussy's two books of *Preludes*, each containing 12 pieces. In notes made early during the composition of his *Makrokosmos*, Crumb cited Debussy's *Preludes* as a model—an influence reflected partly by the fact that both works have an identical number of pieces.

The title *Makrokosmos* was suggested by *Mikrokosmos*, Béla Bartók's six-volume collection of piano studies. Though more obviously didactic, Bartók's collection nonetheless belongs to the same tradition as the other forerunners to Crumb's music. Its 153 separate pieces seem to represent a summation of Bartók's language in respect to style, compositional technique, and exploration of the piano's idiomatic resources.

Since the *Makrokosmos* volumes occupy a critically important position in Crumb's catalog, a study of these works will enable us to understand more clearly his approach to the craft of composition (and the thought process behind that approach) and perhaps even offer clues to the evolution of his very personal musical language. We can observe the genesis of these volumes in the nearly 150 pages of Crumb's sketches and drafts which were the product of two years of work, beginning in 1971. For convenience sake, this material may be divided into three groups: (I) The sketches and drafts for the various pieces constituting *Makrokosmos I*; (II) those for *Makrokosmos II*; (III) a series of outlines which record the composer's development of the final overall design of each volume. So important, conceptually, is the internal organization of each volume, that we must first consider the evolution of that organization as reflected in those outlines.

Crumb's original conception for *Makrokosmos* differs considerably from the final version. Initially he planned to compose three volumes, each containing ten pieces. It is clear that he gradually began to narrow his focus, as a later plan contains well-developed outlines for the first two volumes, but only minimal annotations for the third. As Crumb's planning continued, he presented the third volume in outline only once more. To this he later appended the annotation "Volume III a possibility for later composition?!" Subsequently, Crumb did in fact compose a third work in the series, the *Music for a Summer Evening*, scored for two pianos and percussion and using material originally intended for the concluding movements ("Epilogues") of Volumes I and II. However, since *Makrokosmos III* differs considerably from the solo volumes in scale, architecture, and compositional intent, we shall turn our attention exclusively to the earlier two works.

Crumb began to compose several of the individual pieces of *Makrokosmos* even as he was developing his overall architecture. He began at least two pieces in July of 1971, including the one ultimately entitled "The Mystic Chord" (*Makrokosmos II* #2). However, he did not finish the final designs for the volumes until February, 1972. The composer has stated that he attaches special significance to the "psychological curve" of each volume—to the broad dramatic contour to which each piece will in turn contribute either increasing tension or gradual release. Thus, while he may have tentatively sketched and arranged material for an individual piece, and defined its formal context, he postponed the final version until he had determined its proper place within each volume.

Progress towards an appropriate architectural design for the two volumes can be traced through no fewer than eleven charts on which the composer mapped his thoughts. During this part of the compositional process, Crumb changed the number of pieces to be included in each volume from ten (nine pieces plus an Epilogue) to thirteen (twelve plus an Epilogue) (Illustration 1). Later, when he decided to use the Epilogues' music in another volume entirely, he settled on twelve pieces as the appropriate number for both *Makrokosmos I* and *II*.

As the number of pieces varied, so also did other aspects of the ground-plan. The pieces were grouped to give the performer the option of playing only a portion of either volume. The size of these groupings changed as the number of pieces changed: from three groups of three pieces, to four groups of three, to, finally, three groups of four. Only in the final draft of the overall design did Crumb replace his working title "Fantasy Pieces" with the present title "Makrokosmos." Previously, "Makrokosmos I" had served as the title of the third piece of the first volume, while "Makrokosmos

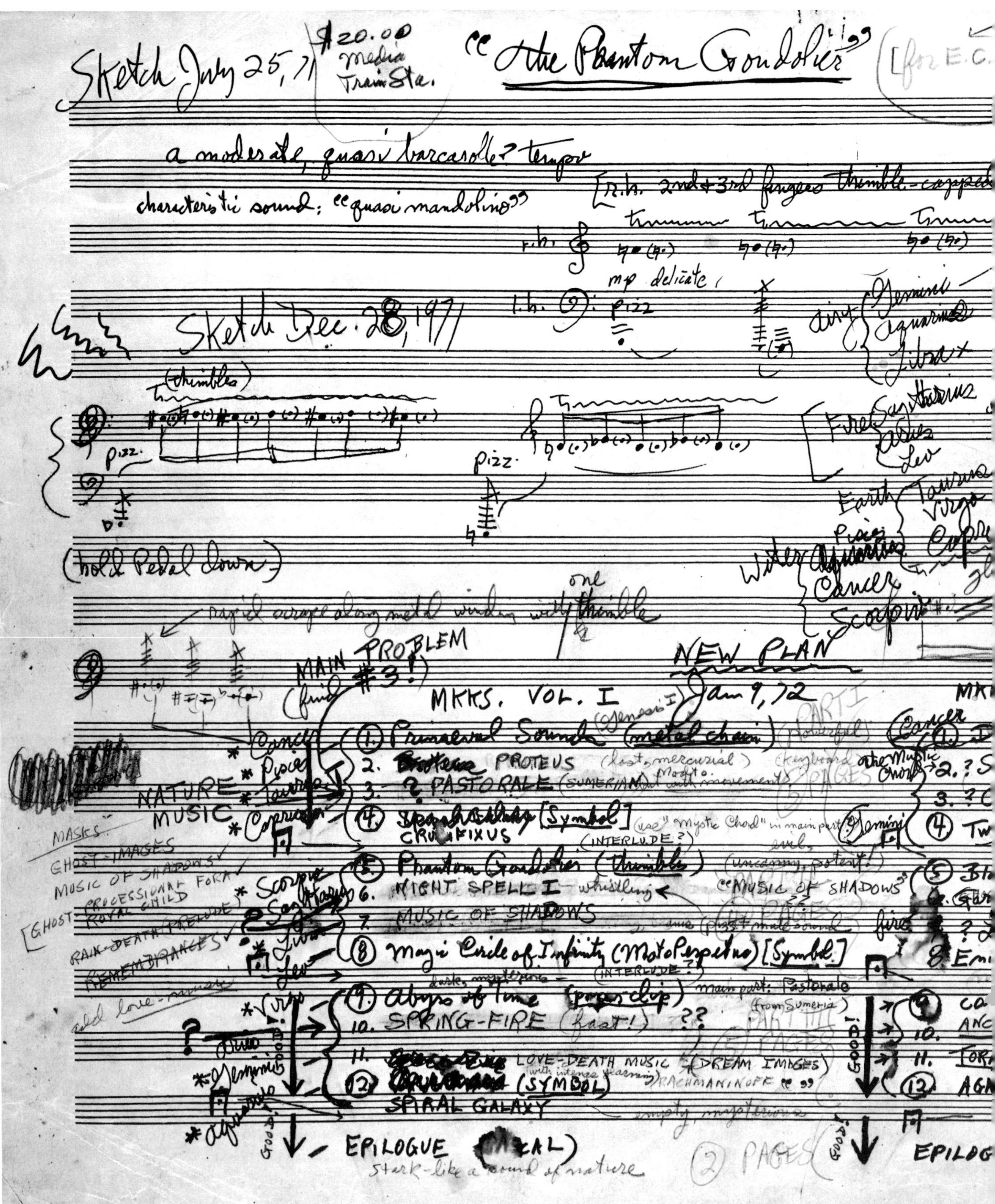
Sketch July 25, 71
$20.00 media Train Sta.
"The Phantom Gondolier"
a moderate, quasi barcarolle? tempo
characteristic sound: "quasi mandolino"
r.h. 2nd + 3rd fingers thimble-capped
r.h.
l.h.
mp delicate
pizz
Sketch Dec. 28, 1971
(thimbles)
pizz.
airy
Gemini
Aquarius
Libra
Fire
Sagittarius
Aries
Leo
Earth
Taurus
Virgo
Capricorn
Water
Pisces
Cancer
Scorpio
(hold Pedal down)
rapid scrape along metal winding with thimble
one
MAIN PROBLEM
(find #3!)
NEW PLAN
Jan 9, 72
MKKS. VOL. I
1. Primeval Sounds (Genesis I) (metal chain)
2. PROTEUS (fast, mercurial)
3. ? PASTORALE (SUMERIAN)
4. CRUCIFIXUS [Symbol] (INTERLUDE?)
use "Mystic Chord" in main part
5. Phantom Gondolier (thimbles) (uncanny, potent!)
6. NIGHT SPELL I whistling
"MUSIC OF SHADOWS"
7. MUSIC OF SHADOWS
8. Magic Circle of Infinity (Moto Perpetuo) [Symbol] (INTERLUDE?)
main part: Pastorale (from Sumeria)
9. Abyss of Time (paper clip)
10. SPRING-FIRE (fast!) ??
11. LOVE-DEATH MUSIC (DREAM IMAGES)
12. (SYMBOL)
SPIRAL GALAXY
RACHMANINOFF " "
empty, mysterious
EPILOGUE
stark - like a sound of nature
(2) PAGES
NATURE MUSIC
MASKS
GHOST-IMAGES
MUSIC OF SHADOWS
PROCESSIONAL FOR A ROYAL CHILD
[GHOST
RAIN-DEATH PRELUDE
REMEMBRANCES
GOOD
PART I
PART II
PAGES
MKKS
EPILOG

1)

1) Sketch of the ground-plan of *Makrokosmos*.

II" identified the eighth piece of the second. During one stage of composition, the composer had entitled each volume "The Mysterious Universe: 13 'Fantasy Pieces' for Piano." Later, "Makrokosmos" identified the Epilogues, at that time the thirteenth piece of each volume. Each Epilogue was associated with a literary quotation: Volume I with an excerpt from the *Pensées* of Blaise Pascal, Volume II with a quotation from Ranier Maria Rilke. The composer later transplanted these quotations, along with their associated musical material, to *Music for a Summer Evening* (*Makrokosmos III*).

During this time Crumb decided upon the character and locations of symbolically notated movements such as "Spiral Galaxy," "Crucifixus," and "The Magic Circle of Infinity," each of which employs the striking graphic notation for which he later became well-known. In addition, he changed the titles and locations of pieces from plan to plan. All of this work was directed towards the shaping of his "psychological curve."

In composing the individual pieces, Crumb was similarly preoccupied with formal perfection, as a study of the sketch material makes abundantly clear. In an article about him published in *Musical America*, he remarks that "the sophisticated forms are no longer viable . . . but the primitive forms are still workable."[1] As students of Crumb's music are aware, clearly delineated formal structures, often quite simple ones, are a basic element of his style. In constructing his "primitive forms," Crumb relies on a number of self-contained but potent motives which must serve as the basic building blocks of the musical structure. The "crystallization" of these basic motivic cells and their logical sequence are problems which are tackled in the sketching process.

The raw material of *Makrokosmos I* and *II* may be divided into two categories. The first consists of fragmentary and isolated motives, textures, and harmonic structures, as well as brief memoranda about the desired ambience of each piece, its appropriate sonority, and its relationship both to adjacent pieces and to the whole volume. Such material may be identified strictly as "sketches." The second category consists of subsequently written "continuity drafts," as we might identify them, in which the composer began the task of arranging and developing in a formal setting his previously sketched ideas. These drafts are rarely complete in their earliest versions, however. They customarily contain open spaces separating the initial and concluding measures, which had usually been completed first. One encounters one or more motives set down within the open spaces to serve as the composer's "landmarks" or intermediate goals directing him to the next goal. No matter how diverse the musical materials become, Crumb's procedure remains the same throughout the twenty-four pieces of *Makrokosmos*.

Crumb followed his initial "continuity drafts" with more finished ones that contain few, if any interruptions in the sequence of musical ideas. While he may add, alter, or drop an occasional bar, he will otherwise leave the piece virtually intact. Often in the second or (rarely) third continuity draft, one sees evidence that the composer was already thinking ahead to the final "fair copy" which would be used for the published facsimile edition. For instance, an arrow in red ink may link the beginning of a particular bar to the note "start 3rd system." Reference to the published score reveals that, as Crumb had indicated, the third system of that piece *does* begin at that point.

Although George Crumb believes that serious creative work depends on a routine of daily work sessions, his teaching schedule necessarily limits his time during the academic term. Thus, it is not surprising that the most sustained and dramatic progress on *Makrokosmos* occured during the summer and Christmas vacation periods. Such was the case in late July, 1971, when he began to sketch four pieces of Volume I: the first sketch of "Proteus" (#2) is dated July 21, that of "Night-Spell I" (#6), July 24, and those of "Music of Shadows" (#7) and "The Magic Circle of Infinity" (#8), July 25.

The sketch and drafts of "Proteus," on which we will concentrate our attention, provide representative examples of Crumb's compositional process at different stages. The three stages are reflected in (1) a sketch, (2) an incomplete draft, and (3) a finished version on which Crumb could trace the final copy of this piece as it appears on pages 7 and 8 of the printed edition of *Makrokosmos I* (Edition Peters 66539a).

The first sketch (Illustration 2) shows the earliest stage of work on the piece. Crumb formulated several different components of "Proteus" at this time: tempo, form, the primary melodic material, and the "ambience" (provided by sympathetically vibrating bass strings). A survey of all of Crumb's *Makrokosmos* sketches indicates that he worked from the top of the page down, breaking off work when progress had stopped. With that normative process in mind, one can deduce that tempo and sonority were the germinal ideas for the piece. We first read "prestissimo scherzo. . . everything 4/♪ ? = fast (or 4/♪ ?)" in the top margin of the manuscript. Crumb immediately decided that 4/♪ was preferable: it appears at the beginning of the three-stave system, together with a notation for the silently depressed forearm cluster.

To the right of the clefs and cluster appear three melodic fragments evenly distributed along the top system. These motives must have represented the most important elements of the piece, for they appear in this first sketch in a more finished form than any of the other ideas seen lower down on the page. Each is given a metrical context: while the first and third occupy single measures, the middle one is distributed over parts of two measures. Labelled by Crumb *A*, *B*, and *C*, these motives are markedly distinct from each other. *A* is a linear idea containing thirteen pitches; *B* consists of the reiterated pitch g′, ornamented by its adjacent semitones transposed up one octave;[2] *C* is an example of one of the composer's well-known notational devices, a written-out accelerando, involving in this case a chordal figure, in which the chord loses a pitch with each repetition. It is interesting that only the "gesture" is outlined—the specific pitches are not yet fixed.

Although these three motives clearly constitute the essence of "Proteus," the composer instinctively realized that additional, albeit subordinate, elements would be needed to flesh out the composition. A survey of the rest of this sketch page shows three new ideas, sketched in bold strokes, and subsequently identified as *D*, *E*, and *F*. Motive *E* is of special interest not only because of its singular occurence in "Proteus," but also because of its derivation from the rhythm and contour of *A*.

Several other motivic fragments occupy the periphery of this middle portion of the sketch. At the left, just below the cluster, is a brief, lightly sketched idea with the caption, "2nd bar?." Despite the tentative character of the handwriting, this idea does eventually appear in the second measure of the piece, where it functions like a consequent to the antecedent *A*. Balancing it, on the extreme right of the page, are two ideas: the first, seen above and to the right of *E*, disappears from later drafts; the second, directly below the conclusion of *E* presents the trill figure found in measures 10 and 39 of the final version.

At the bottom of the page, Crumb made a provisional outline of the structure of "Proteus" by arranging the six principal motives of his sketch (identified by their letters *A* to *F*). While even at this stage he wished to create a logical order for his material, Crumb consciously avoided making a Procrustean bed of incompatible motives. That he regarded the arrangement as tentative is made very clear by the question mark after the word "form" and also by the cross-outs and reworkings of the sequence of letters. The incompleteness of the later draft shows even more clearly that Crumb had not yet made a permanent commitment to a definite design. Despite the fact that there were many loose ends to tie up, he must have decided that the material in this sketch showed promise—a fact borne out by his comment in red at the right: "Good sketch."

The two pages of the first continuity draft (Illustration 3) are no less revealing of Crumb's procedures than the "Good sketch" of July 21, 1971. Undated but identified in the upper left as the "2nd Draft," it clearly shows that despite obvious progress, much work remained. A brief comparison with the earlier sketch shows that the bass forearm cluster now has specific limits. Crumb has revised the performance direction to "Very fast; volatile, Protean," and begun to consider the appropriate metronome mark.

In this draft, Crumb was immediately concerned with delineating the physical space "Proteus" would occupy. After having laid out six systems over two pages as the probable format, he filled in a concluding pair of measures (these measures, however, do *not* conclude the piece in the final draft) and worked further on the opening measures. Crumb has stated that he often will "frame the musical canvas" before attempting to articulate the form of a piece in any detail.

The first twelve measures of this draft include Motive *A* (with the added second measure) along with Motives *B* and *C*, but not in the order outlined in the sketch. The eighth and ninth measures, which contain variants of *A* and *B*, have been crossed out and replaced by two measures of rest. The resultant extension of the top system into the margin strongly suggests that Crumb set down Motive *C* (seen in the draft at the beginning of the second system) before he revised the preceding measures, for he drew it in carefully with a ruler, and added dynamic and other expressive indications. This motive must have been the composer's first intermediate goal in the formal direction of the piece. Perhaps Crumb also crossed out the fourth measure at this time (the second continuity draft shows a full measure's rest at this point—the second of two such measures). He may have decided to preface Motive *C* with two measures of silence because he had already placed rests in measures 3 and 4, or perhaps his procedure was the reverse. In any case, the prevalence of rests allows the echoing sympathetic resonances to emerge more perceptibly.

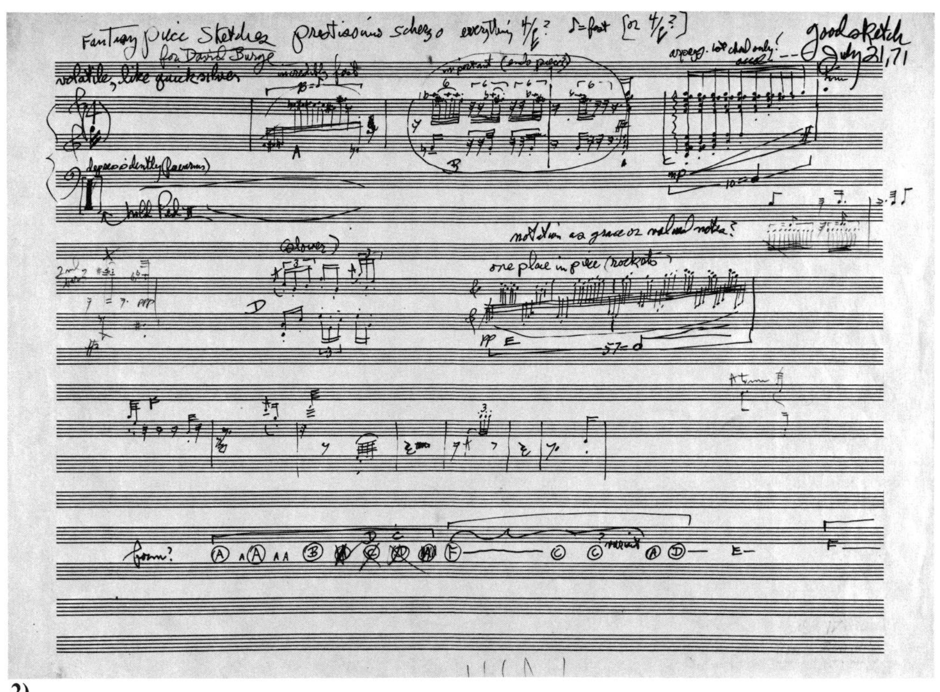

2)

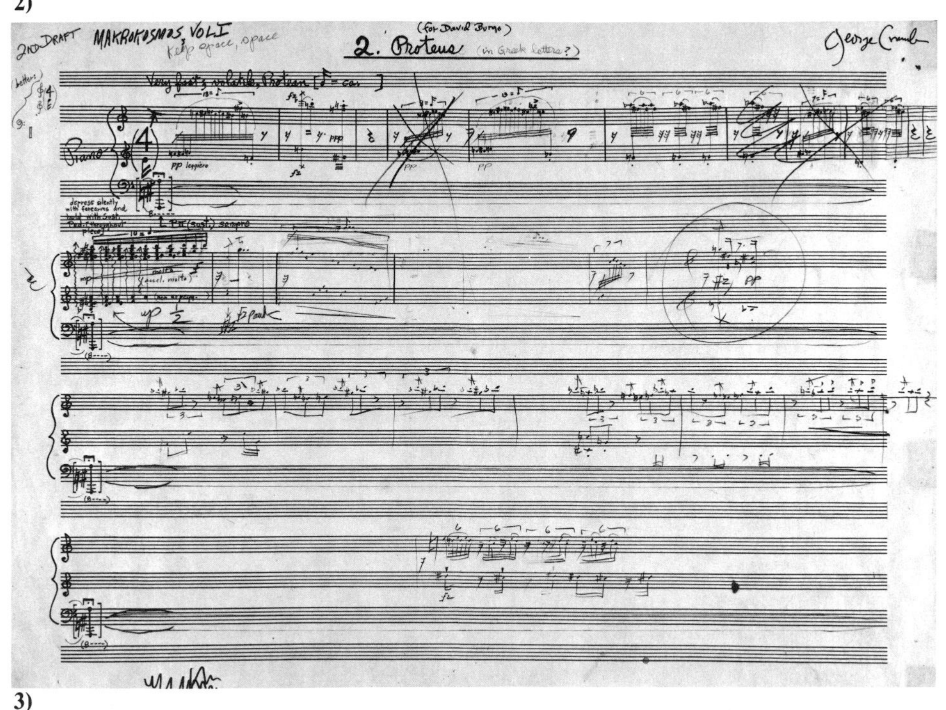

3)

4)

2) First sketch of "Proteus."

3,4) "Continuity draft" of "Proteus."

5)

5,6,7) Second "continuity draft" of "Proteus."

6)

7)

After Motive *C* and the following trill-figure (unlabelled in the sketch), Crumb found progress on "Proteus" more difficult. The third measure of the second system contains another idea: a descending figure possibly derived from Motive *A*, but never completed. The contents of the next two measures were erased. Another, shorter variant of Motive *A* then follows, after which a variant of measure 2 appears. This variant, drawn in haste with its own pair of treble clefs and encircled in red, appears as an intruder in the draft. The remaining two materials on the first page are an extended version (later rejected) of Motive *D* and, on the bottom system, Motive *B*. Crumb appears now to be breaking off the draft, with the problem of continuity unresolved.

The second page suggests the uncertainty even more dramatically. Though we see below a very complete extended version of Motive *E*, we also see that Crumb's work on other pieces of *Makrokosmos* may have distracted him from the completion of "Proteus." The few notes on the top staff at the left will eventually appear at the beginning of "Music of Shadows (for Aeolian Harp)," the seventh piece of Volume I. References also appear to three other pieces being composed simultaneously: "Love-Death" (later retitled "Dream Images"), "Night-Spell," and "Spring-Fire."

This intermediate draft of "Proteus" is undated. Later drafts of "Music of Shadows" and "Night-Spell," dated July 28, 1972, suggest that an entire year passed between the earliest sketching and the final drafting of these pieces and we can assume that the timetable for "Proteus" was no different. Among Crumb's sketches for *Makrokosmos* appears a log of his activities from April to July, 1972. It shows that this was a time of intense work on both solo volumes as well as on *Music for a Summer Evening*. He finished the final drafts of Volume I that summer, working on several of the pieces concurrently, as had been his procedure with the earlier sketches.

The second draft of "Proteus" (Illustration 4) more clearly deserves the title "continuity draft" than the first, although it is by no means a "fair copy." In this draft, Crumb worked intensely on the purely formal aspects of the composition. One sees that he was now also at work on the volume as a whole: the first page of "Proteus" is actually the second page of a six-page fascicle containing continuity drafts of the first four compositions of *Makrokosmos I*: "Primeval Sounds (Genesis I)," whose conclusion appears above the beginning of "Proteus" (Illustration 4, page 1); "Proteus" itself; "Pastorale (from the Kingdom of Atlantis, ca. 10,000 B.C.)"; and the cross-shaped "Crucifixus," the first of the symbolically notated pieces.

As in the first continuity draft, Crumb carefully laid out the opening and closing sections of "Proteus." The first page of Illustration 4 contains the first ten measures (with the revisions of the previous draft); the second page shows the continuation from measures 11 to 38, at which point the music breaks off. So close is this material to Crumb's final version, both in content and distribution on the page, that all his reworkings seem at first glance to represent a kind of "worrying" of the text, with no further substantive changes appearing. A closer examination reveals that this "fine tuning" had a point.

After the second measure of the second page, Crumb considered inserting a measure's rest, which would, in effect, displace the next four measures. He then debated deleting the measure of rest following these four measures. In the second system, he crossed out the second measure, eliminating an "echo" of the previous measure and thereby tightening the composition. Revising further, he struck out the eighth and ninth measures (of the second system). The ninth measure was then reinstated and the eighth was recast with alternate material (sketched in above and below the system). To remind himself of these revisions when later preparing the final ink copy, he numbered the sixteen measures starting from the inserted measure of rest after measure 12 and concluding at the end of the second system.

Even these modifications did not entirely satisfy Crumb. A rethinking of the passage prompted still another numbering of measures, this time in blue pencil. Beginning with the fourth measure of the second system, the new revision covered ten measures, concluding in a measure's rest written in the right margin.

The third system was barely touched. Apart from eliminating the second measure, Crumb merely corrected the figure indicating the number of notes in the four-measure "velocissimo" passage (Motive *E* of the sketch), which now assumed a precise rhythmic duration of a triple-dotted half note.

After drafting the first four measures of the bottom system, Crumb realized that he had overestimated the length of "Proteus." He pencilled in the double barline at the end of this page; however, to avoid the trouble of recopying, he simply drew an arrow in blue pencil to connect the music of this page to the concluding four measures on the following page. With this done, the composition of "Proteus" was finished.

As his sketch and drafts reveal, George Crumb's compositional method involves a slow and laborious struggle to achieve "significant form." Even though his music projects an aura of spontaneity (and can even sound improvisatory), close analysis shows a logical and organic structure based on "classical" principles. He is concerned with elegantly shaped phrases, properly balanced proportions, and clear distinctions between expository, developmental, transitional, and recapitulatory functions. His insistence on the highest degree of integration on all levels is evident throughout the sketching process. Although "Proteus," like several of the *Makrokosmos* pieces, might be described superficially as a mosaic design of tiny motivic cells, the critical aspect is the composer's technical command of his materials: these basic cellular ideas are elaborated into seemingly inevitable larger phrases which in turn coalesce into a total form for the piece. And finally, the piece as a unit must function organically within the formal hierarchy of the entire volume.

One sees everywhere that Crumb sought the most concise and economical expression of his ideas. Extraneous materials and redundancies are rigorously excluded and every piece is carefully worked out so that each detail contributes to the whole. Given the extraordinary vitality of the germinal ideas, the result of this process of distillation is music of distinctive character and exceptional quality expressed in a unique musical language.

---

[1]Shirley Fleming, "George Crumb. Musician of the Month," *Musical America* (September, 1968).

[2]Crumb introduced this figure in his *Five Pieces for Piano* (1962).

The Element of Sound in *Night of the Four Moons*

Stephen Chatman

George Crumb's *Night of the Four Moons* for Alto, Alto Flute (doubling Piccolo), Banjo, Electric Cello, and Percussion, manifests his delight in exploring the realm of sound in its manifold aspects—texture, density, dynamics, and most importantly, timbre. Although I am here concerned primarily with these sound elements, I will also discuss certain related stylistic traits including basic pitch structures, rhythmic procedures, structural forms, notation, text and mood.

Night of the Four Moons, composed during the Apollo 11 flight (July 16–24, 1969), is based on fragments dealing with the moon taken from various Federico García Lorca texts. These fragments were carefully chosen and magnificently pieced together to form a four stanza sequence of related lines, each stanza constituting one of the four movements of the work.

The Lorca texts:

I La luna está muerta, muerta; pero rescucita en la primavera.	The moon is dead, dead; but it is reborn in the springtime.
II Cuando sale la luna, el mar cubre la tierra y el corazón se siente isla en el infinito.	When the moon rises, the sea covers the earth, and the heart feels like an island in infinity.
III Otro Adán oscuro está soñando neutra luna de piedra sin semilla donde el niño de luz se irá quemando.	Another obscure Adam dreams neuter seedless stone moon where the child of light will be kindling.
IV "¡Huye luna, luna, luna! Si vinieran los gitanos, harían con tu corazón collares y anillos blancos." "Niño, déjame que baile. Cuando vengan los gitanos, te encontrarán sobre el yunque con los ojillos cerrados." "¡Huye luna, luna, luna! que ya sienta sus caballos." "Niño, déjame, no pises mi blancor almidonado."	"Run away moon, moon, moon! If the gypsies should come, they will make of your heart necklaces and white rings." "Child, let me dance. When the gypsies come, they will find you on the anvil with your little eyes closed." "Run away moon, moon, moon! for I hear now their horses." "Child, leave me, do not step on my starched whiteness."
¡El jinete se acercaba tocando el tambor del llano! Dentro de la fragua el niño tiene los ojos cerrados.	Drumming the plain, the horseman was coming near! Inside the smithy the child has closed his eyes.
¡Por el olivar venían, bronce y sueño, los gitanos! Las cabezas levantadas y los ojos entornados.	Along the olive grove the gypsies were coming, bronze and dream! Heads high and eyes half-closed.
Cómo canta la zumaya, ¡ay, cómo canta en el árbol!	How the owl hoots! Ah, how it hoots in the tree!
Por el cielo va la luna con un niño de la mano.	Through the sky goes the moon holding a child by the hand.

Although the text can be interpreted freely, it certainly conveys a wish to leave the moon inviolate, untouched by man. Translated into terms approximating our modern day sensibilities, the "child" might be seen as symbolizing spacemen or the beginnings of space exploration; the "smithy" (IV; line 15), as the spaceship; the "gypsies" (IV; line 2), as a microcosm of the human race. Lines such as "Child, leave me, do not step on my starched whiteness" (IV; lines 11–12), express this feeling of "violation" in an especially poignant image.

The listener is constantly aware that Crumb's primary emphasis is on sound and, more specifically, timbral exploitation. *Night of the Four Moons* illustrates his strong interest in utilizing many different vocal and instrumental techniques to create a unique world of sound. Crumb, who enjoys improvising and devising new timbral techniques on whatever instruments he can smuggle into his workroom, regards composition as a similar activity—"improvising on paper." Undoubtedly this improvisatory approach adds to the uncontrived and extraordinarily fresh, innovative character of *Night of the Four Moons*.

Aside from coloristic elements, Crumb generally emphasizes rhythm, form, and linear construction but seems less concerned with any elaborate development of pitch and harmony. Although his pitch structures are well organized, they are exceedingly economical and not as complex as those of many other present day composers. In the light of the strong linear emphasis and the predominance of one and two-part structures in *Night of the Four Moons*, vertical or harmonic analysis tends to be unprofitable. One can only cite the frequent use of major ninths, major seconds, octaves (relatively rare in Crumb's music), and unisons, in addition to French augmented sixth chord-types.

Crumb's imaginative, almost *outré*, choice of instrumentation implies in itself a unique coloristic potential—the alto voice, alto flute, piccolo, banjo, and electric cello provide strongly contrasting timbral values. And in addition the composer requires an odd assortment of percussion instruments—Tibetan prayer stones, alto African thumb piano (Mbira), bongo drums, castanets, tambourine, Chinese temple gong and tam-tam. A contact microphone attached to the body of the cello yields the only electronic element in the work. The microphone generates curious tone qualities which complement the sounds produced by the wide variety of cello techniques; moreover, it makes all of the effects clearly audible. Because of his predilection for live performers, Crumb prefers electrifying instruments to using synthesized or computerized sounds.

Crumb's instrumentation is sparse and tenuous throughout nearly the entire work. In Movement I, the texture is never more than two-part, punctuated by an occasional single percussion sound. The many solo passages in this movement alternate three times between alto flute, bongo drums, and alto voice, each developing its own solo material. Movement II, although essentially a quartet consisting of alto voice, alto flute, banjo, and Tibetan prayer stones, has a texture which, again, never exceeds two parts and quite often reduces to one. In Movements III and IV, Crumb for the first time enlarges the texture to three and four parts, which enables him to achieve many beautiful simultaneities of color. Throughout the work he employs the same or slightly varying instrumentation for similar sections (i.e. *A*, *A'*, *A''*) and uses a contrasting instrumentation and texture for each of the other sections (i.e. *B*, *C*, *D*). In this way timbre assists him in the articulation of form.

In addition to his basic palette of colors, Crumb utilizes many unusual timbral effects throughout the work. He employs them in an organized set for the pre-chosen instruments in each movement, thus creating unique and differentiated gestures of sound. Such timbral effects are never used gratuitously, but always function as an integral part of the composition.

†All the musical examples appear at the end of the article.

In Movement I, special effects for the alto flute include a slow, wide vibrato; and the "speak-flute" effect (See Figure 1). The banjo sounds are differentiated timbrally by: metal plectrum *sul pont.*, plectrum *modo ord.*, or plucking with the fingers. Likewise in the electric cello we find: plectrum *sul pont.* or pizz. *modo ord.* Other characteristic sounds are provided by tongue clicks, two-plate finger cymbals (see Figure 2), and Chinese temple gong (see Figure 1). Most of these effects are employed in specific passages, in individual notes or motives, or for the appropriate times, such as between or at the beginnings or ends of ideas. For example, the tongue clicks (see Figure 2) are produced throughout the movement solely by the alto flutist and always occur in the A sections, at the beginning of that particular motive; the Chinese temple gong is struck once during each of the alto solos and in the coda, during the "speak-flute" solo (see Figure 1).

Crumb introduces new timbral effects in Movement II, which, in general, are much softer and more delicate than those in Movement I, but are just as well organized and appropriate to the particular mood. The electric cello quarter-tone trill over an extended *arco sul ponticello* glissando, along with the scraping of a nail over the surface of a tam-tam (see Figure 5), provide an introductory gesture for the movement. The first harmonics to appear in the work, the banjo pizzicato harmonics on A and G, are imitated by the electric cello pizzicato harmonics on E and D (see Figure 3). Other striking timbral elements are the "bottleneck technique" of the banjo (see Figure 4), which results in quarter-tone pitch bending and quarter-tone trills, and the unique indefinite pitched timbre of the Tibetan prayer stones (see Figure 5). At the conclusion of the movement, the prayer stones are imitated by percussive key clicks on the alto flute, produced in a novel manner (by entirely covering the mouthpiece with the mouth in order to yield pitches down to a full octave below the normal range of the instrument).

Crumb does not exploit the timbres of instruments as much in Movement III as in the two previous movements. Although the only effects are flutter-tonguing in the piccolo, "rapid tremolo on D-sharp string (scordatura) with two thimble-capped fingers" in the banjo, and cello and banjo harmonics, Crumb introduces several new percussion instruments and combines them with the principal instruments to produce fresh colors. The movement opens with the unique timbral combination of glockenspiel, piccolo, and African thumb piano mixed with electric cello harmonics. As in the other movements, all of these effects and special instrumental combinations are organized and employed for specific sections: the glockenspiel and piccolo combination, as well as the cello harmonics, appear only in sections *A* and *A′*; the piccolo flutter-tonguing appears only in section *B*.

Timbral effects introduced in Movement IV include electric cello glissandi "with extremely fast tremolo" in sections *A* and *A′*; the striking of the tambourine membrane with a soft stick, the drumming of fingertips on the banjo membrane, and the rapping of knuckles on the body of the cello in sections *B* and *B′*; and in section *C*, at the climactic moment of the entire work, the score calls for the incisive sound of Japanese Kabuki blocks. Again, Crumb associates timbres and special effects with specific sections within the form.

Sensitivity, precision, and contrast characterize Crumb's use of dynamics. For example, Movement I, although predominantly loud, contains sharp contrasts between the strong crescendi of the solo bongo drum passages and the pianissimo alto voice passages, as well as lesser contrasts in the form of diminuendi, crescendi, and variations in dynamic markings within the loud sections (see Figure 2). Markings vary throughout the movement from *pppp* to *ffff*. Attacks are also precisely indicated by sforzando, staccato, and accent markings, and Crumb frequently couples descriptive Italian words to the given dynamic abbreviations, e.g. *sempre*, *deciso*, *subito*, *molto*, *poco*, *meno*, *al niente*, *eco*, and *possibile*. Considering the more gentle second and third movements, the general dynamic spirit of *Night of the Four Moons* might be described as a wide range of delicate soft sounds dominating, but in alternation with an equally wide range of contrasting forceful loud sounds.

Crumb's unique notation is essential to the success of the work. It is neat, clear, precise, at times complex, and above all, innovative. Inasmuch as many sections are unmetered or spatially notated, requiring the performers to see spatial relationships between instruments, it is necessary to read from the complete score. Consequently, the score is large enough to be read easily, completely transposed, and contains "cut-away" measures of rest which make it easier to read. The rhythmic notation is unusual in its preference for small units of measurement and minute beat divisions. Meter denominators are predominantly 𝅘𝅥𝅯 or 𝅘𝅥𝅯., and beat divisions of 𝅘𝅥𝅰, 𝅘𝅥𝅱, and even 𝅘𝅥𝅲 are prevalent. These are often grouped into quintuplets and septuplets, or into *accelerando-ritardando* motives (see Figures 6, 7, and 8). In the "senza misura" sections, rhythms are sometimes very freely notated (see Figures 3,4). Pauses or holds are frequently notated in terms of seconds of time (see Figures 3, 5, and 9). In unmetered or spatial sections, the performers are, at times, assisted by vertical arrows, which indicate exact entrances in relation to other parts (see Figure 3).

Crumb's verbal instructions for the performers are necessarily explicit in order to ensure the realization of his frequently unprecedented timbral effects. He likewise seeks perfection in the realization of the expressive and affective aspects of his musical conception; therefore, many of his instructions concern the prevailing mood and spirit of the music. Examples of this kind are tempo markings such as "Hesitantly, with a sense of mystery" (Movement III), "Lentamente e con eleganza" (Movement IV), and "Boldly, with rhythmic élan" (Movement I). Interpretive directions, directed mostly toward the alto, also demonstrate Crumb's concern for the definitive mood, e.g. "shrill, metallic," "coquettish, sensual," "tenderly, with warmth" (all in Movement IV), and "chastely" (Movement I).

The first movement of *Night of the Four Moons*, "La luna ésta muerta, muerta. . ." ("The moon is dead, dead. . ."), may be used as an example to illustrate Crumb's treatment of form, pitch, and rhythm. The general form is made up of four distinct but related sections, and each section, except section 4, contains three subsections (see Figure 10). Sections 2 and 3 are basically developments and extensions of section 1, while 4 (a short restatement of *A* material and *C* material) serves as a kind of coda, the last phrase, *C‴* (see Figure 1), being the real closing gesture.

The pitch structure of Movement I, as well as of the entire work, is based on the intervals of the tritone, second (usually major), and third. In particular, Crumb bases the movement on the scale G/A/C-sharp/E-flat/G-flat, which contains the G/G-flat (major/minor 3rd step) alternation (see Figures 1 and 2). The *C* sections contain only the basic scale, while the *A* sections contain the basic scale and some of its transpositions. (The *B* sections are of indefinite pitch.)

The first scale transposition F-sharp/G-sharp/C/D/F, superimposed on the original scale, occurs in section 2*A′* (see Figure 11). The second transposition, this time a retrograde-inversion transposition (E-flat/G-flat/A-flat/C/D), occurs in section 3*A″* (see Figure 12). Two pitches later, the melodic interval of a minor second appears for the first time. The pattern which contains it, C/D/F/G-flat/F/D, is developed through the transpositional sequence F-sharp/G-sharp/B/C/B/G-sharp at the climactic moment of the first movement. Section 4*A‴* returns to the original scale and the concluding *C‴* is a simple restatement of it. One additional pitch element—a minor 9/perfect 5 motive (see Figure 13), present throughout the entire work, occurs twice in this movement, although it does not center around any particular pitches.

In Movement I, marked "Boldly, with rhythmic élan [♪. = 92]", the meter denominator [♪.] remains constant, while the numerator varies from section to section. All of the rhythms in the *A* sections can be regarded as developments through fragmentation, augmentation, diminution, and repetition, of the motive in measure 1 (see Figure 2). The unmeasured *B* sections [♪ = ♪] are based primarily on two characteristic motives, ♬ and ♬ . The *C* sections, marked "più lento [♪. = 60]," are characterized by thirty-second note triplet groupings with occasional grace-note decorations. The time signatures of the *C* sections, unlike those of the *A* sections, change with each occurrence (sections C, C′, C″, and C‴ are measured as 5/♪. , 6/♪. , 8/♪. , and 7/♪. , respectively). Another rhythmic idea, introduced in this movement but not fully developed until later movements, is the quintuplet figure, which is sometimes notated as an accelerando (see Figure 8).

Crumb is imaginative and resourceful in his setting of the Lorca texts and fully realizes in musical terms the evocative qualities and vivid imagery implicit in the poetry. The vocal writing, which alternates between syllabic and melismatic styles, is always sensitive to the special phonetic qualities of the Spanish language. Even the notational style seems influenced by the spirit of the poetry: in Movement II ("Languidly, with a sense of loneliness"), the text is set in spatial time duration to project a kind of "suspended" feeling; and in Movement IV ("Intense, breathlessly!"), the vocal line is melodically improvised, conveying a wild, excited mood, appropriate for the line "Run away moon, moon, moon!" Imaginative effects, such as trilled r's, prolonged n's, whispers, hisses, and glissandi, enhance the emotive meaning of the text and help to create an intimate, sensual quality, as in the "Quasi danza spagnola" sections of Movement IV.

Night of the Four Moons is a mixed-media work in that it possesses both visual and dramatic qualities. The composer has recommended a specific seating plan for the performers on the stage; he creates a highly dramatic effect by directing them (in Movement IV) to walk gracefully, one by one, to the single crotale (placed at edge of stage), sharply strike it, and then exit to an offstage position (see Figures 14 and 16). Other dramatic characteristics are the highly stylized "roles" of the child and the moon, sung by the alto (in Movement IV), and the dramatic feelings expressed through the performer's interpretations of Crumb's directions.

The work projects a colorful and exotic Spanish flavor. In addition to the Spanish costume worn by the alto, as directed by Crumb, the music itself is influenced by the spirit and musical sound of the Spanish text. The traditional Spanish Flamenco style is suggested by the inclusion of castanets and tambourine, the extensive use of ♬ and ♬ (in Movement IV), the many embellishments in the vocal writing, and the implications of Phrygian mode (lowered seconds and sevenths) in many passages. The Flamenco style, alluded to throughout the work, becomes especially overt in the "Quasi danza spagnola" music of Movement IV (see Figure 15).

In addition to the Spanish quality, a degree of exotic oriental tone color is evoked by the Tibetan prayer stones, Chinese temple gong, and Japanese Kabuki blocks. African or Afro-American tone colors are represented by the bongo drums, thumb piano (Mbira), and banjo.

Perhaps the most hauntingly beautiful and conceptually most astonishing music in *Night of the Four Moons* occurs in the concluding "apotheosis" section, which, in its metaphysical implications, seems to encapsulate the total sense of the work.* Crumb here presents a simultaneity of two contrasting musics—a "Musica Mundana" (a remote and ethereal quasi-pentatonic music, played by the cellist solely in harmonics), and a "Musica Mundana" (a tonal "in stile Mahleriano" music played offstage by the other performers) (see Figure 16). The "Musica Humana" ("Epilogue: Farewell-music as Berceuse"), which intermittently emerges and fades like a "radio signal," is couched in the tonality of F-sharp Major. The composer has indicated that this tonality was chosen because of its association with Haydn's "Farewell Symphony," in which the performers, as also in this work, leave the stage one by one until the piece has ended. After the last fragile statement of the "stile Mahleriano" music, the static "Musica Mundana," which has already been sustained in the background for several minutes, provides an eerie and extraordinarily effective conclusion to the work.

In all of his compositions—among which I consider *Night of the Four Moons* to be unsurpassed—Crumb stands in the forefront of those composers who are profoundly involved in the exploration of the sound-dimension. George Crumb's creative gift and painstaking craft have produced musical sounds more striking and beautiful than those most other composers have been able to achieve through electronic or improvisatory techniques. He has developed his own unique musical style and language while maintaining a strong link with musical and humanistic tradition.

---

*See Music Plate, page 44

This article originally appeared in *Music and Man* (June, 1974), and is here reprinted, with revision, by kind permission of Gordon and Breach Science Publishers Ltd.

1)

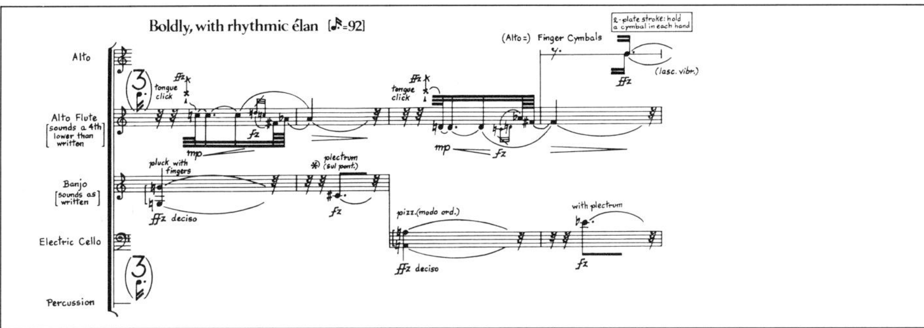

2)

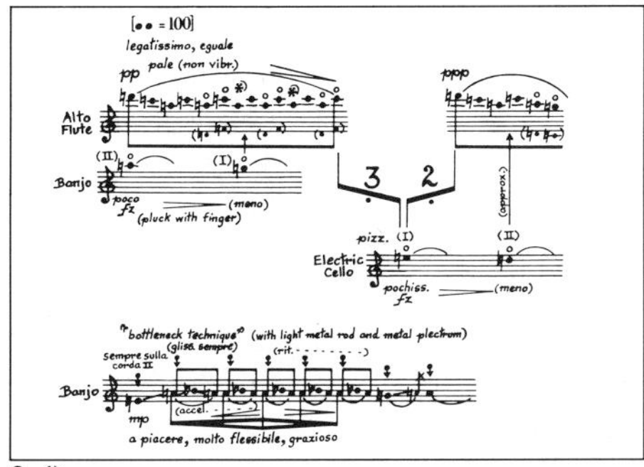

3,4)

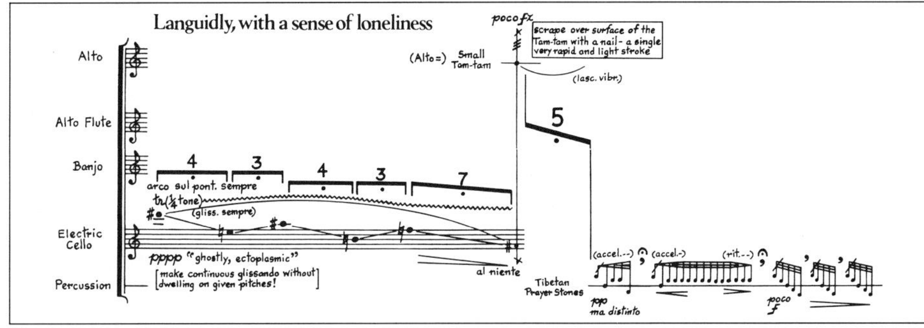

5)

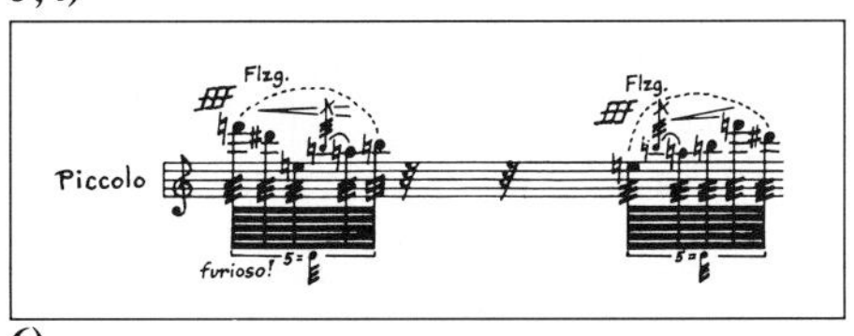

6)

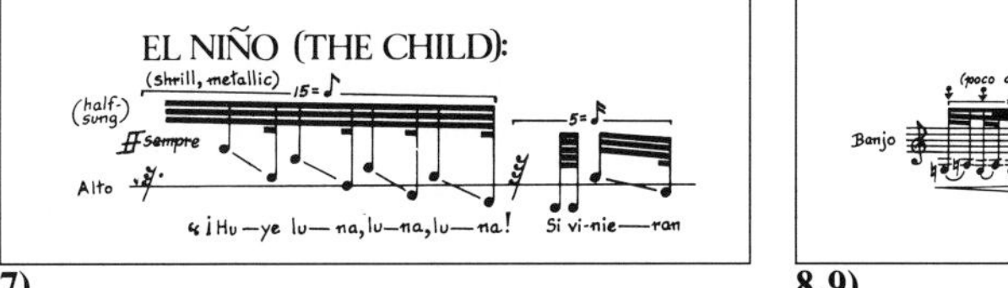

7)

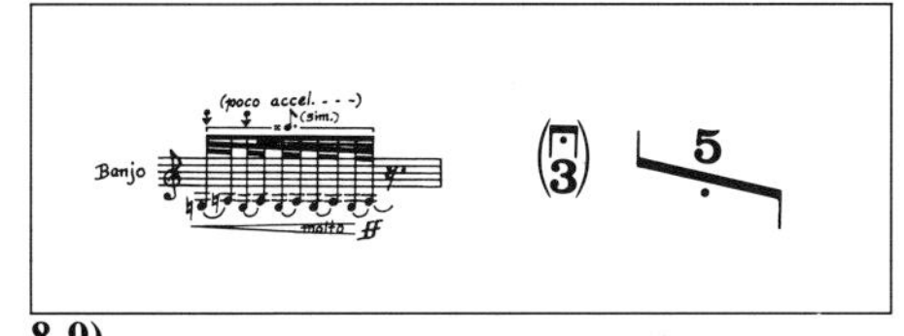

8,9)

10,11)

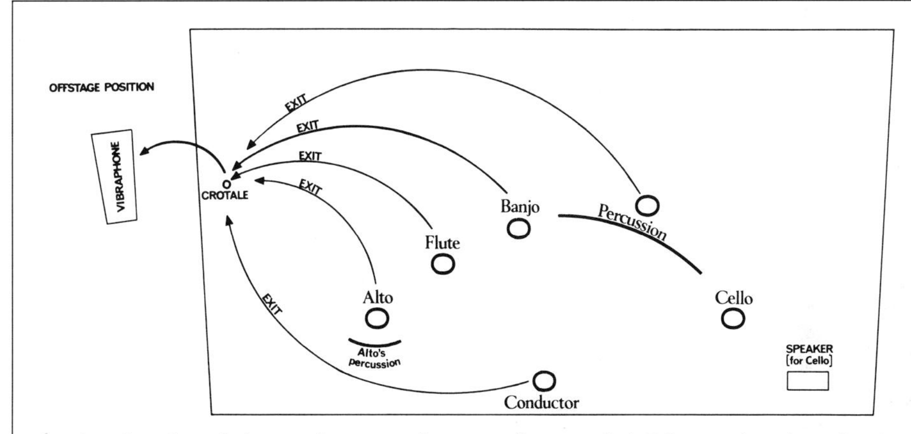

14)

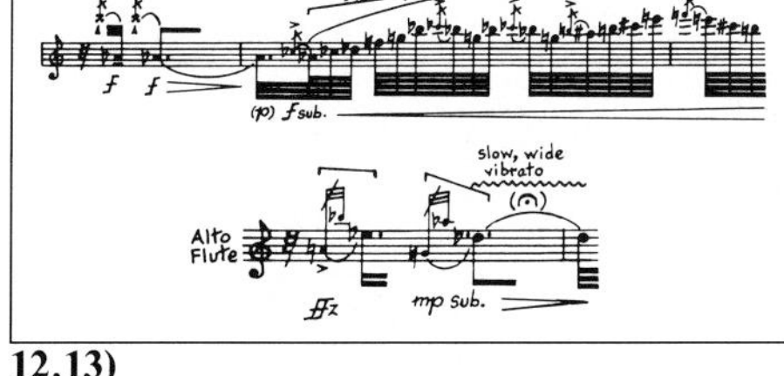

12,13)

(Note: Alto Flute sounds a fourth lower than written!)

1) "Speak-flute" effect.

2) Timbral effects, Movement I (beginning).

3) Harmonics, Movement II.

4) "Bottleneck technique," Movement II.

5) Timbral effects, Movement II (beginning).

6 and 7) Examples of complex small units of measurement.

8) Accelerando motive.

9) Notation of pauses.

10) Form analysis, Movement I.

11) First scale transposition, Movement I.

12) Second transposition, Movement I.

13) Minor 9/perfect 5 motive.

14) Recommended placement of performers on stage.

15) Spanish influence, Movement IV.

16) "Musica Mundana" and "Musica Humana," Movement IV.

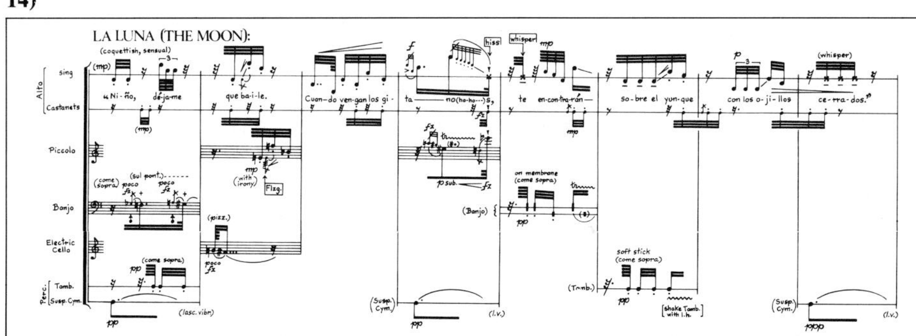

15)

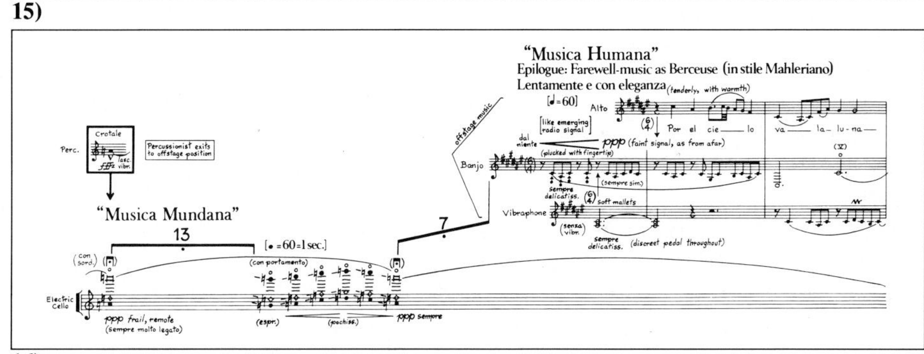

16)

George Crumb: Friend and Musical Colleague

Richard Wernick

They call him "Bun." At least his mother and younger brother do. And it is told that in his childhood days he blew the door off a neighbor's garage in Charleston while testing his homemade fireworks for the Fourth of July. I guess George lost the knack with gunpowder, after he made it big as a composer. For years the Crumbs and the Wernicks would get together every Fourth, George loaded down with all kinds of chemicals which he would mix and blend on the desk in my studio, and then with a sly small-town kind of grin remove from a plain paper bag all the additional ingredients and implements that went into making fireworks. All this display of course was for the "tots" ("tot" in the Crumb lexicon being anyone under 21). After all, if big people wanted to shoot off fireworks there were still plenty of places close by to get them illegally. But it would be more fun for the "tots" to make our own. The "tots" ' attitude was typical ("when the fireworks are ready, let us know"), and they went off to create their own mischief while George and I and usually Gene Narmour, whose family generally joined us for these occasions, covered ourselves with sooty black gunpowder. The wives were worried, but only the first year, because, as I said, George had lost the knack. We made an awful lot of smoke and very, very little noise, and as the years went by the "tots" became more and more disinterested and the wives became considerably less worried, because we all knew that George's bombs were going to leave a lot of smoke in my backyard and a lot of soot on my desk and that was all. . .

But as George's talent for pyrotechnics was failing, his capacities as a composer were increasing at an exponential rate. One of course had nothing to do with the other, but it certainly has been fun to watch.

George and I first met in the fall of 1964. We arrived in Buffalo, N.Y. at about the same time together with our families. George was invited to be pianist/composer for the Center of the Creative and Performing Arts at the University of Buffalo, and I was joining the faculty of the music department there for what I thought was a fairly conventional academic appointment "with minor administrative responsibilities." These minor responsibilities turned me into the keeper of the most unbelievable musical zoo ever assembled. The details of that year of madness need not be recapitulated here. Suffice it to say that there were times when the Crumb/Wernick clans truly felt that we were the only sane people in Buffalo. Beyond this siege mentality into which we were forced, George and I had an immediate liking for one another, our wives were both at the same stage of pregnancy, and our other children were the same ages. It was a familial rapport that was immediate and lasting.

I was not really prepared for my first visit to the Crumb household. I had no prior acquaintance with George's music, and even the name meant nothing. The George Crumb I met was very quiet and self-effacing; his slight stoop and slow West Virginia drawl seemed antithetical to my Northeastern idea of what a composer should look like. (We still tease his wife Liz for being the only person we know who needs three syllables to pronounce her daughter Ann's name!) So it was somewhat of a surprise and a revelation to walk into George's studio for the first time. The Buffalo quarters being temporary, George had converted the dining room into a studio, and the

2)

THE NEW YORK TIMES

3)

1) With son David and "Tammy," Media, 1968.

2) Finishing *Echoes of Time and the River,* Media, 1966.

3) George Crumb, 1974.

THE TORONTO STAR

4)

BRUCE STROMBERG

5)

4) Jocular demonstration of tuned crystal goblets, Toronto, 1974.

5) Richard Wernick, George Rochberg and George Crumb ("The Penn Troika"), 1977.

first impression was that of entering a small art gallery. The oversized pages of George's latest piece were all tacked to the dining room walls. They were in various stages of completion, some with only a very few notes, others nearly all filled in. Their immediate effect was unforgettable: they were immaculate and they were beautiful, and it was obvious that I had entered a musical world which was original and profound. The first impulse was to look at them from a distance, the same way I would look at paintings in a gallery, and then to examine more closely the ones that were the most intriguing. But I also realized that I was viewing the physical manifestation of a unique compositional process. All the pages of the piece were there; there was even a double bar at the end of the final page, although there were hardly any notes on that page at all. The piece was "composed"; the structure was there; the phrases were apparent; the sense of "time" was in complete control; now only the pitches were needed. It was clear, just from seeing those incomplete pages, that George had a sense of color and timbre that was unique and personal, but it was not until I heard the rehearsals and performance of *Night Music I* a few weeks later that I truly understood the nature of George's gift. Not only does George have a pitch sense which is extraordinarily finely tuned, he has perhaps the best sense of timing of any composer I know. When events change in a Crumb piece they change at exactly the right moment. It is a remarkable instinct for the manipulation of time, combined with an expression of poetry in music that is truly profound.

The Crumbs and the Wernicks did survive their year in Buffalo. Thank heaven it was only one! George went off to the University of Pennsylvania, and I went off to the University of Chicago, but we did keep in close touch. The timing of my arrival in Chicago was not only good for me; it turned out to play a significant role in George's career as well. The Chicago Symphony Orchestra, then under the direction of Jean Martinon, had just agreed to perform four weeks of contemporary music at the University of Chicago, and through a grant from The Rockefeller Foundation was prepared to commission a small number of new works. When I put George's name on the list of prospective composers it happened that he was by far the least known. However, the committee agreed to look at his work, and then agreed that he should be given one of the commissions. The work he composed for us was *Echoes of Time and the River*, which of course won the Pulitzer Prize, and from that point on George's star rose rapidly.

In the summer of 1967 our family was invited to visit the Crumbs in Media. It was during that time that George introduced me to George Rochberg who was then Chairman of the music department at Penn. Shortly after my return to Chicago, Rochberg invited me to join the Penn faculty, and I realized I'd been "set up" by Crumb, who obviously had a bit more political savvy than I'd given him credit for. I joined the Penn faculty in 1968, and George and I have been colleagues in the same department now for sixteen years.

George has been at the peak of his creative powers during these years. He has composed a succession of works which are truly remarkable, and in the process become one of the most imitated composers in America. Yet the composers, particularly the very young ones, who imitate George, really show little understanding of

George or his music, or of an even more important facet of his musical personality: namely that George, more than any other composer I know, lives deep within a world of musical self-creation into which no one else is invited—not even his closest friends and associates. He is the musical solipsist par excellence. He lives in an inner world that is dark and mysterious, a world that is primeval and atavistic. The great Lorca cycle is but one manifestation of this world, as is *Black Angels*. His world is impenetrable, and he would surely be a miserable failure at psychoanalysis. Whereas all the rest of us in the music department, composers and scholars alike, have had to endure the drudgery of at least a single term as chairman, it wouldn't occur to any of us to expect George to emerge from his very private cosmos long enough to get the staffing or the budget straight for a single semester. Perhaps long enough to make some failed fireworks or a huge snow fort for the "tots" when they were young enough, but not long enough to be a chairman.

I am reminded of a discussion I had with a colleague years ago in Aspen. We had recently returned from a magnificent performance of the *St. Matthew Passion*, and I remarked that perhaps the two most inspired bars in the piece were those toward the end where the chorus sings "Truly this was the Son of God." I argued that only a composer of deep religious faith, as Bach was, could have composed those bars in the context in which they appeared. My friend argued the opposite: that the deep religious fervor of those measures was a matter of technique, stagecraft and dramatic effect, and could have just as easily been composed by an atheist. I disagreed then, and still do.

My view of George's music is similar. The outward trappings are easy to simulate because the technique required to simulate them is rather negligible. A few plucked harmonics inside the piano, a bowed vibraphone or cymbal, the flutist striking a delicate crotale note from time to time, a slow harmonic rhythm, and you have the "shell" of a Crumb piece. Other styles are much more difficult to imitate. It requires an enormous amount of compositional craft to imitate the polyphony in a Bach fugue or a development in the style of Beethoven. But a close look at Crumb's music reveals a minimal use of either polyphony *or* development, two aspects of music which have generally been associated with compositional craft. It would be a great mistake to ignore the sonoric aspects of George's music, because sheer virtuosity of sound and color are highly elevated parameters of his music. But it would also be a mistake to attribute so much to that aspect that the architectural, formal and melodic aspects are ignored. All the parts are integral, and their fusion creates one of the truly great musics of our time. And what is equally important to understand is the fact that George truly dwells in a musical world of his own, a world which is almost like a "time warp," parallel to the real world, but not really of it.

George's musical sensitivity embraces the standard 18th and 19th century repertoire as well as the 20th. He perceives music in general in a way that is unique. He talks about music in a way that no one else does; he is never pedantic (hardly!) or even terribly analytical. But when George says, "Gee, garsh, look at how Beethoven does . . ." it is almost guaranteed that he has perceived something in a way that is original and different. I love to talk about music with George as much as I love to play music with him. It is a never-ending source of delight to me to see him approach the keyboard: a sense of anticipation that most conductors would (or should) envy, combined with a physical "embrace" of the keyboard (*and* the music) that is deeply moving. We have played a lot of music together, four hands, as well as even an occasional eight hands, sober and not-so-sober (George's timing with the gin bottle being not quite as refined as his timing with his notes). After a series of George's libations, my piano playing (if you want to call it that) gets better while his deteriorates, and sometimes we end up almost even.

George and I have had much to share, from the joy of music to the anguish of watching our youngest sons, who share the same name, struggle with serious illness. I am truly indebted to those vagaries of time, place and coincidence which brought us together twenty years ago, and which have created between us an indissoluble bond of friendship.

Photographs

1) Family music-making, 1971.
Left to right: Cindy, William, David (partially visible) and George Crumb.

2) Daryl D. Dayton, United States Information Agency Music Advisor, in Caracas, 1976.

3) With son Peter, Philip West and Jan DeGaetani (Mrs. Philip West), Media, 1977.

1)

2)

3)

4)

5)

6)

4) At the Parthenon, Athens, 1978.

5) Robert Miller with family and friends. Left to right: David Crumb, Vickie and Robert Miller, Rolf Schulte, Elizabeth Crumb. Front: Christopher Miller.

6) George and Elizabeth Crumb at The Dome of the Rock, Jerusalem, 1980.

7) Gilbert Kalish and George Crumb after the premiere of *The Sleeper,* New York City, December, 1984.

8) At C. F. Peters Corporation with Series Editor Don Gillespie.

9) George Crumb at The University of Western Australia, Perth, August, 1984 (before Kaare K. Nygaard's sculpture of Percy Grainger).

G. STEVE JORDAN

7)

MARGOT McCARTHY

8)

9)

10)

11)

12)

10) On the way to the New York premiere of *Gnomic Variations*, March, 1984. Left to right: George Crumb, Gretchen and Ross Lee Finney.

11) With Lewis Kaplan of the Aeolian Chamber Players.

12) At William Paterson College, New Jersey, 1980.

Epilogue

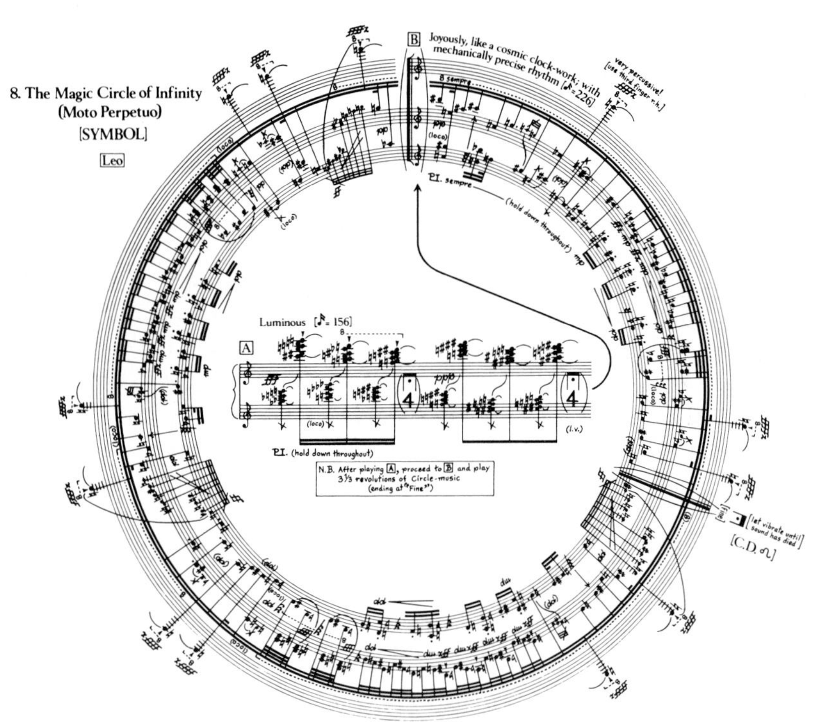

De Oraculo Crumbi

The Contexts of Science and Art in the Twentieth Century*

Eugene Narmour

In the beginning, it appeared to physicists that space, populated by physical matter, and time, through which such matter changed, existed independently. Similarly to humanists and scholars, there seemed to be visual art on the one hand and temporal art on the other. Later on, scientists gradually discovered—much to our astonishment—that space and time were relativities, that they were two aspects of the same thing.

To artists and composers this raised a very real, parallel possibility that visual and temporal experiences were themselves *relativities of some one fundamental emotional and perceptual condition. Thus, many contemporary composers and artists sought to create artworks that explored a perceptual-cognitive relativity based upon the assumption of an aesthetic continuum between temporal and visual art, between time and space, so to speak. We thus have on the one hand the paintings of Seurat, Duchamp, and Klee, which capture time as space, and on the other the compositions of Debussy, Ives, and Bartók, which capture space as time. Such works, coterminous with the revolution in physics, were offered not just as analogical or virtual metaphors of the space-time continuum but rather as real, actualized representations of it.*

Feeling that even this did not go far enough, some composers in the late twentieth century—they may be called "radical transcendentalists"—went the whole philosophical distance. They were not satisfied with musical analogies or musical metaphors or with real representations of the time-space relation but rather argued vice versa through their compositions: that time and space actually *embodied music. Their cry was that music, in its most fundamental and non-metaphysical state, was present with all other relativities at the creation, before living, sentient perceivers ever existed. To them the distinction between natural fact and man-made artifact seemed basically spurious.*

What kind of an aesthetic did such a pluralistic, relativistic world generate—where mind and matter fused, where mental and physical life existed symbiotically? Ironically, the relativistic world of the transcendentalist invoked aesthetic beliefs similar to those that existed prior to the birth of modern science. For the radical transcendentalists perforce re-embraced certain pre-scientific, medieval unities (such as musica mundana *and* musica humana*) since, if music suffused all creation, the unified cosmos must be capable of making* its *own music—the solar wind whistling through the celestial branches, the galactic bells pealing throughout the macrocosm.*

Neo-medieval too was the radical transcendentalists' aesthetic belief about the relationship between heaven and earth. Enveloping both the perfection of the macrocosm and the imperfection of life here on earth, space-time to them was set in motion and regulated by a dualistic theism. In the works of the radical transcendentalists, God and Devil stand in splendid opposition, a Biblical confrontation

*Editor's note: Embedded within this article are more than seventy references to Crumb's musical compositions, his writings, and his thought. Moreover, the form of the article parallels that of Crumb's *Processional* for piano.

portending an apocalyptical finale. Since some music is good, there must be a primal creative force behind the universe operating on its behalf; but since some is evil, there must also exist a powerful antagonism. The two struggling forces play out their foreordained roles, each having its own functionally specialized music, like all the other elements of the macrocosm.

To the neo-medievalist, the echoes of this macrocosmic Dies Irae, *of course, also reverberate throughout* musica humana, *though with much greater ambiguity. The sounds of the black angels beguile us constantly. The earth is an ambivalent dreamworld to the radical transcendentalist composer, a haunted landscape, set in mythic time and populated by ghosts, Druids, gnomes, and gargoyles—mystical medieval apparitions with mysterious voices whose menacing, magical lyrics seem indicative of some deeper, albeit perplexing, truth. On earth, only the ancient voices of children equal the music of the* Lux Aeterna. *Through them life is rekindled and order reintroduced. Redemption seems possible despite death's unending drones and refrains.*

In addition to the space-time discovery, which paralleled the rebirth of certain aspects of medieval aesthetics, there also occurred in this century, though much later, another scientific revelation that the radical transcendentalist composer could not escape from. For just as the space-time dualism turned out not to be what it originally and scientifically seemed, so the biological absolutism between plant and animal also blurred. For it was discovered that one same genetic substance—DNA—drives and possesses all living things. The positivistic barrier erected between the animate and the inanimate thus no longer appeared so certain.

Moreover, the biological discoveries blurring the categories between plant and animal ramified in every direction—historical, sociological, and cultural—as Darwin's and Wallace's theories had a century earlier. The success of evolution, for instance, now attested only to man's relative chances of survival; evolution by DNA supported no presumption of inherent historical value. Similarly, the idea of social and cultural progress—of an innate manifest destiny inherent only in the descendents of the white European race of Homo sapiens*—was demolished completely by the advances of microbiology. In short, Western science irreparably undercut Western man's self-proclaimed pinnacle of evolutionary superiority. And it undercut much of what Western man had traditionally believed about his history, his society, his culture, and the nature of his art in general.*

Just as the hypothesis of a time-space unity in physics corresponded to the assumption of a temporal-visual unity in the arts, so the revolution in biological genetics was paralleled in music by Western composers searching for a new aesthetic. Ironically again the radical transcendentalist composer ended up embracing aesthetic philosophies that predated modern science by several centuries. For African and Eastern cultures, which flowered to full blossom while Europe lay in the Dark Ages, had, after all, found music throughout the cosmos, as did the later medievalists and the twentieth-century transcendentalists. These cultures, for example, perceived music in the moon's nocturnal changes, in the cyclicity of night and day, and in the subtle shifting of the seasons. Following the logic of their aesthetic, the radical transcendentalist composer could thus envision summer and autumn as being literally vibrant with music.

In addition to these planetary rhythms, African and Eastern cultures also endowed the animal and plant kingdoms with their own music. To the radical transcendentalists who embraced this aesthetic, the buzzing of insects, the screech of seagulls, and the cries of the whale formed an integral part of musica natura. *It was not just that the "found sonic objects" of the plant and animal kingdoms produced interesting sounds to these Western composers but rather that the natural musical acoustic was heard in and of itself as inherently aesthetic. Beating a log produced* in esse *the music of the tree; the tapping of one mineral compound by another was* viva voce *the music of the rock; the snap of the jaw created* in rerum natura *the music of the bone. All this worked its way into the musical mind of the radical transcendentalist.*

The real contribution of the radical transcendentalist composer, however, was to recognize that neither the physical or the biological upheaval in the sciences nor the incorporation of neo-medieval philosophies and non-Western aesthetics into contemporary music necessarily meant a wholesale rejection of the more recent Western artistic tradition. The musics of Bach, Beethoven, Schubert, Chopin, Mussorgsky, Mahler, Strauss, Ravel, Berg, and Stravinsky lost none of their power in the transcendentalist assimilation; they simply ceased functioning as the cultural goals of a bankrupt Hegelian history, becoming rather an integral material of the pluralistic collage. Similarly, there was no reason why traditional forms—madrigals, suites, passacaglias, marches—could not continue to function as vehicles of expression. Likewise, traditional Western instruments as well as traditional ensembles could all retain their culturally endowed potential as viable modes of communication for the transcendentalist composer. Indeed, some composers were wise enough to sense that it was only *the assimilation of the near-Western past into the heady admixture of medieval philosophy and Eastern-African aesthetics that prevented radical transcendental music from degenerating into an empty, pan-aesthetic eclecticism.*

But if all the highly-evolved traditions of Western music were not necessarily eclipsed in light of the radical transcendentalist's adoption of non-Western aesthetics and the primal instruments of nature, then folk instruments too—the dulcimer, the musical saw, and the banjo—could be allowed to take their place in the pantheon of a post-scientific, post-teleological, post-historical aesthetic pluralism. Indeed, in the aesthetics of radical transcendentalism musical instruments are not either "developed" or "natural" or "folk" since any of these classes melds into, while simultaneously embodying, all the others. Like space-time and plant-animal, the radical transcendentalist composer could conceive atavistic vocal utterances and the highly evolved, precise increments of pitch on the keyed flute as emanating fundamentally and irrevocably from the same source: the music of the universe. The song of the rock smelted to make wire and the song of the tree felled to make a sounding board constitute, so to speak, the musical DNA of the modern grand piano. In the world of the radical transcendentalist, all instrumental and human voices belong ultimately and absolutely to one, and only one, music. And to the transcendentalist composer all such music itself belongs to one, and only one, time.

After all, from the perspectives of both composition and science, the earth is but a tiny space-time vessel, borne along by a ceaseless river, which, in no contradictory sense, nonetheless also has a beginning and an end, just as space is simultaneously both infinite and finite, just as life is both organic and inorganic.

Like the corpuscles and waves of light from the heavens, the procession of time appears to us in various guises. It dances frenetically, marches majestically, moves stolidly, stands suspended, lies frozen. Ultimately, however, we now know that all space-time collapses. Like imploding stars, time echoes only remembrances of itself.

Can we perceive and comprehend these echoes? Who will guide our space-time ark through the echoing waves of this river? What flora and fauna will survive the voyage?

Who shall be our gondolier?

Contributors

David Burge is internationally known as a concert pianist, recording artist, lecturer, journalist, teacher and advocate of twentieth-century music. Since 1975 he has been Chairman of the Piano Department of the Eastman School of Music.

Gilbert Chase, the celebrated music historian, has recently completed the Third Edition of his pioneering survey *America's Music: From the Pilgrims to the Present*. Mr. Chase resides in Chapel Hill, North Carolina.

Composer **Stephen Chatman** is Associate Professor of Music at the University of British Columbia and President of the Vancouver New Music Society. His works have been commissioned and performed by major Canadian orchestras and choirs and have been published and recorded internationally.

David Cope has composed over 70 works for varying media and is the author of three books on contemporary music: *New Directions in Music*, *New Music Composition* and *New Music Notation*. He currently teaches composition and theory at the University of California at Santa Cruz.

Esteemed for her versatile artistry, mezzo-soprano **Jan DeGaetani** appears internationally in lieder recitals, chamber music concerts, oratorio, opera, and with orchestra. Renowned for her presentation of contemporary music, she is a Professor of Voice at the Eastman School of Music and spends her summers as Artist-in-Residence at the Aspen Music Festival.

Formerly a professor of music and orchestra administrator, **Suzanne Mac Lean** is currently a professional astrologer and counseling psychologist in Santa Fe, New Mexico. She conducts the Santa Fe Women's Ensemble, and composes.

Eugene Narmour, Associate Professor of Music at the University of Pennsylvania, is the author of *Beyond Schenkerism* as well as articles on musical hierarchies, analytical symbologies, and music performance. He is currently writing books on melody and harmony.

Robert Shuffett holds a doctorate in composition from the Peabody Conservatory and is currently active as a free-lance composer in the Washington area. Together with David Cope, he has compiled a book of interviews with George Crumb.

Following an early career as pianist, **Teresa Sterne** worked for Columbia and Vanguard Records, and was director of Nonesuch Records (1965–1980) and music director for WNYC-FM (1981–1982). She is currently active as an independent record producer.

Composer-conductor **Richard Wernick** teaches at the University of Pennsylvania where he holds the position of Professor of Music and Music Director of the Penn Contemporary Players. Recipient of the 1977 Pulitzer Prize in Music, Mr. Wernick also serves as the Consultant for Contemporary Music to the Philadelphia Orchestra.

Christopher Wilkinson, Associate Professor of Music at West Virginia University, holds a doctorate in musicology from Rutgers University. In addition to his research in twentieth-century music, he also specializes in studies of sacred music of the early baroque.

Special thanks are due to the following for their assistance towards the completion of this project: George Crumb, Hank Haffner, Mrs. Walter Hinrichsen, Lynn Ozer, Thomas Pritchett, Pamela Tucker, Peters Edition, Ltd., London, and C. F. Peters Musikverlag, Frankfurt.

Bibliography

Music might be defined as a system of proportions in the service of a spiritual impulse.

George Crumb

Bibliography

WRITINGS ABOUT GEORGE CRUMB

Books & Magazine Articles

Ågren, Lennart. "Crumbrapport fraan Oerebro." *Nutida Musik* (Sweden). No.4, 1981/82.

Alcaraz, J.A. *George Crumb-entrivista y comentarios*. Mexico City: Ediciones de la Biblioteca Benjamin Franklin, 1977.

"American Composer: George Crumb." *The West Virginia Hillbilly* (Richwood,WV). July 20, 1968.

Baker's Biographical Dictionary of Musicians. Seventh Edition (1985). Revised by Nicolas Slonimsky.

Barrett, Nick. "Crumb's Sound-World." *The Listener* (England). November 2, 1978.

Baur, John. *Music Theory Through Literature*. Englewood Cliffs, NJ: Prentice-Hall, Inc., 1984 (re: *Ancient Voices of Children*).

Blatter, Alfred. *Instrumentation/Orchestration*. New York: Longman, Inc., 1980.

Borroff, Edith. "George Crumb," in *The New Grove Dictionary of Music in the United States* (forthcoming).

Borroff, Edith. *Three American Composers* (Fischer, Finney, Crumb). Unpublished typescript. (State University of New York at Binghamton .

Borroff, Edith, and Irwin, Marjory. *Music in Perspective*. New York: Harcourt Brace Jovanovich, Inc., 1976.

Borwick, Doug. "The Instrumental Theater Piece—An Introduction to Form and Analysis." *Woodwind World, Brass and Percussion*. July, 1976.

Brandeis, Fanny, ed. *Louisville Orchestra Program Notes for "Echoes of Time and the River."* November 20, 1970.

Broeck, Jan L., ed. "The Composer: Between Man and Music: George Crumb." *Interface: Journal of New Music Research* (Netherlands). IX, 1980.

Burge, David. "Best Pieces of the '70s." *Contemporary Keyboard*. November, 1979.

Burge, David. "Contemporary Piano Repertoire, Part III: George Crumb." *Contemporary Keyboard*. May/June, 1976.

Burge, David. "George Crumb and I." *Contemporary Keyboard*. August, 1976.

Burge, David. "George Crumb's *Five Pieces*." *Keyboard*. July, 1983.

Burge, David. "George Crumb's *Gnomic Variations*." *Keyboard*. November, 1983.

Burge, David. "Performing the Piano Music of George Crumb." *Contemporary Keyboard*. August, 1976.

Burkhart, Charles. "George Crumb" in *Anthology for Musical Analysis*. New York: Holt, Rinehart and Winston, Inc., 1972.

Chase, Gilbert. *America's Music*. Revised Third Edition. Urbana: University of Illinois Press. (forthcoming).

Chatman, Stephen. "George Crumb: 'Night of the Four Moons,' The Element of Sound." *Music and Man* (England). Spring, 1974 (contained herein).

Chatman, Stephen. "George Crumb's *Madrigals Book III*: A Linear Analysis." *In Theory Only* (University of Michigan). Dec/Jan, 1975–76.

Chlopecki, Andrezej. "George Crumb. Musica humana-musica mundana." *Ruch Muzyczny* (Poland). May, 1976.

Clark, Robert S. "American Composers Now." *Hudson Review*. Spring, 1978.

Clarke, Garry E. *Essays in American Music*. Westport, CT: Greenwood Press, Inc., 1977.

Cooper, Paul. *Perspectives in Music Theory*. Second Edition. New York: Harper & Row, 1981.

Cope, David. *New Directions in Music*. Fourth Edition. Dubuque, Iowa: William C. Brown Co., 1984.

Cope, David. *New Music Composition*. New York: Schirmer Books, 1977.

Cope, David. *New Music Notation*. Dubuque, Iowa: Kendall/Hunt Publishing Co., 1976.

"George H. Crumb," *Composers of the Americas* 15: 55–9 (1969). (Published by the Organization of American States).

"George Crumb." *Current Biography*. New York, December, 1974.

"George Crumb." *Pan Pipes*. January, 1969.

"George Crumb," in *West Virginia Songbag*. Edited and published by Jim Comstock, Richwood, West Virginia, 1974.

"George Crumb." *Who's Who in America, 1982/83*.

"Crumb is Praised." *BMI Many Worlds of Music*. Winter/Spring, 1974.

Daniel, Oliver. "George Crumb." Brochure of Broadcast Music, Inc., 1975.

Davis, William D. "An Analysis of 'No piensan en la lluvia y se han dormido' from *Madrigals, Book I* by George Crumb." *The American Society of University Composers Monograph Series*. No. 12, Summer, 1984.

Dayton, Daryl. "American Music in the 1970's," Typescript. Available from the United States Information Agency, 1974.

Dayton, Daryl. "Czarni Aniolowie" ("Black Angels"). *Nowa Muzyka, America*. United States Information Agency, 1975.(Polish).

Dayton, Daryl. "George Crumb: American Musical Picasso." United States Information Agency *Backgrounder*, 1976.

Dayton, Daryl. "Muzica Intră pe Noi Făgasuri." Brochure in Romanian published by the United States Information Agency, 1975.

Dayton, Daryl. "Na Nowchy Drogach w Muzyce." *Nowa Muzyka, America*. United States Information Agency, 1975. (Polish).

Dayton, Daryl. "Scores for the New Music—*Black Angels*," Typescript. Available from the United States Information Agency, n.d.

Dayton, Daryl. "Twentieth-Century Music—USA," Typescript. Available from the United States Information Agency, n.d.

Derhen, Andrew. "Brooklyn Philharmonia." *Musical America*. June, 1980.

Diehl, George K. "Variazioni." *Notes for Philharmonic Hall* (Lincoln Center, NYC). January, 1973.

Dobay, Thomas R. de. "The Evolution of Harmonic Style in the Lorca Settings of George Crumb." *Journal of Music Theory*. Vol. 28, 1984.

Downes, Edward, ed. "Ancient Voices of Children." *New York Philharmonic Program Notes*. January, 1973.

Drăgănoiu, Ioan. "Cu George Crumb despre Muzica americană contemporană." *Tribuna* (Romania) (1975).

"Echoes of Time and the River." *Program Notes of the Cleveland Orchestra*. Twenty-Second Program, April 3-5, 1969.

Ewen, David. *American Composers: A Biographical Dictionary*. New York: G. P. Putnam's Sons, 1982.

Faidley, Jan. "Treatment of Woodwind Timbre in the Compositions of George Crumb." *National Association of College Wind and Percussion Instructors Journal*. Winter, 1983-84.

Feldman, Mary Ann, ed. *Program Notes of the Minnesota Orchestra*. Subscription Concert No. 1. September 24-26, 1975. (re: *Echoes of Time and the River*.)

Fleming, Shirley. "George Crumb: Musician of the Month." *Musical America*. September, 1968. Reprinted in *ASCAP Today*. December, 1968.

Foster, David. "George Crumb," in *The Encyclopedia of World Biography*. New York: McGraw-Hill Inc. (forthcoming)

Fowler, Charles B. "American Composer Sketches: George Crumb." *Music Educators Journal*. April, 1967.

Francombe, Leona. "The Eternal Triangle: Composer, Performer and Audience in George Crumb's Music." *Banff Letters* (Alberta, Canada). Spring, 1985.

Frankenstein, Alfred. "The Contemporary Musical Experience." *Musical America*. December, 1972.

Freed, Richard. "Notes to 'Star-Child'." *Philadelphia Orchestra Program Notes*. May 17-19, 1979.

Godfrey, Naomi, and Weinstein, Michael. "Faculty Profile: George Crumb." *Columns* (University of Pennsylvania). Fall, 1979.

Godwin, Joscelyn. *Schirmer Scores*. New York: Schirmer Books, 1975. pp. 1073-75.

Hamilton, David. "Music." *The Nation*. January 25, 1975.

Hamilton, David. "Three Composers of Today." *Musical Newsletter*. January, 1971.

Hansen, Peter S. *Introduction to Twentieth-Century Music*. Fourth Edition. Boston: Allyn and Bacon, Inc. 1977.

Henahan, Donal. "Crumb, The Tone Poet." *New York Times Magazine*. May 11, 1975. Reprinted in abridged form in *Dialogue*, Vol. 9, No. 2, 1976 as "George Crumb: The Poetry of Music."

Hentoff, Nat. "The Sounds of Love, Wind and Sea." *Cosmopolitan*. January, 1975.

Hertzog, Christian, ed. "Music of George Crumb." *Notes of the Contemporary Directions Ensemble* (University of Michigan). December 4/5, 1981.

Hickok, Robert. *Exploring Music*. Third Edition. Reading, MA: Addison-Wesley Publishing Co., 1979. (re: *Vox Balaenae*).

Hiller, Lejaren. "The Avant Garde String Quartet in the U.S.A." Accompanying Brochure to Vox Record Album SVBX 5306, 1973.

Hitchcock, H. Wiley. *Music in the United States: A Historical Introduction*. Second Edition. Englewood Cliffs, NJ: Prentice Hall, Inc., 1974.

Hoffer, Charles R. *The Understanding of Music*. Fifth Edition. Belmont, CA: Wadsworth Publishing Co., 1984 (re: *Night of the Four Moons*).

Holland, James. *Percussion*. New York: Schirmer Books, 1978.

"Information." *The World of Music* (UNESCO). Summer, 1971.

The International Cyclopedia of Music and Musicians (Thompson's). Eleventh Edition. New York: Dodd, Mead & Co., 1985.

Irashkin, A. *Program Notes* on George Crumb and "Ancient Voices of Children." (Russian). Tchaikovsky Hall, Moscow. Subscription Series No. 64. 1983/4.

"Jesienne refleksje. . .Skrzynska" (Reflections on the Autumn Festival). *Ruch Muzyczny* (Poland). 19: 5-7, No. 24, 1975.

Johnson, Bengt Emil. "Ekon ur tystnader. Om George Crumbs Musik till Federico García Lorcas dikter." *Nutida Musik* (Sweden). No. 4, 1975/76.

Johnson, Bengt Emil. "Hans Lyssnar efter ljuden från andra sidan. . .Erinringar och Synpunkter betraffende George Crumb." *Nutida Musik* (Sweden). No. 1, 1982/83.

Kamien, Roger. *Music: An Appreciation*. Third Edition. New York: McGraw Hill Book Co., 1984 (re: *Ancient Voices of Children*).

Kastendieck, Miles. "George Crumb." *The Many Worlds of Music* (Broadcast Music, Inc.). July, 1972.

Kerman, Joseph. *Listen*. Second Edition. New York: Worth Publishers, Inc., 1976.

Klein, Elisabeth. "George Crumb's Klavervaerker." *Norsk Musikk Tidsskrift*. December, 1977; January, 1985.

Kolodin, Irving. "Music to My Ears." *Saturday Review*. May 25, 1968.

Korall, Burt, ed. "Composers in Focus: George Crumb." *The Many Worlds of Music* (Broadcast Music, Inc.). Winter, 1976.

Kostka, Stefan, and Payne, Dorothy. *Tonal Harmony*. New York: Random House, Inc., 1984.

Kowal, Roman. "Crumb-Lorca." *Ruch Muzyczny* (Poland). March 13, 1977.

Kowal, Roman. "George Crumb—*Ancient Voices of Children*. (Polish). Musicological Pamphlet published by the Conservatory of Music, Kraków, 1977.

Kraglund, John. "Canadian Chronicles." *The Canada Music Book*. Autumn/Winter, 1974.

Kuzmich, Natalie. *Musical Growth: A Process of Involvement*. Toronto: Gordon V. Thompson Ltd., in preparation.

Lange, Art. "George Crumb and the Art Ensemble of Chicago: Moving Parallel in Separate Worlds." *Parachute* (Chicago). June, 1977.

Laretei, Käbi. "Sfärernas Klanger." *Nutida Musik* (Sweden). No. 4, 1980/81.

Lee, Douglas. "Current Chronicle: Penderecki and Crumb at Wichita State." *Musical Quarterly*. February, 1975.

Lewis, Robert Hall. "Younger American Composers. George Crumb: *Night Music I*." *Perspectives of New Music*. Spring/Summer, 1965.

Lipman, Samuel. *The House of Music*. Boston: David R. Godine, 1984.

Machlis, Joseph. *The Enjoyment of Music*. Fifth Edition. New York: W. W. Norton & Co., 1984.

Machlis, Joseph. *Introduction to Contemporary Music*. Second Edition. New York: W. W. Norton & Co., 1979.

Mayer, William. "Live Composers, Dead Audiences." *New York*

Bibliography — Books & Magazine Articles (Continued)

Times Magazine. February 2, 1975.

McLaughlin, Patricia. "Three Penn Composers." *Pennsylvania Gazette*. December, 1977.

Mead, Philip. "George Crumb: The Approachable Avant-Garde." In Pitchford, Roy, ed. *Sixth Form Occasional Papers: No. 5 Music*. Cambridgeshire College of Arts and Technology (England), 1981.

Meyers, Mary Ann. "A Composer Who Doesn't Take Orders from the Musical Establishment." *Pennsylvania Gazette*. October, 1968.

Miller, Samuel D. "Can Selections for Children Be Avant-Garde?" *Music Educators Journal*. October, 1981. (re: *Makrokosmos II*).

Moevs, Robert. "Reviews of Records." *Musical Quarterly*. April, 1976.

Morgan, Robert P. *An Anthology of Twentieth-Century Music*. New York: W.W. Norton & Co., 1985. (re: *Night of the Four Moons*).

Morgan, Robert P. "Reviews." *High Fidelity*. June, 1974.

Morgan, Robert P. "Sonic Innovations for the String Quartet." *High Fidelity*. October, 1972.

"Music As Pollution?" *Musical America*. December, 1979.

Orkis, Lambert. "Performing with a Personal Touch." *Smithsonian Performing Arts Notes* (Washington, D.C.). November/December, 1980.

Ortiz, Carlos Barreiro. "Imagen Parcial de la Obra de George Crumb." *Centro Colombo-Americano* (Bogotá). July, 1983. 52-page booklet containing also interview by Alcaraz (see: Interviews), "Algunas Opiniones," and Crumb's essay "Does Music Have a Future?" (Spanish).

Ottman, Robert. *Advanced Harmony: Theory and Practice*. Third Edition. Englewood Cliffs, NJ: Prentice-Hall, Inc., 1984. pp. 391–92.

Parsons, Arrand, ed. "Echoes of Time and the River." *Chicago Symphony Orchestra Program Notes*. October 24, 1968.

Pearlman, Leonard A. "George Crumb," in *The New Grove Dictionary of Music & Musicians*, 1980.

Plush, Vincent. "George Crumb in Australia." *Stereo FM Radio* (Sidney). August, 1976.

Plush, Vincent. "The World of George Crumb." *Stereo FM Radio* (Sidney). August, 1976.

Porter, Andrew. "Musical Events: Notes on Notes on Notes." *New Yorker*. January 20, 1975.

Porter, Andrew. "Musical Events: Stars." *New Yorker*. November 25, 1974.

Porter, Andrew. "Review." *High Fidelity*. October, 1975.

"Pulitzer Prize-Winning Composer Returns to Campus." *Illinois Alumni News* (Urbana). March, 1981.

Rasmussen, Karl Aage. "George Crumb." *Dansk Musiktidsskrift* (Denmark). December, 1975.

Rasmussen, Karl Aage. "George Crumb." *Dansk Musiktidsskrift* (Denmark). March, 1978.

Rasmussen, Karl Aage. "Night of the Four Moons," (Danish), *Program Notes for the Royal Danish Theatre*. April, 1982.

Reuter, Rocky J. "Symmetrical Structures in George Crumb's *Five Pieces for Piano*." *Journal of the Graduate Music Students at The Ohio State University*. 9 (1985).

Reynolds, Charles. "Ancient Voices of Children." *Joy Magazine* (Alaska). November, 1972.

Riemann Musik-Lexikon. Mainz: B. Schott's Soehne, 1975.

Robertson, Alan. "Minnesota Dance Theatre's Newly Completed George Crumb Trilogy." *Dance Magazine*. September, 1978.

Ruder, Poul. "Introduktion af den amerikanske Komponist George Crumb's *Ancient Voices of Children*." *Dansk Musiktidsskrift* (Denmark). April, 1976.

Sable, Barbara Kinsey. "On Contemporary Notation and Performance." *NATS Bulletin*. May, 1976.

Sachs, Joel. "Notes for a George Crumb Retrospective Concert." *Stagebill* (Lincoln Center, NYC).XI, No. 6. February, 1984.

Salzman, Eric. "American Composer George Crumb." *Stereo Review*. September, 1971.

Salzman, Eric. *Twentieth Century Music*. Second Edition. Englewood Cliffs, NJ: Prentice-Hall, Inc., 1974.

Samana, Leo. "La Rochelle en de Amerikanen." *Mens en Melodie* (Holland). September, 1976.

Saylor, Bruce, and Smith, Patrick J. "Crumb's *Makrokosmos II* — New Vision or Dead End?" *Musical America*. February, 1975.

Saylor, Bruce. "Looking Backwards: Reflections on Nostalgia in the Musical Avant-garde." *Centerpoint* (NYC). 1:5, No. 3, 1975.

Schindler, Allan. *Listening to Music*. New York: Holt, Rinehart and Winston, 1980.

Schneider, John. *The Contemporary Guitar*. Berkeley: University of California Press, 1984.

Shirley, Wayne D. "Music Meets Theater." *Stagebill* (Kennedy Center). XIII/2, October, 1984. (re: *Night of the Four Moons*).

Smith, Christopher S. "An Analysis of George Crumb's *Black Angels (Images I): Thirteen Images from the Dark Land*." Unpublished paper (State University of New York, Potsdam). 1982.

Smith, Patrick J., and Saylor, Bruce. "Crumb's *Makrokosmos II* — New Vision or Dead End?" *Musical America*. February, 1975.

Steinitz, Richard. "George Crumb." *BBC Promenades Concerts Prospectus*. 1979.

Steinitz, Richard. "George Crumb." *Contact. Today's Music* (England). No. 15. Winter 1976/77.

Steinitz, Richard. "George Crumb." *Musical Times*. October, 1978.

Steinitz, Richard. "The Music of George Crumb." *Contact. Today's Music* (England). No. 11. Summer, 1975.

Sterne, Teresa. "Recording Contemporary Music." *Peters Notes*. Fall/Winter, 1978/79 (contained herein).

Stone, Kurt. "Current Chronicle." *Musical Quarterly*. October, 1965.

Stone, Kurt. *Music Notation in the Twentieth Century: A Practical Guidebook*. New York: W. W. Norton & Co., 1979.

Suber, Charles. "The First Chorus." *Down Beat*. October 21, 1976.

Sullivan, Jack. "The Music of Terror." *Keynote*. August, 1985.

Sullivan, Jack, ed. *The Encyclopedia of Horror and the Supernatural*. New York: Viking Press, 1985.

Terry, Kenneth. "George Crumb: Makrokosmic Cartographer." *Down Beat*. October 21, 1976.

Thomson, William. *Music for Listeners*. Englewood Cliffs, NJ: Prentice-Hall, Inc., 1979. (re: *Ancient Voices of Children*).

Trotter, Herman, ed. "Echoes of Time and the River." *Buffalo Philharmonic Program Notes*. October 27, 1968.

Trotter, Herman. "June in Buffalo: Second Annual Contemporary Festival Features Xanakis, Crumb." *Musical America*. October, 1976.

Turetzky, Bertram. "Vocal and Speech Sounds—A Technique of Contemporary Writing for the Contrabass." *Composer* (USA). I: No. 3, 1969.

"2 Top Intl Awards to 'Ancient Voices'." *Billboard*. August 28, 1971.

Vyverberg, Henry. *The Living Tradition: Art, Music and Ideas in the Western World*. New York: Harcourt Brace Jovanovich, Inc., 1978.

Warburton, Thomas. "New Piano Techniques for Crumb's Piano Music." *Piano Quarterly*. Fall, 1974.

Webster, Daniel. "Decomposing." *Philadelphia Magazine*. February, 1970.

Wennerstrom, Mary H. *Anthology of Musical Structure and Style*. Englewood Cliffs, NJ: Prentice-Hall, Inc., 1983 (re: *Ancient Voices of Children*).

Wernick, Richard. "George Crumb," in Vinton, John, ed. *Dictionary of Contemporary Music*. New York: E. P. Dutton & Co., Inc., 1974.

Whealton, Stephen Allen. "The Stark Delicacy of George Henry Crumb." *The Unicorn Times* (Washington, D.C.). n.d. [1976].

White, John D. *The Analysis of Music*. Second Edition. Englewood Cliffs, NJ: Prentice-Hall, Inc., 1984.

White, John D. "Systematic Analysis for Musical Sound." *Journal for Musicological Research*. V: 1/2, 1984.

Winn, Steven. "Sympathy in Sound." *Daily Pennsylvanian*. (Philadelphia). *34th Street Magazine* insert. February 10, 1972.

Newspaper Articles

Åhlén, Carl-Gunnar. "George Crumb—ende 70-talisten," *Svenska Dagbladet* (Stockholm), October 20, 1978.

Albaugh, Edwin. "George Crumb: Far-Out Music with Overtones of Appalachia," *Washington Evening Star*, August 15, 1973.

Alter, Allan. "New Crumb Piano Work in Free Recital by Burge," *The Daily Pennsylvanian* [University of Pennsylvania], October 31, 1973.

Amacker, Walt. "A Whale of a Tale." *Richmond News Leader*, October 18, 1975.

Armstrong, George. "Crumb Opposing Composer Cults," *Charleston Daily Mail* [WV], March 9, 1979.

Armstrong, George. "Staging the Scene," *Charleston Daily Mail* [WV], February 28, 1979.

Babcock, Charles R. "The Sound of Music. . .Includes Thunking a Gong Inside a Tub of Water," *Louisville Courier-Journal*, November 20, 1970.

Barras, Rick. "Composer Pens Winning Score in Family Room," *Philadelphia Inquirer*, September 6, 1970.

Bretz, Lynn. "Pieces of Crumb," *Lawrence Journal-World* [KS], February 24, 1980.

Britton, David. "Words to inspire. . .," *West Australian* (Perth), July 16, 1984.

Caldwell, Larry. " 'Hope of a Few Good Pages' Drives Composer Crumb," *Boulder Sunday Camera*, July 8, 1979.

Cardona, Patricia. "George Crumb, Creador del Sonido 'Micrócosmico'," *Uno más Uno* (Mexico City), April 21, 1979.

Carr, Tim. "3 C's of American Music to Be Featured in Twin Cities Events," *Minneapolis Tribune*, April 30, 1978.

Cera, Stephen. "Composer Gets to Face His Own Music," *Baltimore Sun*, December 14, 1970.

Close, Roy M. " 'Echoes' To Be Visual, Aural Happening," *Minneapolis Star*, September 24, 1975.

"Composer Delves Avant Garde," *Wichita Eagle and Beacon*, February 2, 1975.

"Composer Gets $10,000 Grant," *Philadelphia Evening Bulletin*, September 2, 1977.

"County Composer Gets Pulitzer Prize," *Delaware County Daily Times* [PA], May 29, 1968.

Covell, Roger. "The Daring of Diffidence," *Sidney Morning Herald* [Australia], March 15, 1976.

"George Crumb." Biographical Sketches of Persons Selected for the Pulitzer Prizes for 1968, *New York Times*, May 7, 1968.

Culver, Anne M. "Unique Program by Pianist Highly Enjoyable," *Rocky Mountain News* [Denver], January 23, 1975.

Deegan, Cecily. "George Crumb Makes Music with Poetry and Unusual Sounds," *Baltimore News American*, December 16, 1979.

Dubow, Steve. "Music Prize-Winner Crumb Looks 'Beyond Awards'," *The Daily Pennsylvanian* [University of Pennsylvania], December 8, 1975.

Emert, Harold. "US Composer Visits Rio," *Brazil Herald* [Rio de Janeiro/São Paulo], October 14, 1982.

Ennis, Bayard F. "George Crumb Jr. Receives Pulitzer Prize," *Charleston Gazette-Mail* [WV], May 19, 1968.

Ennis, Bayard F. "'Echoes of Time' Stirring up Controversy," *Charleston Gazette-Mail* [WV], September 29, 1968.

Ennis, Bayard F. "Music-Stage," *Charleston Gazette-Mail* [WV], April 17, 1966.

Ennis, Bayard F. "Pulitzer Winner Completes Another Music Composition," *Charleston Gazette-Mail* [WV], November 26, 1968.

Ennis, Bayard F. "State Musicians Contribute to Modern Times," *Charleston Gazette-Mail* [WV], December 8, 1968.

Ennis, Bayard F. "West Virginians for 1968," *Charleston Gazette-Mail* (Magazine Section) [WV], January 5, 1969.

Ericson, Raymond. "A 'King' for Atlanta," *New York Times*, May 24, 1968.

Fagin, Steve. "Even a Paper Clip Comes in Handy When Modern Composer Is at Work," *The Day* [New London, CT], November 13, 1983.

Felton, James. "George Crumb's Manner Belies His Passionate Nature," *Philadelphia Evening Bulletin*, February 13, 1973.

Feyerherm, Joel. "Jeffrey Jacob and George Crumb: 'Together They Make a Team'," *The College Reporter* [Franklin & Marshall College], March 15, 1983.

Finn, Robert. "Crumb: The Man and His Music," Cleveland *Plain*

Bibliography—Newspaper Articles (Continued)

Dealer, October 23, 1981.
Finn, Robert. "Delicate 'Voices' Is Masterpiece," Cleveland *Sunday Plain Dealer*, October 19, 1975.
Finn, Robert. "Ear-filling Treat Will Echo at Severance," Cleveland *Plain Dealer*, November 3, 1968.
Frazier, Michael. "George Crumb: He Composes Dreams," *The Steel City Star* [Pittsburgh], February 8, 1979.
Freeman, R. G. "A Modern Composer Finds Fame, Fortune Are Hard to Attain," *Wall Street Journal*, August 15, 1974.
Gagnard, Frank. "Now For Something Completely Different," New Orleans *Times-Picayune*, January 21, 1973.
Gelles, George. "A Special Homage to Leviathan," *Washington Star*, March 23, 1975.
George, Earl. "Hurray—And Alas! Crumb Likes Concert with Pupil, But Feels Older," *Syracuse Herald-Journal*, March 6, 1984.
Ginsberg, Linda. "Sounds & Silences of Contemporary Music," *The Penn Paper* [University of Pennsylvania], January 10, 1985.
Godfrey, Peter. " 'Almost Heaven' in London. 'Our George' Now Leading Composer," *Charleston Daily Mail* [WV], January 31, 1974.
Greenberg, Gene. "Media Composer Hopes Someone Is Listening," *Delaware County News* [PA], April 11, 1973.
Greiff, Otto de. "George Crumb en Bogotá," *El Tiempo* (Bogotá), March 23, 1984.
Greiling, Franziska L. "Avant Garde: Detroit Already Knows George Crumb," *Detroit News*, October 20, 1978.
Guinn, John. "Crumb Can Compose in Circles," *Detroit Free Press*, October 27, 1978.
Guinn, John. "Crumb's Special Effects Light Up a Music-Filled Week," *Detroit Free Press*, December 7, 1981.
Gwin, Adrian. "George Crumb Jr. Pulitzer Winner," *Charleston Daily Mail*, May 7, 1968.
Haskell, Harry. "Composer to Stage Own Melodic Event," *Kansas City Star*, February 17, 1980.
Haskell, Harry. "Music Master's Fame Deserved," *Kansas City Star*, March 2, 1980.
Haskell, Harry. " 'Star-Child': Exotic Parable," *Kansas City Star*, April 2, 1978.
Henahan, Donal. "The Avant-Groove: We're All in It," *New York Times*, July 7, 1968.
Henahan, Donal. " 'One of the Gentle People,' " *New York Times*, December 13, 1970.
Henahan, Donal. "What a Sock in the Midriff Did for Jan," *New York Times*, January 14, 1973.
Henry, Pat. "Composer George Crumb Creates Musical Magic," *Lubbock Avalanche* [TX], January 29, 1976.
Highwater, Jamake. "How Modern Is Modern?," *Soho Weekly News* [NYC], April 7, 1977.
Holst, Gail. "A Dog's Breakfast, Or Festival Fruitsalad," *Nation Review* [Australia], March 19, 1976.
Horowitz, Joseph. "Music: Brooklyn Philharmonia Plays a Modern American Bill," *New York Times*, February 23, 1980.
Horta, Luiz Paulo. "George Crumb traz à Sala a Poesia Musicala de Lorca," *Jornal do Brasil*, October 16, 1982.
Hume, Paul. " 'Clang, Bang, Hmmm, Sffzzz' You Can Tell by the Sound When George Crumb Is Around," *Washington Post*, July 9, 1978.
Hume, Paul. "Composer George Crumb: He (Sort of) Has the Whole World (of Such and Such) in His Hands," *Washington Post*, August 15, 1973.
Hume, Paul. "Modern Work That Matters," *Washington Post*, March 19, 1972.
"Inspiration in Music of Maoris, Aborigines," *Otago Daily Times* [Dunedin, N Z], March 10, 1976.
Kelly, Frederic. "Awaiting Debut of New Film," *Baltimore Sun*, June 4, 1978.
Kraglund, John. "A Sellout for Crumb?," Toronto *Globe and Mail*, March 29, 1974.
Kress, Dorothy W. "Profile of the Week: George Crumb. The Sound of Music," *Town Talk* (Media, Pa), June 13, 1968.
LaFave, Kenneth. "Afraid to Call the Emperor Naked," *The Daily Wildcat* [University of Arizona], April 11, 1974.
Lague, Louise. " 'Human' Music Coming, Four Composers Agree," *Washington Star*, September 1, 1972.
Loft, Kurt. "Give This Theatrical, Avant-garde Group a Chance," *Tampa Tribune*, January 17, 1985.
Lyon, Raymond. "Palmares de la Tribune Internationale des Compositeurs et Tribune de L'Asie," *Le Courrier Musical de France*, 35: 146, 1971.
MacCluskey, Thomas. "George Crumb, Unique Man," *Rocky Mountain News* [Denver], February 4, 1973.
McHugh, Gretchen. "Composer George Crumb Taps Into Life's Essence," *Birmingham Observer and Eccentric* [MI], November 2, 1978.
McLellan, Joseph. "Welcome to 'Pretty' Modern Music," *Washington Post*, February 18, 1976.
"[Melvin] Strauss to Introduce 2 Works Here," *Buffalo Courier-Express*, October 20, 1968.
Moor, Paul. "Berlin: The Music Festival That Wouldn't Shut Down," *International Herald Tribune* [Paris], October 20, 1976.
Morrow, Bruce. "The Composed Style of George Crumb," *Minnesota Daily* [Minneapolis], February 5, 1981.
"Mother Is Proud of Son's Pulitzer," *Charleston Gazette* [WV], May 8, 1968.
Neff, R. Bretton. "Crumb—Space-Music Collision," *The Sunflower* [Wichita State University], February 3, 1975.
Oliva, Mark. "Weighty Modern Composer," *Nevada State Journal* [Reno], October 3, 1976.
Oliver, Gerry. "Pulitzer Prize Winner Defines Circular Music," *Delaware County Daily Times* [PA], May 29, 1968.
Ortiz, Carlos Barreiro. "Los críticos y la música de George Crumb," *El Espectador* (Bogotá), March 18, 1984.
Ortiz, Carlos Barreiro. "George Crumb: La poética en partituras," *El Pueblo* (Cali, Colombia), March 25, 1984.
Parmelee, Paul. "CU Composer George Crumb Receives Rockefeller Grant," *Boulder Daily Camera*, August 9, 1964.
Pincus, Andrew L. "A Famous Crumb for Lunch," *Berkshire Eagle*

[Pittsfield, MA], August 13, 1976.
Pincus, Andrew L. "George Crumb Composition Is Gaining Recognition," *Berkshire Eagle* [Pittsfield, MA], August 8, 1975.
Pniewski, Tom. "Explorations in Sound," *TV & Entertainment News* [Hong Kong], January 24, 1979.
Porter, Andrew. "George Crumb," *Financial Times* [London], May 20, 1975.
Portzman, Bob. "George Crumb—Music for Tibetan Prayer Stones and Dancers on Trapezes," *Minneapolis Tribune*, May 25, 1978.
Rasky, Frank. "Composer Spends Lunch with a Glass of G Sharp," *Toronto Star*, March 29, 1974.
Redmond, Michael. "College Draws New Sounds to the State," *Sunday Star Ledger* [Newark], February 24, 1980.
Redmond, Michael. "A Composer Talks About His Work," *Sunday Star Ledger* [Newark], March 30, 1980.
Rhein, John von. "Composer Crumb Just Seeks New Sounds," Akron *Beacon Journal*, July 26, 1973.
Rice, Bill. "Crumb Music Is Unique, Surprising," *Schenectady Gazette*, February 4, 1976.
Robinson, Delmar. "Chamber Music Highlight to Be Work by Crumb," *Charleston Sunday Gazette-Mail* [WV], September 9, 1973.
Rockwell, John. "Crumb, the Academy and Hot-tempered Romanticism," *Los Angeles Times*, March 5, 1972.
Ron, Hanoch. "G. Crumb: To Write Sweet Music," *Yedioth Acharanoth* (Tel Aviv)(Hebrew), November 21, 1980.
Roos, James. "Moving Music: Crumb's Gift to Avant-Garde," *Miami Herald*, February 1, 1981.
Salisbury, Wilma. "Composer Crumb Taps Full Range of Musical Thought," Cleveland *Plain Dealer*, February 25, 1972.
Schertzer, Jim. "Arts School's Performance Pleases Composer," *Winston-Salem Journal*, February 8, 1975.
Schonberg, Harold. "The Sound & Fury of Contemporary Music for Piano," *New York Times*, November 24, 1974.
Simons, Nancy. "George Crumb: Beethoven Meets the Exorcist," *Town Talk* (Media, PA), October 2, 1974.
Singer, Samuel L. "George Crumb Picks Banjo in Moon Flight Music," *Philadelphia Inquirer*, November 22, 1970.
Smith, Martha. "Crumb's Mom Recalls Kitchen Clatter," *Charleston Gazette-Mail* [WV], February 3, 1974.
Steinberg, Michael. Review of Ned Rorem's *An Absolute Gift*, *New York Times*, May 21, 1978.
Stockholm, Gail. "Crumb's Music Causes Stir—In Hearts and Heads," *Cincinnati Enquirer*, April 1, 1973.
Thomson, William. "Learn to Respect Individual Tastes," *The Daily Wildcat* [University of Arizona], April 18, 1973.
Tircuit, Heuwell. "Enviable Record of the Composers' Competition," *San Francisco Sunday Examiner and Chronicle*, May 27, 1973.
"Twentieth Century Music: A Diversity of Style," *Almanac of the University of Pennsylvania*, April 26, 1983.
"U.S. Composer Says Oriental Music Inspiring," *Korea Herald* [Seoul], April 18, 1978.
Vermeulen, Ernst. "Hoog niveau op vertolkersconcours van Gaudeamus," *R.C. Mandelsblaat* [Rotterdam], April, 1976.
Webster, Daniel. "Battling Makes the Music Sweeter," *Philadelphia Inquirer*, October 28, 1971.
Webster, Daniel. "Crumb Plucks Muted Note," *Philadelphia Inquirer*, May 7, 1968.
Webster, Daniel. "George Crumb: Time Gives Him Academy Performance," *Philadelphia Inquirer*, January 21, 1973.
Webster, Daniel. "'New Wave' Music," *Philadelphia Inquirer*, May 5, 1968.
Webster, Daniel. "String Section Rebels over Crumb Cantata," *Philadelphia Inquirer*, May 17, 1979.
West, Barbara. "Bowdoin Series Presents George Crumb's Music," Brunswick *Times Record* [ME], July 25, 1978.
Wilkinson, Christopher. "Native-Born Composer Returns to Residency, Performances," Morgantown *Panorama* [WV], March 4, 1979.
Willis, Thomas. "Pulitzer Music Award a Disquieting Omen," *Chicago Tribune*, June 2, 1968.
"WSU to Host Noted Duo," *Wichita Eagle and Beacon*, January 26, 1975.

Dissertations and Theses about George Crumb

Chun, Yung Hae. "The Extension of Piano Techniques in Compositions by George Crumb for Solo Piano." Doctoral dissertation, University of Wisconsin, 1982.
Cordes, Jean Kunselman. "A New American Development in Music: Some Characteristic Features Extending from the Legacy of Charles Ives." Doctoral dissertation, Louisiana State University, 1976.
DeBaise, Joseph. "George Crumb's *Music for a Summer Evening*: A Comprehensive Analysis." Doctoral dissertation, Eastman School of Music, 1982.
De Dobay, Thomas Raymond. "Harmonic Materials and Usages in the Lorca Cycle of George Crumb." Doctoral dissertation, University of Southern California, 1982.
Dubaj, Mariusz. "Makrokosmos." Masters thesis, Akademia Muzyczna, Gdańsk, Poland, 1985.
Faulkner, Susan Green. "An Analysis of George Crumb's *Makrokosmos, Volume II* and Its Relationship to *Makrokosmos, Volumes I* and *III*." Doctoral dissertation, University of Cincinnati, 1980.
Goter, Arlene. "The Treatment of the Piano in *Night Music I* and *Music for a Summer Evening (Makrokosmos III)*." Doctoral dissertation, Indiana University, 1983.
Harrel, Doris. "New Techniques in Twentieth-Century Solo Piano Music: An Expansion of Pianistic Resources from Cowell to the Present." Doctoral dissertation, University of Texas, Austin, 1976.
Houston, Robert Ewing, Jr. "A Comparative Analysis of Selected Keyboard Compositions of Chopin, Brahms, and Franck as Transcribed for the Marimba by Clair Omar Musser, Earl Hatch, and Frank Mac Callum Together with Three Recitals of Works by Bartók, Crumb, Miyoshi, Kraft and Others." Doctoral dissertation, North Texas State University, 1980.

Mac Lean, Suzanne. "A Study of Constructional Principles in George Crumb's *Makrokosmos, Volume I.*" Masters thesis, American University, 1974.

Matthews, Nell Wright. "George Crumb's *Makrokosmos, Volumes I* and *II*: Considerations for Performance, Including Observations by David Burge, Robert Miller and Lambert Orkis." Doctoral dissertation, University of Oklahoma, 1981.

McCarthy, Mairéad Rita. "Symbols and Creative Transformation in George Crumb's *Black Angels*—an Interdisciplinary Exploration." Masters thesis, University of Western Australia, 1983.

McGee, William James. "An Extended Concept of Timbre and Its Structural Significance, with a Timbral Analysis of George Crumb's *Night of the Four Moons*." Doctoral dissertation, University of Arizona, 1982.

McKay, John Robert. "Notational Practices in Selected Piano Works of the Twentieth Century." Doctoral dissertation, Eastman School of Music, 1977.

Moore, Linda Grace. "Contemporary Cello Techniques from the Twentieth-Century Repertory." Doctoral dissertation, Ball State University, 1976.

Ott, David L. "The Role of Texture and Timbre in the Music of George Crumb." Doctoral dissertation, University of Kentucky, 1982.

Reynolds, Karen. "Japan As a Source for New Wind Sounds." Masters thesis, University of California at San Diego, 1975.

Romeo, James Joseph. "Vocal Parts in the Music of George Crumb." Masters thesis, Michigan State University, 1978.

Rouse, Christopher. "The Music of George Crumb: Stylistic Metamorphosis as Reflected in the Lorca Cycle." Doctoral dissertation, Cornell University, 1977.

Sams, Carol Lee. "Solo Vocal Writing in Selected Works of Berio, Crumb, and Rochberg." Doctoral dissertation, University of Washington, 1975.

Shuffett, Robert V. "The Music, 1971–1975, of George Crumb: A Style Analysis." Doctoral dissertation, Peabody Institute, 1979.

Simoni, Mary. "The Computer Analysis of Atonal Music: An Application Program Using Set Theory." Doctoral dissertation, Michigan State University, 1984.

Synnestvedt, Peter N. "A Study of Three Contemporary American Works for Orchestra." Doctoral dissertation, University of Cincinnati, 1985.

Takenouchi, Aleksei. "Numbers and Proportion in George Crumb's Solo Piano Works." Doctoral dissertation, Northwestern University, 1985.

Timm, Kenneth N. "A Stylistic Analysis of George Crumb's *Vox Balaenae*." Doctoral dissertation, Indiana University, 1977.

Yoshida, Kikuko. "A Study of George Crumb: Music Based on Poetic Images." Masters thesis, Tokyo Geijutsu Daigaku (Tokyo National University of Fine Arts and Music), 1985.

WRITINGS BY GEORGE CRUMB

"Black Angels," *Contemporary Music Newsletter*, September/October, 1972.

"Extension Through Time, Space," *Korea News Review*, October 20, 1979.

"Music: Does It Have a Future?," *The Kenyon Review*, Summer, 1980. (Reprinted herein). Reprinted in Spanish in Ortiz, Carlos Barreiro, "Imagen parcial de la obra de George Crumb." Booklet published by the Centro Colombo-Americano, Bogotá, 1983.

"Percussion: the *Terra Nova* of Contemporary Music." A short article included in *Forum des Percussions*. Paris: Centre Georges Pompidou and the Association Acanthes. (in preparation)

"Peter Westergaard: Variations for Six Players," *Perspectives of New Music*, Spring/Summer, 1965.

"Star-Child," Program Notes Written for the New York Philharmonic, May 5, 1977.

See also: Program notes in the "Annotated Chronological List of Works."

INTERVIEWS WITH GEORGE CRUMB

Alcaraz, José Antonio. "Un Dialogo: George Crumb con José Antonio Alcaraz." Mexico City: Ediciones de la Biblioteca Benjamin Franklin, 1977. (15 page booklet in Spanish). Reprinted in "Imagen parcial de la obra de George Crumb." Published by the Centro Colombo-Americano, Bogotá, 1983.

Duckworth, William. Interview with George Crumb, March 20, 1982, in *The Language of Experimental Music: Interviews with 50 American Composers*. Unpublished typescript.

Dutkiewicz, Andrzej. "George Crumb at the Eastman School of Music," *Ruch Muzyczny* (Polish) XX, No. 10, 1976.

Gagne, Cole, and Caras, Tracy. *Soundpieces. Interviews with American Composers*. Metuchen, NJ: Scarecrow Press, 1981.

Haworth, Roger. *How to Talk About Music*. New York: George Braziller, Inc., 1985.

Hume, Paul, and George Crumb. Video-taped Interview at Wichita State University. February 3, 1975. Copy at University of Oklahoma, Department of Music Theory.

Liebman, Stuart. "Who Is George Crumb and Why Is He Telling All Those Stories?" *Boston Phoenix*, November 12, 1974.

"O mais Importante é a música, que transcende a qualquer movimento," *O Globo* (Rio de Janeiro), October 16, 1982. (Newspaper interview in Portuguese).

Plush, Vincent. Interview with George Crumb. Oral History, American Music, Yale School of Music. Interview 148 in Major Figures in American Music Series, October 10, 1983.

Potter, Keith. "New Music," *Classical Music* (England), November, 1978.

Shuffett, Robert. "Interviews with George Crumb," *Composer Magazine* (ed. David Cope), X–XI, 1980. See also: Interviews with George Crumb in the author's "The Music, 1971–1975, of George Crumb: A Style Analysis," Doctoral dissertation, Peabody Institute, 1979.

Varga, B.A. "Three Questions on Music," *New Hungarian Quarterly* 25: 200, 1984.

Discography

Ancient Voices of Children

Jan DeGaetani, Mezzo-soprano; Michael Dash, Boy Soprano; the Contemporary Chamber Ensemble, Arthur Weisberg, Conductor. *Nonesuch H-71255.*

Nellie Lee, Soprano; Pavlik Sedov, Boy Soprano; Ensemble of Soloists of the Orchestra of the Bolshoi Theatre, A. Lazarev, Conductor. *Melodiya* (USSR). (in preparation)

Apparition

Jan DeGaetani, Mezzo-soprano; Gilbert Kalish, Piano. *Bridge BDG 2002.*

Black Angels

The New York String Quartet; *CRI SD 283.*

Same, *CRI Signature Edition (autographed). CE-2.*

The Concord String Quartet; *Turnabout 34610.*

Same, *Vox SVBS-5306.*

The Gaudeamus String Quartet; *Philips 6500 881.*

Same, "Threnody 1: Night of the Electric Insects" only. *Warner Brothers W 2774* (Music Excerpts from "The Exorcist").

Celestial Mechanics (Makrokosmos IV)

Lambert Orkis and James Primosch, Pianists. *Smithsonian Collection N 027.* Re-released by *Pro Arte Records.*

Peter Degenhardt and Fuat Kent, Pianists. *AMU Records* (Germany). (in preparation)

Dream Sequence

The Aeolian Chamber Players. *Columbia Odyssey Y 35201.*

Dreamtiger. *Merlin Records* (England). (in preparation)

Echoes of Time and The River

The Louisville Orchestra, George Mester, Conductor. *Louisville S-711.*

Chicago Symphony Orchestra, Irwin Hoffman, Conductor. In album "The Outstanding Contemporary Compositions of the United States." *The International Music Exchange, Inc.* ("Frozen Time" only).

Eleven Echoes of Autumn, 1965

The Aeolian Chamber Players. *CRI S-233.*

Same, *CRI Signature Edition (autographed). CE-2.*

University of New South Wales Ensemble. *Music Broadcasting Society of New South Wales MBS 5* (Australia).

Five Pieces for Piano

David Burge, Piano. *Advance FGR-3.*

Ingrid Lindgren, Piano. *BIS LP-261.*

Four Nocturnes (Night Music II)

Paul Zukofsky, Violin; Gilbert Kalish, Piano. *Mainstream MS/5016.*

Same, *Desto DC 6435/37.*

Eric Rosenblith, Violin; David Hagen, Piano. *Columbia Odyssey Y 35201.*

John Harding, Violin; David Stanhope, Piano. *Music Broadcasting Society of New South Wales MBS 5* (Australia).

Gnomic Variations

Jeffrey Jacob, Piano. *Orion ORS 84473.*

A Haunted Landscape

The New York Philharmonic, Arthur Weisberg, Conductor. *New World Records NW 326.*

A Little Suite for Christmas, A.D. 1979

Lambert Orkis, Piano. *Bridge Records BDG 2007.*

Lux Aeterna

Jan DeGaetani, Mezzo-soprano; The Penn Contemporary Players, Richard Wernick, Conductor. *Columbia Odyssey Y 35201.*

Madrigals, Books I/IV

Jan DeGaetani, Mezzo-soprano; University of Pennsylvania Contemporary Players, Richard Wernick, Conductor. *AR-Deutsche Grammophon 0654 085.*

Elizabeth Suderburg, Soprano; The Contemporary Group, University of Washington. *Vox Turnabout TV-S 34523.*

Anne-Marie Mühle, Mezzo-soprano; Musica Varia. *BIS LP-261.*

Makrokosmos, Volume I

David Burge, Piano. *Nonesuch H-71293.*

Robert Groslot, Piano. *Queen Elisabeth International Competition Records 1980 022* (Belgium).

Robert Nasveld, Piano. *Attacca Babel d527-2* (Netherlands).

Makrokosmos, Volume II

Robert Miller, Piano. *Columbia Odyssey Y 34135.*

Robert Groslot, Piano. *Queen Elisabeth International Competition Records 1980 022* (Belgium).

Robert Nasveld, Piano. *Attacca Babel d527-2* (Netherlands).

Music For a Summer Evening (Makrokosmos III)

Gilbert Kalish and James Freeman, Pianists; Raymond DesRoches and Richard Fitz, Percussionists. *Nonesuch H-71311.*

Barbro Dahlman and Ingrid Lindgren, Pianists; Seppo Asikainen and Rainer Kuisma, Percussionists. *BIS LP-262.*

Peter Degenhardt and Fuat Kent, Pianists; Wolfgang Lindner and Karl Peinkofer, Percussionists, *AMU Records ETST 038* (Germany).

Night Music I

Louis Toth, Soprano; Paul Parmelee, Piano/Celesta; David Burge and Thomas MacClusky, Percussion; George Crumb, Conductor. *CRI SD 218.*

Jan DeGaetani, Mezzo-soprano; Orchestra of Our Time, Joel Thome, Conductor. *Candide CE 31113.*

Mary Morrison, Soprano; Marion Ross, Piano/Celesta; John Wyre and John Engleman, Percussion. *CBC SM 148* (Canada).

Night of the Four Moons

Jan DeGaetani, Mezzo-soprano; The Aeolian Chamber Players. *Columbia Masterworks M 32739.*

Discography
(Continued)

Sonata for Solo Cello

Roy Christensen, Cello. *Gasparo GS101.*
Robert Sylvester, Cello. *Desto DC-7169.*
Frans Helmerson, Cello. *BIS LP-65.*

Songs, Drones, and Refrains of Death

Lawrence Weller, Baritone; The Philadelphia Composers' Forum, Joel Thome, Conductor. *Desto DC 7155.*

Variazioni

The Louisville Orchestra, David Gilbert, Conductor. *Louisville LS-774.*

Vox Balaenae

The Aeolian Chamber Players. *Columbia Masterworks M 32739.*
Dreamtiger. *Cameo Classics GOCLP9018(D)* (England).
Cuarteto da Capo. Produced by *Casa Abierta al Tiempo/ Universidad Autonoma Metropolitana* (Mexico).

Reviews of Recordings

Ancient Voices of Children

Boehm, Mary Louise. *Pan Pipes*, January, 1972.
Furie, Kenneth. *High Fidelity*, May, 1975.
Hamilton, David. "Toy Pianos, Musical Saws—And a Great Vocal Tour de Force," *High Fidelity*, August, 1971.
Henahan, Donal. "Crumb's Private Music," *New York Times*, July 4, 1971.
Kinsey, Barbara. *NATS Bulletin*, February/March, 1972.
Kolodin, Irvin. *Saturday Review*, July 31, 1971.
MacDonald, Calum. *Records & Recordings*, February, 1972.
Miller, Philip L. *American Record Guide*, August, 1971.
"1971's Best Lps," *Time Magazine*, June 3, 1972.
Northcott, Bayan. *Music & Musicians* (England), January, 1973.
Price, Theodore. *Rochester Sunday Democrat and Chronicle*, July 25, 1971.
Rich, Alan. "Devils and Ghosts," *New York Magazine*, August 16, 1971.
Roberts, Joe. "Sounds of Today," *Lomita News* (CA), January 12, 1972.
Salter, Lionel. *Gramophone*, February, 1972.
Salzman, Eric. "American Composer George Crumb," *Stereo Review*, September, 1971.
Sterritt, David. "Crumb's Amazing Lorca Cycle," *Christian Science Monitor*, June 25, 1971.
Thorne, Michael. *Hi Fi News* (London), April, 1975.

Apparition

Crutchfield, Will. *High Fidelity*, December, 1983.
Crutchfield, Will. *Keynote* (NYC), January, 1983.
Davis, Peter G. *Ovation* (NYC), February, 1984.
Gerber, Leslie. *Fanfare*, July/August, 1984.
Holmes, Thom. *Recordings of Experimental Music*, February/March, 1984.
Kozinn, Allan. *New York Times*, April 29, 1984.
Passarella, Lee. *The New Records*, December, 1983.
Suzuki, Dean. *OP*, January/February, 1984.

Black Angels

Connolly, Justin. *Tempo*, March, 1976. (Philips)
Frankenstein, Alfred. *Hi Fidelity*, June, 1975. (Philips)
Harvey, James E. *The Flint Journal* (Michigan), May 7, 1972. (CRI)
Henahan, Donal. *New York Times*, April 23, 1972. (CRI)
Jack, Adrian. *Records & Recording*, January, 1976. (CRI)
Kunold, Wulf. *Melos*, September/October, 1977. (Vox)
Mann, William S. *Gramophone*, March, 1976. (CRI)
McLellan, Joseph. "Turntable Crumb," *Washington Post*, September 28, 1975. (Philips)
Morgan, Robert. *High Fidelity*, October, 1972. (CRI)
Morgan, Robert. "The String Quartet Is Alive and Well," *High Fidelity*, November, 1973. (Vox)
"Records: Pick of the Pack," *Time Magazine*, December 11, 1972. (CRI)
Rockwell, John. *New York Times*, June 13, 1973. (Vox)
Rockwell, John. *New York Times*, June 17, 1973. (CRI)
Salzman, Eric. *Stereo Review*, November, 1975. (Philips)
Stimeling, Gary. *High Times*, April, 1978. (CRI)
Trimble, Lester. *Stereo Review*, November, 1972. (CRI)

Celestial Mechanics (Makrokosmos IV)

Jones, Raymond. "Smithsonian Album Reflects Our Times," Newport News *Daily Press* [Va], August 12, 1982.
Kozinn, Allan. *High Fidelity*, November, 1982.

Echoes of Time and the River

Frankenstein, Alfred. *High Fidelity*, November, 1971.
Henahan, Donal. "Crumb's Private Music," *New York Times*, July 4, 1971.
Salzman, Eric. "American Composer George Crumb," *Stereo Review*, September, 1971.
Webster, Daniel. "Prize-Winning 'Echoes' Saved from Limbo," *Philadelphia Inquirer*, August 15, 1971.
Willis, Thomas. *Chicago Tribune*, July 11, 1971.

Eleven Echoes of Autumn, 1965

Boehm, Mary Louise. *Pan Pipes*, January, 1970.
Hamilton, David. *High Fidelity*, May, 1969.
Henahan, Donal. *New York Times*, April 6, 1969.
Henahan, Donal. *Musical Quarterly*, April, 1969.
Jack, Adrian. *Records & Recording*, January, 1975.
Mann, William S. *Gramophone*, July, 1975.
Moore, D. W. *American Record Guide*, September, 1969.
Turok, Paul. *Music Journal*, November, 1969.
Ulehla, Ludmila. *Contemporary Music Newsletter* (NYC), April 17, 1970.
(All above reviews are of CRI S-233.)

Five Pieces for Piano

Cohn, Arthur. "Gilt-Edged Aural Securities," *American Record Guide*, May, 1967.
Salzman, Eric. *Stereo Review*, January, 1968.
Strongin, Theodore. *New York Times*, March 26, 1967.
(All above reviews are of Advance FGR-3.)

Four Nocturnes (Night Music II)

Frankenstein, Alfred. *High Fidelity*, November, 1975. (Vox)
Salzman, Eric. *Stereo Review*, August, 1974. (Mainstream)

Gnomic Variations

Simmons, Walter. *Fanfare*, July/August, 1984.

A Haunted Landscape

Ellis, Stephen W. *Fanfare*, July/August, 1985.
Freed, Richard. *Stereo Review*, November, 1985.
Guinn, John. *Detroit Free Press*, June 2, 1985.
Hall, David. *Ovation*, August, 1985.
Kerner, Leighton. *Village Voice*, June 18, 1985.
Walsh, Michael. *Time Magazine*, June 24, 1985.
Webster, Daniel. *Philadelphia Inquirer*, May 26, 1985.
Wierzbicki, James. *St. Louis Post-Dispatch*, June 29, 1985.

Madrigals, Books I/IV

Bender, William. "Records: Summer's Choice," *Time Magazine*, August 30, 1971. (DGG)
Chittum, Donald. "Reviews of Records," *Musical Quarterly*, July, 1972. (DGG)
Daniel, Oliver. *Saturday Review*, December 26, 1970. (DGG)
Henahan, Donal. "Component Maker Meets Record Company—The AR/DGG Contemporary Music Project," *High Fidelity*, February, 1971.
Henahan, Donal. *New York Times*, January 3, 1971. (DGG)
Mayer, Martin. *Esquire*, May, 1971. (DGG)
Morgan, Robert P. *High Fidelity*, November, 1974. (Vox)
Salzman, Eric. *Stereo Review*, January, 1975. (Vox)
Turok, Paul. *Music Journal*, February, 1975. (DGG)

Makrokosmos, Volume I

Bronston, Levering. *New Records*, May, 1974.
Gill, Dominic. *Financial Times*, May 1, 1975.
Henahan, Donal. *New York Times*, March 10, 1974.
Jack, Adrian. *Records & Recording*, March, 1975.
Kengott, Louise. "George Crumb Provides a Musical Feast," *Milwaukee Journal*, September 21, 1975.
Mann, William. *Gramophone*, May, 1975.
McLellan, Joseph. "Music of the Spheres," *Washington Post*, March 10, 1974.
Miller, Robert. *North Carolina Anvil*, April 13, 1974.
Peterson, Melody. "Nudisks: Of Whistled Ghostliness, Four Organs and the Mushroom Men," *Numus West*, May, 1974.
Salzman, Eric. *Stereo Review*, August, 1974.
Thorne, Michael. "Some Crumbs of Comfort," *Hi Fi News* (England), April, 1975.
(All above reviews are of Nonesuch H-71293.)

Makrokosmos, Volume II

Down Beat, February 10, 1977.
Mark, Michael. *American Record Guide*, December, 1976.
Morgan, Robert P. *High Fidelity*, April, 1977.
Salzman, Eric. "The Avant-Garde: In Love with Easeful Death," *Stereo Review*, February, 1977.
Spieler, F. Joseph. *Harper's Magazine*, June, 1977.
(All above reviews are of Odyssey Y 34135.)

Music for a Summer Evening (Makrokosmos III)

Chapman, Robb. "Crumb's 'Makrokosmos'," *Yale Review*, October 28, 1975.
Contemporary Keyboard, September/October, 1975.
Covell, Roger. "A Crumb of Comfort in the Mystery of Space," *Sydney Morning Herald* (Australia), November 22, 1975.
Culver, Anne M. Denver *Rocky Mountain News*, October 19, 1975.
Dolmetsch, Carl. *The Virginia Gazette* (Williamsburg), July 25, 1975.
Dufford, Barb. *Syracuse Guide* (NY), April, 1976.
Freed, Richard. *Stereo Review*, December, 1975.
Harvey, James E. *Flint Journal* (MI), August 17, 1975.
Jack, Adrian. *Records & Recording*, October, 1975.
Kenngott, Louise. "George Crumb Provides Musical Feast," *Milwaukee Journal*, September 21, 1975.
McLellan, Joseph. "Music for Interstellar Space," *Washington Post*, September 21, 1975.
Moevs, Robert. "Reviews of Records: George Crumb," *Musical Quarterly*, April, 1976.
Philippot, Michel P. *Diapason* (France), January, 1976.
Porter, Andrew. *High Fidelity*, October, 1975.
Simon, Jeff. *Buffalo Evening News*, September 6, 1975.
Tircuit, Hewell. *San Francisco Chronicle*, February 15, 1976.
Wells, Tilden. *Columbus Dispatch*, August 24, 1975.
Wierzbicki, James. *Cincinnati Post*, January 30, 1976.
(All above reviews are of Nonesuch H-71311.)

Night Music I

Boehm, Mary Louise. *Pan Pipes*, January, 1969. (CRI)
Davis, Peter G. *New York Times*, September 16, 1979. (Candide)
Ditsky, John. *Fanfare*, November/December, 1979. (Candide)
Flanagan, William. *Stereo Review*, July, 1968. (CRI)
Kolodin, Irving. *Saturday Review*, June 29, 1968. (CRI)
Monson, Karen. *High Fidelity*, October, 1979. (Candide)
Potter, Keith. *Records & Recording*, January, 1977. (CRI)
Smoley, Lewis M. *American Record Guide*, January, 1980. (Candide)
Tircuit, Hewell. *San Francisco Chronicle*, December 21, 1979. (Candide)
Whittall, Arnold. *Gramophone*, March, 1977. (CRI)

Sonata for Violoncello Solo

Frankenstein, Alfred. *High Fidelity*, June, 1975. (Desto)
Freed, Richard. *Stereo Review*, October, 1975. (Desto)
Homfray, Tim. *Records & Recording*, July, 1979. (BIS)
Moore, David W. *American Record Guide*, October, 1979. (BIS)

Songs, Drones, and Refrains of Death

Morgan, Robert P. *High Fidelity*, March, 1974.
Tircuit, Heuwell. *San Francisco Chronicle*, June 30, 1974.

Variazioni for Orchestra

Ellis, Stephen W. *Fanfare*, November/December, 1981.
Morgan, Robert P. *High Fidelity*, March, 1982.
Shupp, Enos E., Jr. *New Records*, September, 1981.

Vox Balaenae

Clarke, John. "Not Man Apart," Published by Friends of the Earth Foundation. League of Conservation Voters. July, 1974. (Columbia)

Reviews of Printed Music

Composite Reviews

Key: AV = Ancient Voices of Children; **BA** = Black Angels; **DS** = Dream Sequence; **11E** = Eleven Echoes of Autumn, 1965; **ETR** = Echoes of Time and the River; **4N** = Four Nocturnes; **LA** = Lux Aeterna; **MBI/IV** = Madrigals, Books I to IV; **MK I/II** = Makrokosmos, Volumes I/II; **MSE** = Music for a Summer Evening; **N4M** = Night of the Four Moons; **NMI** = Night Music I; **SDR** = Songs, Drones, and Refrains of Death; **VB** = Vox Balaenae.

Bennett, Myron. "George Crumb's Music Means Magic and Beauty," *Cincinnati Enquirer*, September 24, 1971. AV/ETR

Carroll, Jim. *Crawdaddy*, March, 1975. BA(Vox)/4N(Vox)/MBI/IV(Vox)/MKI(Nonesuch)/N4M/SDR/VB(Columbia)

Connolly, Justin. *Tempo*, March, 1976. BA(Philips)/MSE(Nonesuch)

Ditsky, John. *Fanfare*, July/August, 1979. DS/4N/LA(Odyssey)

Gill, Dominic. "Crumb of America," *Financial Times* (London), April 22, 1976. BA(CRI)/ETR/MSE(Nonesuch)/NMI(CRI)

Hamilton, David. *Musical Newsletter*, January, 1971. NMI(CRI)/11E(CRI)

Henahan, Donal. "Crumb's Private Music," *New York Times*, July 4, 1971. AV/ETR

Henahan, Donal. "New American Music—Plain and Fancy," *New York Times*, April 21, 1974. N4M/VB(Columbia)

Henahan, Donal. "Neglected Crumb, with Jan DeGaetani," *New York Times*, March 29, 1979. DS/4N/LA (Odyssey)

Lange, Art. *American Record Guide*, June, 1979. DS/4N/LA (Odyssey)

McLellan, Joseph. "Music of the Spheres," *Washington Post*, March 10, 1974. MKI(Nonesuch)/N4M/VB(Columbia)

Morgan, Robert P. *High Fidelity*, June, 1974. 4N(Mainstream)/MKI(Nonesuch)/N4M/VB(Columbia)

Oliva, Mark. *Nevada State Journal*, October 3, 1976. MKI(Nonesuch)/MKII(Odyssey)/MSE(Nonesuch)

Rich, Alan. "Report from Inner Space," *New York Magazine*, September 24, 1979. DS/4N/LA (Odyssey)

Roberts, Joe. *Michigan Daily News*, January 12, 1972. AV/ETR/NMI(CRI)

Salzman, Eric. *Stereo Review*, August, 1979. DS/4N/LA (Odyssey)

Salzman, Eric. *Stereo Review*, April, 1974. N4M/SDR/VB(Columbia)

Simon, Jeff. "Is Top Composer George Crumb America's Genius of New Music?", *Buffalo Evening News*, April 15, 1972. ETR/11E(CRI)/NMI(CRI)

Terry, Ken. "Crumb's Works Accessible on Pair of LPs," Schenectady *Kite*, March 10, 1976. AV/N4M/VB(Columbia)

Ancient Voices of Children

Fennelly, Brian. *Notes* of the Music Library Association, March, 1973.

NATS Bulletin, May/June, 1972.

Black Angels

Odegard, Peter S. *Notes*, March, 1973.

Eleven Echoes of Autumn, 1965

Fennelly, Brian. *Notes*, December, 1973.

Five Pieces for Piano

Clavier, February, 1974.

Four Nocturnes (Night Music II)

Burge, David. *Notes*, March, 1979.

Musical Opinion, February, 1979.

Lux Aeterna

Burge, David. *Notes*, March, 1980.

Madrigals, Books I/IV

Hill, Jackson. *Notes*, March, 1975.

Schweizerische Musikzeitung, November/December, 1974.

Makrokosmos, Volume I

Clavier, January, 1975.

Lusk, Larry. *Notes*, September, 1974.

Makrokosmos, Volume II

Clavier, September, 1976.

Lusk, Larry. *Notes*, September, 1975.

Mandel, Alan. *Piano Quarterly*, Summer, 1977.

Music for a Summer Evening (Makrokosmos III)

Lusk, Larry. *Notes*, December, 1975.

The Musical Times, October, 1978.

Songs, Drones, and Refrains of Death

Fennelly, Brian. *Notes*, March, 1973.

Frank, Andrew. *Notes*, March, 1977.

Selected Reviews of Performances

Ancient Voices of Children

Armstrong, George. "History to Treat Composer Kindly," *Charleston Daily-Mail* (WV), February 11, 1974.

Barrett, Larry. "The Contemporaries Repeat a Miracle," *Washington Evening Star*, March 25, 1972.

Bernheimer, Martin. "L. A. Hears 'Ancient Voices,' " *Los Angeles Times*, December 12, 1973.

Bowen, Meirion. "Sinfonietta," *The Guardian* (London), October 24, 1972.

"Carter & Kiernan Review," *The Prince George's Post* (MD), March 17, 1977.

Commanday, Robert P. "Big Night for New Music," *San Francisco Chronicle*, January 15, 1974.

Commanday, Robert P. "Memorable New Music," *San Francisco Chronicle*, March 27, 1974.

Condé, Gérard. "Les détours de l'Itinéraire," *Le Monde*, March 16, 1978.

Delden, Lex van. "Componist Crumb een ontdekking." *Het Parool* (Amsterdam), March 14, 1972.

Douglass, Robert. "Symphony Gives Merit to Long Work of Crumb," *Fort Worth Star-Telegram*, March 29, 1976.

Ericson, Raymond. "20th Century Works Performed at Philharmonic 'Rug Concert'," *New York Times*, June 16, 1973.

Ericson, Raymond. " 'Voices of Children' Repeats Success," *New York Times*, January 21, 1973.

Eureka, Leonard. "Odd Materials Work in Museum Concert," *Fort Worth Star-Telegram*, March 19, 1976.

Finn, Robert. "Delicate 'Voices' Is Masterpiece," Cleveland *Plain Dealer*, October 19, 1975.

Fried, Alexander. "Avant-garde Music with Both Far-out and Traditional Appeal," *San Francisco Examiner*, January 14, 1974.

Fried, Alexander. "Chamber Music Finds the Other Half," *San Francisco Examiner*, March 26, 1974.

Giffin, Glenn. "Crumb's 'Ancient Voices' Vivid, Intense," *Denver Post*, January 31, 1972.

Giffin, Glenn. "Rocky Mountain Contemporary Music Festival," *Musical America*, September, 1979.

Grabovsky, L. "Sincerity, Sociability, Depth," (Russian). *Soviet Music*, December, 1984.

Griffiths, Paul. "Music in London," *Musical Times*, December, 1972.

Harrison, Max. "London Sinfonietta," *The Times* (London), October 24, 1972.

Hawthorn, Maggie. " 'A Breath Held for Eternity'," Seattle *Post-Intelligencer*, January 31, 1974.

Henahan, Donal. "Concert: Crumb's 'Voices'," *New York Times*, April 17, 1981.

Henahan, Donal. " 'Voices of Children', Crumb's Full-Blown Masterpiece," *New York Times*, November 2, 1970.

Hughes, Allen. "Boulez Leads the Philharmonic in Final of Its 'Encounter' Series," *New York Times*, February 20, 1972.

Hughes, Allen. "Concert: New Music Unit," *New York Times*, April 27, 1980.

Hume, Paul. "Coolidge Festival. 11 World Premieres," *Washington Post*, November 2, 1970.

"Internationale Musikfestwochen Luzern," *Neue Zürcher Zeitung*, August 28, 1973.

Jack, Adrian. "London Sinfonietta," *Music & Musicians* (England), February, 1973.

Jacobson, Bernard. "Wide Variety in 3 New Works," *Chicago Daily News*, January 30(?), 1973.

Johnson, Harriett. " 'Ancient Voices' Magic," *New York Post*, April 17, 1981.

Johnson, Harriett. "Philharmonic in 'Ancient Voices'," *New York Post*, January 19, 1973.

Johnson, Wayne. " 'Ancient Voices' Deeply Moving," *Seattle Times*, January 31, 1974.

Joslyn, Jay. "Musica Nova Apt Addition to Arts Center," Milwaukee *Sentinel*, September 25, 1975.

Kenngott, Louise. "Visible Music Fills Art Center," *Milwaukee Journal*, September 25, 1975.

Kenyon, Nicholas. *New Yorker*, May 25, 1981.

Kerner, Leighton. "Clang, Wail, Scrape," *Village Voice*, March 2, 1972.

Kotschenreuther, Hellmut. "Reiz unter vielen Reizen. Berliner Philharmonisches Orchester mit Zubin Mehta," *Der Tagesspiegel* (Berlin), June 15, 1983.

Kriegsman, Alan M. "Varied Music: Theatrical, Fervent and Bubbly," *Washington Post*, March 12, 1977.

Kristan, Pamela. "'Ancient Voices' Is Unique Musical, Visual Experience," *Boulder Daily Camera*, January 30, 1972.

Leon, Garby. "New Music: Ancient Voices," *The Phoenix* (Boston), August 3, 1971.

Lowens, Irving. "Crumb's 'Voices' Glitters," *Washington Evening Star*, November 2, 1970.

Lowens, Irving. "Music: Today's Composers Fail to Draw," *Washington Star*, March 14, 1977.

MacCluskey, Thomas. "A Marvelous Way to Explore Sound," Denver *Rocky Mountain News*, January 30, 1972.

Mann, William. "Nash Ensemble/Friend," *The Times* (London), September 8, 1976.

Mootz, William. "U of L Series Has Spell-binding Finale," *Louisville Courier-Journal*, April 14, 1976.

Müry, Albert. "Musica Nova aus Amerika," *Basler Nachrichten* (Switzerland), August 27, 1973.

"News Notes," Boletin Interamericano de Musica" (Washington, D.C.), No. 84, July/October, 1972.

Northcott, Bayan. "London Sinfonietta," *Financial Times*, October 25, 1972.

Northcott, Bayan. "A Compleat Singer," *Music & Musicians* (London), January, 1973.

Porter, Andrew. "Musical Events: O Ces Voix d'Enfants. . . ," *New Yorker*, January 27, 1973.

Rich, Alan. "How to Rear an Audience," *New York Magazine*, July 9, 1973.

Roca, Octavio. " 'Fantasy' In Bleeps & Toots," *Washington Post*, May 5, 1981.

Rothbart, Peter. "Ensemble Measures up to the Music," *Ithaca Jour-*

nal, October 12, 1984.
Schertzer, Jim. "Total Stage, Dance," *Winston-Salem Journal*, February 7, 1975.
Schonberg, Harold C. "Music: Brilliant and Eclectic, Yet with Personality," *New York Times*, December 19, 1970.
Schubert, Irena. "Muzyka w Służbie Humanizmu pokoju i przyjaźni miedzy narodami," *Ruch Muzyczny* (Poland), No. 18, 1984.
Schultze, Wolfgang. "Tanz der alten Erde zur singenden Säge," *Berliner Morgenpost*, June 15, 1983.
Schwamn, Nicola. "London," *Music Journal*, January, 1973.
Seelmann-Eggebert, Ulrich. "Festwochen-würdiges am Rande," *National-Zeitung* (Basel), August 28, 1973.
Smith, Martha. "Crumb Work Draws Varied Response," *Charleston Gazette* (WV), February 11, 1974.
Steinberg, Michael. " 'Ancient Voices' Is Superbly Effective," *Boston Globe*, July 27, 1971.
Steinberg, Michael. "Musica Viva Opens Season with 'Ancient Voices'," *Boston Globe*, October 4, 1973.
Steinberg, Michael. "New Chamber Music. Crumb Shines at Coolidge Festival," *Musical America*, March, 1971.
Stuckenschmidt, H. H. "Alte und junge Stimmen," *Frankfurter Allgemeine Zeitung*, July 7, 1983.
Stuckenschmidt, H. H. "Ausgepichte Modernismen und viel Dur-Geschmetter: Internationales Musikfestival in Moskau," *Frankfurter Allgemeine Zeitung*, July 4, 1984.
Tallián, Tibor. "Századunk zenéje a rádióban" (Music of our Century on the Radio), *Muzsika* (Budapest), XX/10, October, 1977.
Unterecker, John. "An Altogether Compelling Performance. Interarts Opens Summer," *Honolulu Star-Bulletin*, June 7, 1980.
Willis, Thomas. "A Masterpiece of Musical Beauty," *Chicago Tribune*, January 29, 1973.
Woolsey, F. W. "Superb Performances Mark Sparsely Attended Concert, in U of L Series," *Louisville Times*, April 14, 1976.

Apparition

Henahan, Donal. "Recital: Jan DeGaetani," *New York Times*, January 14, 1981.
Henken, John. "DeGaetani Sings Crumb Premiere," *Los Angeles Times*, March 16, 1983.
Irby, Francisco. "Pilgrim's Singing Delights Audience," *Colgate Maroon* [NY], March 1, 1983.
Kerner, Leighton. "Lilacs in Bloom," *Village Voice*, January 28, 1981.
Kohlhaarz, Ellen. "Brahms, der Fortschrittliche, Schönberg, der Bewahrer," *Frankfurter Allgemeine Zeitung*, December 17, 1982.
Schweizer, Klaus. "Kammermusikalisches Gipfeltreffen im Badenweiler 'Römerbad' Hotel," *Basler Zeitung*, November 17, 1982.
"Sieben Fantasien," *Süddeutsche Zeitung*, December 4, 1982.
Smith, Patrick J. "Jan DeGaetani, Mezzo-soprano: Crumb's 'Apparition'," *Musical America*, April, 1981.
Swed, Mark. "DeGaetani, Kalish: Polished Teamwork," *Los Angeles Herald Examiner*, March 15, 1983.

Black Angels

Barnes, Clive. "The Dance: Premiere of 'Black Angels'," *New York Times*, April 2, 1973.
Bloomfield, Arthur. "Absorbing Music Program at Mills," *San Francisco Chronicle*, March 8, 1971.
Borroff, Edith. "U Festival Shows Appreciation of 'New Music' Broadening," *Ann Arbor News*, October 29, 1970.
Brown, Mark. "Mozart Concert by Kronos Quartet Is Enjoyable for All." *Mustang Daily* (San Luis Obispo, CA), February 8, 1983.
Cadieu, Martine. "Deuxième Concert de l'Itinéraire," *Nouvelle l'Horaire* (Paris), January 1, 1975.
Chion, Michael. "Paris," *Guide Musical* (France), March, 1975.
Coleman, Tim. "Moderns," *Music & Musicians* (England), February, 1974.
Commanday, Robert P. "Music and Game Plans at Big Mills Festival," *San Francisco Chronicle*, March 9, 1971.
Felton, James. "Concert Spotlights Penn Teacher-Composers," *Philadelphia Evening Bulletin*, October 28, 1971.
Felton, James. "Judging Music's Meaning," *Philadelphia Bulletin*, April 8, 1971.
Finn, Robert. "Crumb Unveils Eerie Sound Effects," Cleveland *Plain Dealer*, October 19, 1971.
George, Collins. "Electric String Quartet a Lovely Shocker," *Detroit Free Press*, October 19, 1971.
Griffiths, Paul. "Gaudeamus Quartet," *Musical Times*, January, 1974.
Gumberts, William. "Ohio Quartet Gives Music New Twist," *Evansville Press* [IND], November 3, 1971.
Henahan, Donal. "A George Crumb Work Bows, and No Tone Is Left Unturned," *New York Times*, November 16, 1971.
Hughes, Allen. "Music: Hampshire Quartet," *New York Times*, May 30, 1985.
Lambert, John W. "Singing Strings," *The Spectator* [Duke University], February 7, 1985.
Lindsay, Noel. "Acoustics Deaden Sound," *The Daily Journal* (Caracas), June 16, 1973.
Littler, William. "Modern Music Workshop a Stimulating Experience," *Toronto Daily Star*, August 2, 1971.
Löhlein, Heinz-Harald. "Auf der Suche nach dem verlorenen System," *Neue Musikzeitung* (Regensburg), April, 1984.
Mila, Massimo di. "Da Varsavia," *Nuova Rivista Musicale Italiana*, July/September, 1975.
"Musique. DePablo, Vaillant et Crumb à l'Itinéraire," *Le Monde*, December 23, 1974.
Pehrson, Joe. "A Little Here. . .A Little There," *The Michigan Daily* (Ann Arbor), October 27, 1970.
Putnam, Tom. "1971: Music at Home in Historic Church," *Buffalo Courier-Express*, July 31, 1971.
Rockwell, John. "Concord Quartet," *New York Times*, June 13, 1973.
Trotter, Herman. "'Angels' Dominates UB Recital," *Buffalo Evening News*, March 11, 1972.
Trotter, Herman. "Shaw Festival: Music of the Now in Setting of Past," *Buffalo Evening News*, July 31, 1971.
Vincent, Richard. "Philarte Quartet Displays Skills in Connoisseur Concert," Albany *Times-Union*, August 2, 1972.

Selected Reviews of Performances (Continued)

Wagner, Rainer. "Die Lehren der Väter, die Leere der Söhne," *Hannoversche Allgemeine Zeitung*, January 31, 1985.

Ward, Mark. "Soul's Surrealistic Voyage," *Charleston Sunday Gazette-Mail* (WV), February 12, 1984.

Webster, Daniel. "Music by Composer at Penn Has Rich Orchestral Palette," *Philadelphia Inquirer*, October 28, 1971.

Celestial Mechanics (Makrokosmos IV)

Caruso, Michael. "Penn Contemporary Players Render Fine Finney Quartet," *News of Delaware County* (PA), February 28, 1980.

Cera, Stephen. "Finney Work Given World Premiere," *Baltimore Sun*, March 10, 1980.

Considine, J. D. "Mixed Review for the Chamber Concert," *Baltimore News American*, March 10, 1980.

Fleming, Shirley. "Out of World Pianistic Experience," *New York Post*, November 19, 1979.

Gudger, William D. "Contemporary Music Programmed," *Charleston Evening Post* (SC), May 29, 1980.

Holland, Bernard. "Crumb and Carter by Contemporary Group," *New York Times*, May 10, 1981.

Jarrell, Frank P. "20th Century Consort: Musical Experimenters," *Charleston News and Courier* (SC), May 29, 1980.

Micklin, Bob. "Music Review: George Crumb," *Newsday* (Long Island), November 20, 1979.

Porter, Andrew. "Tributes," *New Yorker*, December 10, 1979.

Roca, Octavio. "20th Century Consort," *Washington Post*, December 9, 1980.

Schonberg, Harold C. "Music: Chamber Society Plays New Crumb Work," *New York Times*, November 19, 1979.

Smith, Patrick J. "Chamber Music Society: Crumb Premiere," *Musical America*, March, 1980.

Dream Sequence

Brasch, Norv. "Modern Classics Brought to Appreciative Audiences," Colorado Springs *Sun*, January 29, 1978.

Cerf, Steven. "Bowdoin's Contemporary Music Festival," *Musical America*, April, 1977.

Feder, Susan. "Aeolian Chamber Players," *Musical America*, June 2, 1982.

Hardy, Owen. "Aeolian Players Play Expressively," *Louisville Courier Journal*, March 3, 1980.

Horowitz, Joseph. "Music: Crumb's 'Sequence'," *New York Times*, April 1, 1977.

Lee, Clayton. "Chamber Music with a Difference," *Edmonton Journal*, February 2, 1978.

Lowens, Irving. "Music: at the Library, a Pleasant 'Dream'," *Washington Star*, December 10, 1977.

Reinthaler, Joan. "The Sound—Aeolian Chamber Players," *Washington Post*, December 10, 1977.

Rich, Alan. "Innovations and Ovations," *New York Magazine*, April 18, 1977.

Warden, Carol. "Maine," *Music Journal*, December, 1976.

Webster, Daniel. "Museum Showcases Crumb's Virtuosity," *Philadelphia Inquirer*, April 1, 1977.

Echoes of Time and the River

Bernheimer, Martin. "Mixed Reactions to Pulitzer Winner," *Los Angeles Times*, March 11, 1972.

Close, Roy M. "Crumb's 'Echoes' Leads Orchestra Fare," *Minnesota Star*, September 25, 1975.

Constantine, Peggy. "Concert Produces 'Interesting Sounds'," *Chicago Sun-Times*, May 27, 1967.

Davis, Peter G. " 'Echoes' by Crumb Played by Juilliard," *New York Times*, November 1, 1970.

Dettmer, Roger. "Mandel Concert Was Swell(tering)," *Chicago's American*, May 27, 1967.

Dyer, Richard. "BSO in All-American Program," *Boston Globe*, February 6, 1976.

Finn, Robert. "Antithetical Music Fine Side by Side," Cleveland *Plain Dealer*, April 4, 1969.

Fried, Alexander. "Symphony's Strange Doings," *San Francisco Examiner*, December 8, 1971.

Harrison, Max. "BBC SO. Albert Hall," *The Times* (London), September 6, 1972.

Henahan, Donal. "Chicago," *Musical Quarterly*, January, 1968.

Henahan, Donal. " 'Echoes' a Hit in Premiere," *Chicago Daily News*, May 27, 1967.

Henahan, Donal. "Festival of Contemporary Works at Tanglewood Is Led by Ozawa," *New York Times*, August 16, 1976.

Henahan, Donal. "Music: Moderns' Orgy," *New York Times*, August 18, 1970.

Henahan, Donal. "Skrowaczewski Opens Juilliard's Moderns," *New York Times*, January 24, 1982.

Highwater, Jamake. "Music Needs More Rainbows," *Soho Weekly News* (NYC), March 11, 1976.

Hofmann, Will. "Katzen-Miau und seltsame Geräusche," *Hamburger Anzeiger und Nachrichten*, November 3(?), 1972.

Hume, Paul. "Milwaukee Music," *Washington Post*, May 14, 1972.

Jack, Adrian. "The Autumn in Warsaw," *Music & Musicians* (England), December, 1972.

Jacobsen, Bernard. " 'Echoes of Time' Gets Welcome Symphony Airing," *Chicago Daily News*, October 25, 1968.

Jenkins, Speight. "Ozawa Offers Rare Fare," *New York Post*, February 12, 1976.

Knapp, Peter M. "Musical Melting Pot," *Patriot Ledger* (Quincy, MA), February 9, 1976.

Loft, Kurt. "Crumb's 'Echoes' an Explosive Adventure in Sight and Sound," *Tampa Tribune*, December 15, 1984.

Luhring, Alan A. "Music Festival Closes with Brilliant Concert," *Boulder Daily Camera*, March 10, 1968.

MacCluskey, Thomas. "Concert Is Called Disappointment," Denver *Rocky Mountain News*, February 29, 1972.

MacCluskey, Thomas. "Variety Highlights Musical at CU," Denver *Rocky Mountain News*, March 9, 1968.

Marrocco, W. Thomas. "Firkusny's Performance Absolutely Memorable," Eugene *Register-Guard*, April 14, 1984.

Micklin, Bob. "Music: A Sonic Boom," *Newsday* (Long Island), February 12, 1976.

"Miscellany," *Composer* (London), No. 30, Winter, 1968–69.

Monfried, Walter. "Pianist, Schermerhorn in Full Accord," *Milwaukee Journal*, April 30, 1972.

Morner, Kathleen. "Odd Goings-On for Symphony in Prizewinner," *Chicago Sun-Times*, October 25, 1968.

Northcott, Bayan. "Modern Proms," *Music & Musicians* (England), November, 1972.

Pfeifer, Ellen. "A Difficult Evening for BSO Listeners," *Boston Herald American*, February 6, 1976.

Putnam, Thomas. "Orchestra Good in Crumb's Music," *Buffalo Courier-Express*, October 28, 1968.

Reyher, Loren. "Symphony Eclectic, Beautiful," *Wichita Eagle*, February 3, 1975.

Sanson, Kenneth. "Reaching Far Out for 'Echoes'," *Chicago's American*, October 25, 1968.

Schonberg, Harold. "Ozawa Leads Boston in Complex Program," *New York Times*, February 12, 1976.

Simmons, David. "Promenade Concerts," *Musical Opinion*, November, 1972.

Sly, Allan. "Crumb, Bernstein, Ives: BSO Offers Unusual Program," *Jewish Advocate* (Boston), February 12, 1976.

Smith, Helen C. "Symphony Does the Unexpected," *Atlanta Constitution*, January 16, 1976.

Spingel, Hans Otto. "Klangsplitter und Klangflächen," *Die Welt*, November 4, 1972.

Tircuit, Heuwell. "Oakland Symphony: Not a Typical Yule Program," *San Francisco Chronicle*, December 9, 1971.

Vermeulen, Ernst. "Holland Festival presenteert Amerikaanse Musiek," *Mens en Melodie*, June, 1976.

Wagner, Klaus. "Nachruf und Echo," *Frankfurter Allgemeine Zeitung*, November 13, 1972.

Webster, Daniel. " 'New Wave' Music," *Philadelphia Inquirer*, May 5, 1968.

Webster, Daniel. "Orchestra Presents, In Past and Present, a Fine Toast to Time," *Philadelphia Inquirer*, January 1, 1983.

Webster, Daniel. "Soloist Kang's Playing Is Sound but Doesn't Mesh with Orchestra," *Philadelphia Inquirer*, January 15, 1983.

Willis, Thomas. "Music Lesson Misses," *Chicago Tribune*, October 25, 1968.

Willis, Thomas. "Unusual Works Premiere," *Chicago Tribune*, May 27, 1967.

Eleven Echoes of Autumn, 1965

Bar-Am, Benjamin. "Original and Subtle Work," *Jerusalem Post*, June 24, 1971.

Blanks, Fred. "Method, Madness in a Melange," *Sydney Morning Herald* (Australia), May 31, 1976.

Bloomfield, Arthur. "Walk-on Livens Concert," *San Francisco Examiner*, October 31, 1968.

Charvonia, David M. "Modern Chamber Works Show Richness & Variety," *Washington Times*, April 19, 1983.

Commanday, Robert. "'Ping' a Visual Musical Excitement," *San Francisco Chronicle*, October 31, 1968.

Cunningham, Carl. "Audience Warms to Chamber Works," *Houston Post*, January 23, 1970.

DeRhen, Andrew. "Aeolian Chamber Players," *Musical America*, July, 1972.

Ennis, Bayard F. "Crumb Work Offers New Pattern," *Charleston Gazette-Mail* (WV), February 2, 1969.

Felton, James. "Avant-Garde Concert Is Praised," *Philadelphia Evening Bulletin*, April 22, 1967.

Grebe, Karl. "Neue Musik—artistisch," *Die Welt*, September 11, 1970.

Greenfield, Edward. "Pierrot Players," *Manchester Guardian*, October 11, 1968.

Henahan, Donal. "Aeolian Ensemble Marks Milestone," *New York Times*, March 23, 1972.

Hughes, Allen. "Aeolian Players at Carnegie Hall," *New York Times*, December 3&4, 1966.

Katzenstein, Larry. "Contemporary Chamber Players at UMSL," *Saint Louis Post Dispatch*, March 28, 1978.

Kraglund, John. "Hawkins: An Exceptional Stylist," Toronto *Globe and Mail*, March 15, 1971.

MacCluskey, Thomas. "Concert Is Aural Delight," Denver *Rocky Mountain News*, March 18, 1969.

Mintz, Donald. "AU Chamber Group Offers Two Outstanding Programs," *Washington Evening Star*, April 21, 1969.

Monson, Karen. "Eclectic 'New People' a Nice Gift," *Los Angeles Herald-Examiner*, February 16, 1972.

Orga, Ates. "English & American Moderns," *Music & Musicians* (England), December, 1968.

Rockwell, John. "Valentine's Day Program," *Los Angeles Times*, February 15, 1972.

Schiffer, Brigitte. "Kammermusikalische Klangspiele in London," *Melos*, January, 1969.

Simmons, David. "London Music," *Musical Opinion*, November, 1968.

Steinfirst, Donald. "2 Musical Works Shock Audience," *Pittsburgh Post-Gazette*, November 4, 1969.

Wagner, Klaus. "Interpretation und Exaltation—Hamburg eröffnet die neue Konzertsaison," *Melos*, November, 1969.

Webster, Daniel. "Contemporary Works Played by Two Groups," *Philadelphia Inquirer*, April 20, 1967.

Five Pieces for Piano

Boyd, Jack. "Large Crowd Hears David Burge," *Boulder Daily Camera*, October 10, 1963.

Doerr, Alan. "Burge at National Gallery. Dwindling Crowd Misses Novel Note," *Washington Post*, October 21, 1963.

Feldthusen, Arthur. "Avant garde i øst og vest," *Fyens Stiftstidende* (Odense), April 29, 1970.

Jacoby, Jan. "Ansten for nutiden," *Information* (Copenhagen), September, 1973.

Johnson, Jack F. "Skilled Pianist Praised," Spokane *Spokesman-Review*, November 9, 1963.

Stockholm, Gail. "Jeanne Kirstein Plays Cage, Crumb," *Philadelphia Inquirer*, March 29, 1973.

Strømholm, Folke. "Moderne Klavermusikk," *Verdens Gang* (Oslo), January 26, 1971.

Strongin, Theodore. "Burge Presents 3d Piano Recital," *New York Times*, October 22, 1963.

Trimble, Lester. "Pianist Plays Exciting Recital," *Washington Star*, October 21, 1963.

Four Nocturnes

Dwyer, John. "Artful Modern Trio, 'Ghost' Vibraphone Create Eerie Effects," *Buffalo Evening News*, February 4, 1965.

Felton, James. "Program of Modern Music by 3 Gifted Artists," *Philadelphia Bulletin*, February 6, 1965.

Hayes, Deborah. "Paul Zukofsky Displays Mastery of Technique," *Boulder Daily Camera*, March 3, 1969.

Page, Tim. "Violin Concert: Mary Findley," *New York Times*, June 26, 1983.

Reinthaler, Joan. "20th Century Old Masters," *The Washington Post*, November 19, 1979.

Webster, Daniel. "Styles Range at Music Forum," *Philadelphia Inquirer*, March 19, 1966.

Widdicombe, G. "A Big Night at the Embassy," *Financial Times* (London), December 4, 1969.

Gnomic Variations

Baculewski, Krzysztof. "'Mystery, Cafe & Fugue' for Piano," *Ruch Muvyczny*, January, 1985.

Brandt, Maarten. "Jeffrey Jacob: jong musikaal genie," *Arnhem Zeitungen* (Netherlands), October 4, 1984.

Enfield, Patrick. "Concert of Four British Premieres," Ipswich *Evening Star*, September 26, 1984.

Floyd, Jerry. "Gnomic Noises and Jacob," *Washington Times*, December 14, 1982.

Ganer, Karen Marie. "En utsøkt klaveraften," *Aftenposten* (Oslo), May 26, 1984.

Goldberg, Albert. "Kalish Plays Works of 20th Century," *Los Angeles Times*, February 22, 1985.

Hoffmann, W. L. "US Pianist's Playing of Outstanding Quality," *Canberra Living* (Australia), May 28, 1984.

Holland, Bernard. "Concert: David Burge," *New York Times*, March 20, 1984.

Hoover, Joanne Sheehy. "Gnomic Variations," *Musical America*, April, 1983.

Hoover, Joanne Sheehy. "Jeffrey Jacob," *Washington Post*, December 13, 1982.

Kiørbye, Erik. "Kompetent Pianist," *Vestkysten* (Esbjerg, Denmark), December 10, 1983.

Neesen, Koos. "Jacob zeer begaafde pianist," *Tilburg Zeitungen* (Netherlands), October 2, 1984.

Renkin, Indira. "Pianist Performs," *The College Reporter* (Franklin & Marshall College), March 15, 1983.

Richards, Denby. "Contemporary Enjoyment," *Music and Musicians* (England), November, 1984.

Richards, Denby. "Pianistic Panache," *Hampstead & Highgate Express* (England), September 28, 1984.

Saunders, L. C. M. "Pianist's Skill a Marvel," *NZ Herald* (Auckland, New Zealand), May 30, 1984.

Silsbury, Elizabeth. "Five of the Finest," *The Advertiser* (Adelaide, Australia), May 25, 1984.

Waskowska, Teresa. "Eksklusiv Klaveraften," *Berlingske Tidende* (Copenhagen), December 9, 1983.

White, Michael John. "Purcell Room. Jeffrey Jacob," *The Guardian*, September 29, 1984.

A Haunted Landscape

Aprahamian, Felix. "The Apotheosis of an Orchestra," *The Sunday Times* (London), June 2, 1985.

Blanc, Roger. "Horizons '84," *Perspectives of New Music*, Spring/Summer, 1984.

Cole, Hugo. "New York PO," *The Guardian*, June 1, 1985.

Eckert, Thor, Jr. "New York Philharmonic Finds Promise on the Musical Horizon," *Christian Science Monitor*, June 20, 1984.

Foletto, Angelo. "Per Ravel in technicolor uno scroscio di applausi," *La Stampa* (Milan), June 20, 1985.

Frullini, Andrea. "Dvorak, Ravel, Crumb Entusiasma la Scala in transcinate Mehta," *Il Giornale* (Milan), June 20, 1985.

Goodman, Peter. "A Contemporary Mix," *Newsday* (Long Island, NY), June 9, 1984.

Griffiths, Paul. "NYPO/Mehta," *The Times*, May 31, 1985.

Henahan, Donal. "Philharmonic: Crumb and Knussen Premieres," *New York Times*, June 8, 1984.

Loppert, Max. "Americans Perform American," *Financial Times*, June 1, 1985.

McDonald, William. "Philharmonic Finale: A Touch of Americana," *Scranton Tribune*, May 6, 1985.

Orgill, Roxane. "'New Romanticism': Where the Wild Sounds Are," Bergen County *Record* [NJ], June 11, 1984.

Page, Tim. "Philharmonic New Music in a Festival Rehearsal," *New York Times*, June 9, 1983. (fragment only).

Porter, Andrew. "Gold and Blues," *New Yorker*, July 2, 1984.

Reeve, Stephen. "US Connections in London," *Classical Music*, July 20, 1985.

Rockwell, John. "Music: 'Haunted Landscape'," *New York Times*, April 29, 1985.

Rossi, Luigi. "Con Mehta alla Scala dopo il gelo, il fuoco," *La Stampa* (Milan), June 20, 1985.

Smith, Patrick J. "Horizons '84," *Musical America*, October, 1984.

Stadlen, Peter. "New York Philharmonic," *Daily Telegraph* (London), June 1, 1985.

Swan, Annalyn. "Romantic Longings," *The Atlantic*, November, 1984.

Vail, Chris. "Philharmonic Closes Season," *Wilkes-Barre Citizens' Voice*, May 6, 1985.

Valdes, Lesley. "Crumb: Mood Pieces," *Women's Wear Daily*, June 14, 1984.

Walsh, Stephen. "Michelangeli's Magic Conjuring Trick," *The Observer* (London), June 2, 1985.

Zakariasen, Bill. "Enjoyable Revivals & New Horizons," *Ovation*, August, 1984.

Zakariasen, Bill. "Romance Blooms in New Music," New York *Daily News*, June 9, 1984.

A Little Suite for Christmas, 1979

Ågren, Lennart. "Pianokonst på hög nivå," *Örebro Newspaper* (Sweden), April 9, 1983.

Charvonia, David M. "A Musical Parallel to Nightmares and Dreams," *Washington Times*, December 12, 1983.

Libbey, Theodore W., Jr. "Crumb Work Is Premiered," *Washington Star*, December 15, 1980.

McLellan, Joseph. "Spicing the Season," *Washington Post*, December 31, 1984.

Roca, Octavio. "Holiday Concert," *Washington Post*, December 23, 1981.

Rothstein, Edward. "Review," *New York Times*, March 18, 1984.

Takei, Kōichi. "Chie Roden Piano Recital," *Ongaku no Sekai* (Tokyo), March, 1985.

Waskowska, Teresa. "Ny Klavermusik," *Berlingske Tidende* (Copenhagen), September 23, 1981.

Lux Aeterna

Allsopp, Sidney. "Music," *Richmond Times-Dispatch*, January 17, 1972.

Canick, Michael. "Insects and Syllables," *The Dartmouth*, August 4, 1972.

Hume, Paul. "The Message of the Requiem," *Washington Post*, January 23, 1973.

Johnson, Tom. "Let There Be Lux," *Village Voice*, April 20, 1972.

Lowens, Irving. "George Crumb's Magic—Another World," *Washington Evening Star*, January 23, 1973.

McLellan, Joseph. "The Candle As an Instrument," *Washington Post*, February 11, 1976.

Scarborough, Charles. "Music," *Richmond News Leader*, January 17, 1972.

Madrigals (Books I/IV)

Cole, Hugh. "American Music," *The Guardian*, June 7, 1973. (Bk I)

Commandy, Robert. "Enchanting Chamber Music," *San Francisco Chronicle*, October 22, 1975. (Bks I/IV)

Covell, Roger. "Impassive Mastery and a Speaking Likeness," *Sydney Morning Herald* (Australia), March 31, 1976. (Bk I)

Delden, Lex van. "The Sixth Congress of the International Music Council," *Sonorum Speculum* No. 37, Winter 1968/69. (Bk I)

Fleming, Shirley. "Speculum Musicae," *Musical America*, February, 1973. (Bk I)

Fried, Alexander. "Pillow Program's Musical Rewards," *San Francisco Examiner*, October 21, 1975. (Bks I/IV)

Gelles, George. "Crumb Works Delight at Chamber Concert," *Washington Star*, December 15, 1970. (Bks III/IV)

Gwilt, David. "Group Gives Exciting, Gratifying Performance," *South China Morning Post* (Hongkong), March 6, 1976. (Bk I)

Henahan, Donal. "Music Fete," *New York Times*, August 9, 1972. (Bks I/II)

Hinterberger, John. "New Music Group Gives First Concert," *Seattle Times*, December 5, 1966. (Bk I)

Hughes, Allen. "Ensemble Plays New Composers," *New York Times*, April 12, 1966. (Bks I/II)

Hume, Paul. "Crumb's Miracles," *Washington Post*, February 29, 1972. (Bk III)

Hume, Paul. "Varèse, Crumb, Bartók," *Washington Post*, December 15, 1970. (Bks III/IV)

Johnson, Tom. "Policing the Style Away," *Village Voice*, November 16, 1972. (Bk II)

Johnson, Wayne. "Crumb at U.W.," *Seattle Times*, March 9, 1970. (Bks I/IV)

Lowens, Irving. "Interesting Concert Opens Tawes Center," *Washington Evening Star*, May 11, 1966. (Bks I/II)

Lowens, Irving. "A Persuasive Plea for the Avant-Garde," *Washington Evening Star*, March 12, 1966. (Bks I/II)

Man, Hugo. "Crumb Was Just a Little Too Far Out," *Hongkong Standard*, March 6, 1976. (Bk I)

Maylan, Richard. "Imaginative New American Music," *The Times* (London), June 7, 1973. (Bk I)

Miller, Stephanie. "Contemporary Group in Superlative Concert," *Seattle Post-Intelligencer*, November 11, 1971. (Bks III/IV)

Parris, Robert. "Works Rarely Heard Live," *Washington Star-News*, January 28, 1975. (Bks I/II)

Porter, Andrew. "Musical Events: Catching Up," *New Yorker*, March 21, 1977. (Bk III)

Potter, Keith. "Contemporary," *Music & Musicians* (England), August, 1973. (Bk I)

Putnam, Thomas. "Contemporary Chamber Ensemble Electrifies Scant House at Library," *Washington Post*, March 12, 1966. (Bks I/II)

Reinthaler, Joan. "Underattended 'Renaissance'," *Washington Post*, April 11, 1972. (Bk I)

Rogers, Emmy Brady. "New Works—Colorado," *Music Journal*, June, 1966. (Bk I)

Salzman, Eric. "Chamber Music Finale—Madrigals Stand Out," *New York Herald Tribune*, April 12, 1966. (Bks I/II)

Sinclair, John. "Something Missing," *The Herald* (Melbourne), March 25, 1976. (Bk I)

Singer, Samuel L. "Concert Series Launched on Unusual Note," *Philadelphia Inquirer*, February 21, 1966. (Bk I)

Stromberg, Rolf. *Seattle Post-Intelligencer*, March 9, 1970. (Bks I/IV)

Makrokosmos I

Åhlén, Carl-Gunnar. "Fyra dimensioner," *Svenska Dagbladet* (Stockholm), October 21, 1978.

Arlen, Walter. "Pianist David Burge in Cal State Debut," *Los Angeles Times*, November 17, 1973.

Beck, David L. "Pianist Performs Excellently at U. Concert," *Salt Lake City Tribune*, May 13, 1974.

Bentzon, Niels Viggo. "Musik i verdensklasse," *Politiken* (Copenhagen), October 22, 1978.

Bertsche, Sam. "Lecture-Recital Outstanding," *Manhattan Mercury* (KS), February 2, 1978.

Blechner, Mark. "Bizarre Sounds from Burge," *Chicago Daily News*, February 19, 1973.

Selected Reviews of Performances (Continued)

Bockhoff, Baldur. "Der Abonnentenschreck. Valery Afanassiav im Münchner Herkulessaal," *Süddeutsche Zeitung*, March 18, 1982.

Cable, Susan. "Skillful Burge Plays Piano Inside Out," *Denver Post*, October 25, 1973.

Craig, John. "Concert Season Begins on an Exciting Schedule," *Louisville Times*, September 16, 1978.

"Crumb Is Praised," *BMI Many Worlds of Music*, Spring, 1974.

Culver, Anne M. "Burge, Crumb Together Contenders for Fame," Denver *Rocky Mountain News*, October 25, 1973.

Emmerik, Paul van. "Nasveld duikt tretzeker in piano," *Het Parool*, December 10, 1984. (with Makrokosmos II)

Erickson, Raymond. "Burge Conjures Up a Mystical Collage of Music by Crumb," *New York Times*, November 7, 1973.

Evett, Robert. "Burge Masterful, Crumb Work Dull," *Washington Star-News*, August 15, 1973.

Felton, James. "Pianist David Burge Plays Strong Avant-Garde Fare," *Philadelphia Evening Bulletin*, November 7, 1973.

Finn, Robert. "Burge Shows Off Crumb's Originality," Cleveland *Plain Dealer*, May 18, 1973.

Gamer, Carlton. "Current Chronicle. Colorado Springs, Colorado," *Musical Quarterly*, July, 1973.

Giffin, Glenn. "Pianist Burge Puts Frosting on Crumb," *Denver Post*, February 9, 1973.

Harris, Bill. "Sensitive Touch Carries Pianist," *Kalamazoo Western Herald*, February 23, 1973.

Harvey, James E. "Burge Proves Himself 'Magician' of the Piano," *Flint Journal*, November 4, 1974.

Henahan, Donal. "Music: White Mountains Arts Fete," *New York Times*, August 21, 1973.

Henahan, Donal. "Makrokosmos Volume I," *New York Times*, March 10, 1974.

Hume, Paul. "Contemporary Mix," *Washington Post*, August 15, 1973.

Hume, Paul. "Crumb's 'Makrokosmos' Is Compared to Debussy," *Wichita Sunflower*, February 5, 1975. (with Makrokosmos II)

Hume, Paul. "20th Century Consort," *Washington Post*, February 5, 1979.

Jenkins, Speight. "Zodiac Piano Cycle Receives N.Y. Premiere," *New York Post*, November 6, 1973.

Johnson, Charles. "Burge Interprets George Crumb," *Sacramento Bee*, April 5, 1975.

Lee, Chris. "Master Performance Given by David Burge on Piano," *Woodland Daily Democrat* (CA), April 5, 1975.

MacCluskey, Thomas. "Two Titans of Music Display Their Abilities," Denver *Rocky Mountain News*, February 10, 1973.

McLellan, Joseph. "Makrokosmos," *Washington Post*, May 7, 1974.

Mootz, William. "Concert Premieres Are Remarkable," *Louisville Courier-Journal*, September 16, 1978.

"Ny og gammel musikk," *Kristiansand* (Norway), October 15, 1974.

Orosa-Goguingco, Leanor. "Awardee Faurot," *Manila Bulletin*, July 16, 1976.

Putnam, Thomas. "Amplification Adds Quality of Resonance," *Buffalo Courier-Express*, June 15, 1976. (with Makrokosmos II)

Reyher, Loren. " 'Makrokosmos', Burge A Mind-Blowing Duo," *Wichita Eagle*, February 5, 1975. (with Makrokosmos II)

Rich, Alan. "Mr. Crumb Takes the Cake," *New York Magazine*, November 26, 1973.

Severin, Chris. "Pianist David Burge Goes to Heart of Musical Idea," *Waterloo Courier* (IA), May 5, 1974.

Simon, Jeff. "Crumb Compositions Given Added Scope," *Buffalo Evening News*, June 15, 1976. (with Makrokosmos II)

Singer, Samuel L. "Prize Winner Is Played," *Philadelphia Inquirer*, November 7, 1973.

Skouen, Synne. "Elisabeth Klein," *Arbejderbladet* (Oslo), October 14, 1974.

Stein, H. D. "Unusual Sounds—Pianist Delights Crowd," *The Davis Enterprise* (CA), April 7, 1975.

Walsh, Michael. "Old, New in Fine Concert," *Rochester Democrat and Chronicle*, November 8, 1974.

Winer, Linda. "Pianist Is More Than a Morsel of Musical Worth," *Chicago Tribune*, February 19, 1973.

Makrokosmos II

Bang, Arvid. "En reise i det musikalske verdensrom," *Adresseavisen* (Trondheim), June 10, 1978.

Baucke, Ludolf. "Fantasien über den Tierkreis," *Hannoverische Zeitung*, February 4, 1980.

Borch, Jette. "Fantastike Klangverdener," *Fyens Stiftstidende* (Odense), February 17, 1978.

Commanday, Robert. "Robert Miller at UC: Pianist Reveals Some American Secrets," *San Francisco Chronicle*, May 22, 1978.

Culver, Anne M. "Unique Program by Pianist Highly Enjoyable," Denver *Rocky Mountain News*, January 23, 1975.

Emmerik, Paul van. "Nasveld duikt tretzeker in piano," *Het parool*, December 10, 1984. (with Makrokosmos I)

Finn, Robert. "Pianist Miller Plays Brilliantly with Crumb," Cleveland *Plain Dealer*, September 29, 1975.

Godell, Tom. "Lifschitz Shines with New Works," *Michigan Daily* (Ann Arbor), March 17, 1976.

Harrison, Max. "Philip Mead—Purcell Room," *The Times* (London), October 24, 1977.

Horowitz, Joseph. "Jeffrey Jacob Performs Crumb's 'Makrokosmos'," *New York Times*, February 3, 1980.

Hume, Paul. "Crumb's 'Makrokosmos, Volume II'," *Washington Post*, May 26,1975.

Hume, Paul. "Crumb's 'Makrokosmos' Is Compared to Debussy," *Wichita Sunflower*, February 5, 1975. (with Makrokosmos I)

Jena, Hans-Jörg von. "Sphärenklänge aus dem Klavier," *Spandauer Volksblatt* (Berlin), September 23, 1976.

Johnson, Harriett. "Miller Plays Crumb Premiere," *New York Post*, November 13, 1974.

Karevold, Idar. "Ny Klavermusikk," *Aftenposten* (Oslo), October 16, 1979.

Kerner, Leighton. "Fantasies for a Masochistic Piano," *Village Voice*, December 2, 1974.

Lange, Art. "A New-Breed Virtuoso," *The Reader* (Chicago), February 16, 1979.

Leikvoll, Kjell. "Spennende Konsert," *Bergens Tidende* (Norway),

October 22, 1980.
Morgan, John. "At Sprague Hall: Pianist Robert Miller," *New Haven Register*, January 21, 1977.
Moskvitin, Jurij. "Mirakuløs time," *Politiken* (Copenhagen), May 8, 1980.
"Pianist Violet Lam Brings Music-Making Up to Date," *South China Morning Post* (Hong Kong), February 5, 1979.
Porter, Andrew. "Musical Events. 'Stars'," *New Yorker*, November 25, 1974.
Premate, Zorica. "The Avant-Garde: If You Can't Beat 'em, Join 'em," *Knjizhevne Novine* (Belgrade), May 19, 1983.
Putnam, Thomas. "Amplification Adds Quality of Resonance," *Buffalo Courier-Express*, June 15, 1976. (with Makrokosmos I)
Reinthaler, Joan. "Entertainment/The Arts: Alan Mandel," *Washington Post*, December 16, 1974.
Reyher, Loren. " 'Makrokosmos', Burge a Mind-Blowing Duo," *Wichita Eagle*, February 5, 1975. (with Makrokosmos I)
Rhein, John von. "Miller Brilliant in Offbeat Piece," *Akron Beacon Journal*, September 29, 1975.
Rockwell, John. "Recital By David Burge," *New York Times*, March 23, 1976.
Ryker, Harrison. "Lam's Praiseworthy Venture," *Hong Kong Standard*, February 3, 1979.
Salisbury, Wilma. "Burge Gives Crumb Work Stunning Play," Cleveland *Plain Dealer*, April 27, 1976.
Schonberg, Harold C. "Music: Crumb's 'Makrokosmos II' Bows," *New York Times*, November 14, 1974.
Schultze, Wolfgang. "Mit dem Besen über drei Saiten," *Die Welt*, October 1, 1976.
Simon, Jeff. "Crumb Compositions Given Added Scope," *Buffalo Evening News*, June 15, 1976. (with Makrokosmos I)
Thorpe, Day. "Debussy and Crumb at the Phillips," *Washington Star*, May 26, 1975.
Trishich, Ivana. "A Cure for the Burdensome Dreams of Modern Music," *Politika* (Belgrade), August 27, 1983.
Walsh, Michael. "Burge Perfect for Crumb," Rochester *Democrat and Chronicle*, February 11, 1976.

Music for a Summer Evening (Makrokosmos III)

Breuer, Robert. "Breit aufgefächertes Neuheiten-Quintett," *Melos*, No. I/3, 1975.
Campbell, Karen. "Modern Ensemble Debuts with Percussive Crumb Work," *New Manhattan Review*, May 15, 1985.
Caruso, Michael. "'Music for a Summer Evening' Saves Swarthmore Performance," *News of Delaware County* (PA), February 15, 1979.
Finn, Robert. "Music: Crumb Explores New Worlds," Cleveland *Plain Dealer*, April 18, 1977.
Hamilton, David. "Music," *The Nation*, January 25, 1975.
Henahan, Donal. "Music: Creative George Crumb," *New York Times*, January 15, 1977.
Henahan, Donal. "Music: Crumb's Vision," *New York Times*, January 11, 1975.
Kerner, Leighton. "Five Uneasy Pieces," *Village Voice*, January 20, 1975.
Libbey, Theodore W., Jr. "Freeman, Kalish: Reynolds Premiere," *Musical America*, July, 1979.
Libbey, Theodore W., Jr. "Two New Scores at Library of Congress," *Washington Star*, February 24, 1979.
Manning, Mary. "LA Ensemble," *Las Vegas Sun*, April 27, 1976.
McLellan, Joseph. "Philarte," *Washington Post*, January 20, 1975.
Monson, Karen. "Crumb Gives Concert Class," *Chicago Daily News*, April 22, 1974.
Monson, Karen. "Fromm Concert: Crumb, Ghent," *Musical America*, August, 1974.
Perlmutter, Donna. "Makrokosmos III," *Los Angeles Herald Examiner*, September 21, 1975.
Porter, Andrew. "Musical Events: Notes on Notes on Notes," *New Yorker*, January 20, 1975.
"Salzburger Aspekte," *Das Orchester* (Germany), October, 1982.
Singer, Samuel L. "Penn Turns to Its Own Composers," *Philadelphia Inquirer*, April 28, 1975.
Tatham, David. "New Music Society Warmly Received," *Syracuse Post-Standard*, November 15, 1976.
Trotter, Herman. "June in Buffalo: Second Annual Contemporary Festival Features Xenakis, Crumb," *Musical America*, October, 1976.
Watt, Katherine. "Broad Street to Swarthmore: Concerts Classical, Contemporary," *Philadelphia Evening Bulletin*, April 1, 1974.
Weber, William. "Works by Crumb, Davies at Monday Eve Concert," *Los Angeles Times*, January 14, 1976.
Webster, Daniel. "Crumb, Birtwistle Works Open New Swarthmore Facility," *Philadelphia Inquirer*, April 2, 1974.
Willis, Thomas. "Crumb's 'Summer' Blooms Early," *Chicago Tribune*, April 22, 1974.

Night Music I

Brozen, Michael. *Musical America*, August, 1968.
Cohen, Albert. "Music Festival Opener Pleases," *Ann Arbor News*, March 25, 1965.
Dwyer, John. "New Maestro, Philharmonia on the Way to Unusual Level," *Buffalo Evening News*, February 14, 1976.
Dwyer, John. "UB-Rockefeller Association Make Fine Debut," *Buffalo Evening News*, November 30, 1964.
Ericson, Raymond. "Buffalo Center in Concert Here," *New York Times*, December 2, 1964.
Goldberg, Albert. "Avant-Garde Program Stops Far Short of the Far Out," *Los Angeles Times*, February 9, 1966.
Maguire, Jan. "Unique Chamber Concert Breaks New Ground in Paris," *New York Herald Tribune* (Paris), February 1/2, 1964.
Mayer, Martin. "December's Moderns," *Musical America*, February, 1965.
McLean, Eric. "First Canadian Performance," *Montreal Star*, May 1, 1970.
Rogeri, Alfredo. "New Works—Carnegie Recital Hall," *Music Journal*, January, 1965.
Stone, Kurt. "Current Chronicle," *Musical Quarterly*, October, 1965.

Night of the Four Moons

Bar-Am, Benjamin. "A Retrospective Concert of American Music," *Jerusalem Post*, March 6, 1980.

Evett, Robert. "The Chamber Group: Collection of Talent," *Washington Post*, September 9, 1972.

Henahan, Donal. "Music: Durable Moderns," *New York Times*, April 24, 1974.

Hume, Paul. "Superb Musical Theater," *Washington Post*, February 2, 1972.

Kimball, Robert. "Arthur Weisberg Leads Contemporary Ensemble," *New York Post*, April 24, 1974.

Nazzaro, William J. "Susan Starr Peace Concert Soloist," *Philadelphia Bulletin*, July 13, 1970.

Quinn, Joseph M., Jr. "Premiere Concert Lively," *Delaware County Daily Times* (PA), April 4, 1970.

Rockwell, John. "Music: Wolpe's Quartet, Works by Crumb, Foss," *New York Times*, April 18, 1979.

Rockwell, John. "Music: George Crumb," *New York Times*, June 30, 1983.

Singer, Samuel L. "Composers' Forum Program Both Innovative and Perplexing," *Philadelphia Inquirer*, November 23, 1970.

Tircuit, Heuwell. " 'Bonanza' Was Sterling," *San Francisco Chronicle*, November 6, 1972.

Wierzbicki, James. "Music: George Crumb's Hypnotic Silence," *Cincinnati Post*, April 21, 1976.

Willis, Thomas. "Sounds that Boggle the Ear," *Chicago Tribune*, September 4, 1972.

Pastoral Drone

Belt, Byron. "AGO National Convention San Francisco 1984," *The American Organist*, August, 1984.

Metcalf, Steven. "Communal Feeling Pervades Final Concert of Music Festival," *Hartford Courant*, July 8, 1984.

Processional

Driver, Paul. "Variety on Contemporary Front," *Boston Globe*, July 28, 1984.

Goldberg, Albert. "Kalish Plays Works of 20th Century," *Los Angeles Times*, February 22, 1985.

Kraglund, John. "Flute, Piano and Mezzo Achieve Mixed Results," Toronto *Globe and Mail*, December 12, 1984.

Pincus, Andrew L. "Krosnick-Kalish Team Shines," *Berkshire Eagle*, July 27, 1984.

The Sleeper

Hughes, Allen. "Jan DeGaetani in Carnegie Debut," *New York Times*, December 6, 1984.

Zakariasen, Bill. "From the Sublime to Bloop-bleep," New York *Daily News*, December 5, 1984.

Sonata for Violoncello

Borroff, Edith. "First Modern Music Concert a Mixed Bag," *Ann Arbor News*, October 29, 1971.

"Concert Notes: Chamber," *The Strad* (London), January, 1983.

Henahan, Donal. "Evelyn Elsing, Cellist, Performs Crumb's Sonata," *New York Times*, September 23, 1979.

Jöckle, Rudolf. "Farbenspektrum der Unendlichkeit," *Neue Presse* (Frankfurt), May 30/31, 1984.

Löhlein, Heinz-Harald. "Mahlers Sechste unter Gielen und der Cellist Yo-Yo Ma," *Wiesbadener Kurier*, May 30, 1984.

Mann, William. "Park Lane Group. Purcell Room," *The Times* (London), January 13, 1971.

Porter, Cecelia H. "Cello and Piano Duo Hits High, Low Points," *Washington Post*, November 15, 1966.

Rockwell, John. "Music: Yo-Yo Ma, Cellist," *New York Times*, December 10, 1979.

"Schumann, Crumb und Mahler im Museumskonzert," *Frankfurter Allgemeine Zeitung*, May 30, 1984.

Songs, Drones, and Refrains of Death

Cunningham, Carl. "Music: Syzygy," *Houston Post*, March 8, 1979.

Davis, Peter G. "Foss Leads 2 Local Premieres," *New York Times*, January 28, 1978.

Eckert, Thor, Jr. "A Profile in Search of Good Music," *Christian Science Monitor*, October 10, 1980.

Frankenstein, Alfred. "A Dramatic Satisfying Experience in Color," *San Francisco Chronicle*, April 15, 1975.

Henahan, Donal. "Haunting Crumb Work Caps New Music Series," *New York Times*, April 24, 1972.

Hughes, Allen. "Crumb's 'Songs, Drones, and Refrains'," *New York Times*, April 21, 1973.

Kriegsman, Alan M. "George Crumb," *Washington Post*, October 29, 1975.

Lowens, Irving. "Concert Stars Gifted Group," *Washington Star*, March 11, 1973.

Putnam, Thomas. "Albright-Knox: Gallery's New Music Guest Has Virtuosity," Buffalo *Courier-Express*, April 2, 1973.

Rockwell, John. "Devotees of Crumb Share Chamber Unit's Showcase," *New York Times*, May 7, 1974.

Stockholm, Gail. "Music '73 — Pep Pills to Revitalize the Ear," *Cincinnati Enquirer*, April 4, 1973.

Star-Child

Anthony, Michael. "Composer's Effort Wonderfully Eerie, Moving," *Minnesota Tribune*, March 15, 1979.

Ardoin, John. "DSO Concert Engulfs Audience in Circle of Sound," *Dallas Morning News*, February 4, 1980.

Baruch, Gerth-Wolfgang. "Kochtopfdeckel im Gotteshaus," *Stuttgarter Zeitung*, February 28, 1979.

Bender, William. "Star-Child: Innocence and Evil," *Time*, May 16, 1977.

Breuer, Robert. "Boulez: Abschied von New York," *Oesterreichische Musikzeitschrift*, July/August, 1977.

"Caught," *Down Beat*, September 8, 1977.

Chism, Olin. "'Star-Child' Brings Symphony Audience to Attention," *Dallas Times Herald*, February 4, 1980.

Costa, Peter. "Performance Review: New York," *Percussive Notes*, Winter, 1978.

Diether, Jack. "Crumb's 'Star-Child' Romantic Parable," *The Westsider* (NYC), May 16, 1977.

Felton, James. "'Star-Child' Performed with Clarity, Precision," *Philadelphia Bulletin*, May 18, 1979.

Greenfield, Edward. "Star-Child," *The Guardian* (England), April 28, 1979.

Griffiths, Paul. "Proms," *Music Times*, September, 1979.

Haskell, Harry. "Music Hall Was No Ally of 'Star-Child'," *Kansas City Times*, April 7, 1978.

Hawley, David. "Big! This Minnesota Orchestra Concert g-r-e-w," *St. Paul Pioneer Press*, March 15, 1979.

Henahan, Donal. "Concert: 'Star-Child'," *New York Times*, May 24, 1979.

Henken, John. "Pacific Symphony at Music Center," *Los Angeles Times*, March 2, 1983.

Heyworth, Peter. "Crumb's Portentous 'Child'," *Observer* (England), August, 1979.

Johnson, Harriett. "After Grab for the Stars, Crumb Must Settle for Gazing," *New York Post*, May 6, 1977.

Kerner, Leighton. "The Star-Child's Song Defeats the Apocalypse," *Village Voice*, May 23, 1977.

Lonchampt, Jacques. "'Star Child' et 'Tombeau d'Armor' sous la direction de Pierre Boulez," *Le Monde*, November 5, 1977.

Mayer, Martin. "N.Y. Phil.: Crumb's 'Star Child'," *Musical America*, August, 1977.

Micklin, Bob. "A World Premiere to Rejoice About," *Newsday* (Long Island), May 6, 1977.

Milner, Howard. "Modern Proms," *Music & Musicians* (England), October, 1979.

Piencikowski, Robert T. "Paris," *Schweizerische Musikzeitung*, January/February, 1978.

Porter, Andrew. "Musical Events. Children of the Light," *New Yorker*, May 23, 1977.

Schonberg, Harold C. "Concert: 'Star-Child' by Crumb," *New York Times*, May 7, 1977.

Smith, Patrick J. "New York," *Musical Times*, July, 1977.

Spieler, F. Joseph. "Lost Souls: Star Child," *Harper's*, September, 1977.

Webster, Daniel. "Orchestra and 'Star Child' Explore Sounds and Symbols," *Philadelphia Inquirer*, May 19, 1979.

Variazioni

Boser, Volker. "Fafner lugt aus dem Busch," *Abendzeitung München*, November 2, 1981.

Brachtel, Karl Robert. "Amerikanischer Abend in der Musica Viva," *Münchner Merkur*, November 2, 1981.

del Castillo, Maria Teresa. "Un sinfónico memorable con Crumb, Biava y Villa. *El Espectador* (Bogotá), March 25, 1984.

Commanday, Robert. "Oakland Symphony," *San Francisco Chronicle*, December 9, 1976.

Commanday, Robert. "Colorado Music Festival. Adventure, Skill behind Young Orchestra," *San Francisco Chronicle*, July 9, 1979.

Drezner, Manuel. "Un concierto ejemplar," *El Espectador* (Bogotá), March 26, 1984.

Friend, Alexander. "A Strong Night of Sympathy in Oakland," *San Francisco Examiner*, December 8, 1976.

Greiff, Otto de. "Festival musical de Popayán, y otros," *El Tiempo* (Bogotá), March 26, 1984.

Harrison, May. "Leicestershire SSO/Fletcher," *The Times* (London), May 27, 1981.

Henahan, Donal. "Ehrling Leads 3 U.S. Works at Juilliard," *New York Times*, March 11, 1976.

Henahan, Donal. "Music: The Cincinnati Symphony," *New York Times*, March 15, 1983.

Hume, Paul. "Dorati Speaks, the National Symphony Plays—Beautifully," *Washington Post*, April 21, 1976.

Humphreys, Henry S. "UC Fete Has 'Grand Finale'," *Cincinnati Enquirer*, May 10, 1965.

Lowens, Irving. "New Pieces for National Symphony," *Washington Star*, April 21, 1976.

MacCluskey, Thomas. "Fine Program of 20th Century Works," Denver *Rocky Mountain News*, February 17, 1971.

Marsh, Robert C. "Cincinnati," *Musical America*, August, 1965.

Nazzaro, William J. "Haunting Crumb Work Conducted by Ormandy," *Philadelphia Evening Bulletin*, January 26, 1973.

Rowell, Lewis. "Cincinnati Premieres," *Music Journal Annual*, 1965.

Schonberg, Harold C. "Concert: Philadelphians Play '59 Variazioni by Crumb," *New York Times*, January 31, 1973.

Schreiber, Wolfgang. "Amerika, europaeisch," *Süddeutsche Zeitung*, November 2, 1981.

Webster, Daniel. "George Crumb's 'Variazioni' Glows with an Inner Fire," *Philadelphia Inquirer*, January 26, 1973.

Würz, Anton. "Der Bach-Chor in alter Frische," *Bayerische Staatszeitung* (Munich), November 6, 1981.

Vox Balaenae

Bloomfield, Arthur. "The Whale's Sweet Melody," *San Francisco Examiner*, May 28, 1975.

Bowen, Meirion. "QEH, Dreamtiger," *The Guardian* (London), May 22, 1981.

Caruso, Michael. "'Voice of the Whale' a Thought-Provoking Beauty," *News of Delaware County* (PA), November 16, 1978.

Culver, Anne M. "Pablo Casals Trio Gives Mind-Bending Program," Denver *Rocky Mountain News*, November 2, 1973.

Danner, Peter. "'Extraordinary' New Works in Concert," *Palo Alto Times*, August 4, 1978.

Davis, Peter G. "The Players Three Play Crumb Work," *New York Times*, June 4, 1978.

Erickson, Raymond. "Flutist: Sue Ann Kahn," *New York Times*, March 20, 1980.

Finch, Hilary. "Dreamtiger. Round House," *The Times* (London), November 17, 1980.

Furtwangler, William. "20th Century Consort: Treasure Hunt," *Charleston News and Courier* (SC), May 30, 1980.

Galkin, Elliott. "Old and New in Music Concert," *Baltimore Sun*, November 24, 1975.

Gells, George. "A Special Homage to Leviathan," *Washington Evening Star*, March 23, 1975.

Selected Reviews of Performances (Continued)

Genova, David. "Pablo Casals Trio Lives Up to Its Name," *Denver Post*, November 2, 1973.

Henahan, Donal. "Music: Crumb's Touch," *New York Times*, October 12, 1972.

Henahan, Donal. "Music: Inventive 'Voice of the Whale'," *New York Times*, April 7, 1973.

Henahan, Donal. "Music: Sound of 'Silence'," *New York Times*, April 24, 1975.

Hiemenz, Jack. "Aeolian Chamber Players," *Musical America*, February, 1973.

Hughes, Allen. "Concert: Da Capo Players Give Engaging Program," *New York Times*, November 29, 1974.

Johnson, Lawrence B. "Trio Transforms Song of Whales," *Milwaukee Sentinel*, November 18, 1972.

Kerner, Leighton. "Music," *Village Voice*, October 26, 1972.

Lambert, John W. "Bold Encounters," *The Spectator* [Duke University], March 7, 1985.

Lange, Art. "Modern Music with Emotion," *The Reader* (Chicago), March 2, 1979.

Licata, Ken. "'Evenings for New Music' Commemorating the Future," *Buffalo Spectrum*, October 31, 1973.

Mattos, Ed. "National Musical Arts," *Washington Post*, November 5, 1984.

McLellan, Joseph. "Chamber Music Society of Lincoln Center," *Washington Post*, April 3, 1983.

McLellan, Joseph. "Impressions of (and by) George Crumb," *Washington Post*, March 16, 1976.

"Modern Music Ends Program," *Vineyard Gazette*, Martha's Vineyard (MA), August 29, 1980.

Peters, Holly, and Brousell, Richard. "Philadelphia Soloists," *Franklin and Marshall College Reporter*, October, 1973.

Porter, Andrew. "Musical Events," *New Yorker*, October 21, 1972.

Porter, Andrew. "Potpourri," *New Yorker*, April 28, 1973.

Putnam, Thomas. "Evening for New Music Whips Imaginative Shapes," *Buffalo Courier-Express*, October 29, 1973.

Redmond, Michael. "George Crumb's Chamber Work a Challenge to Montclair Audience," Newark *Star-Ledger*, December 19, 1983.

Reinthaler, Joan. "Voice of the Whale," *Washington Post*, March 18, 1972.

Rhein, John von. "Aeolian Musicians Deliver a Whale of a Sea Theme," *Akron Beacon Journal*, April 18, 1974.

Righi, Leonard. "Philadelphia Soloists Entertain 140 at Lehigh," *The Morning Call*, Allentown (PA), October 4, 1973.

Roca, Octavio. "Aeolian Chamber Players," *Washington Post*, November 23, 1981.

Rothstein, Edward. "Chamber Music Society Plays 'Vox Balaenae'." *New York Times*, April 4, 1983.

Saffle, Michael. "Piece of Crumb Caps Superb Contemporary Concert in Belmont," *Palo Alto Times*, July 9, 1976.

Sears, Lawrence. "Camerata Trio Plays in Dark," *Washington Evening Star*, March 18, 1972.

Steinberg, Michael. "A Weekend of Cheering for Tanglewood," *Boston Globe*, August 16, 1976.

Thorpe, Day. "Crumb's New Sounds Sound Strangely Familiar," *Washington Star*, March 25, 1975.

Tircuit, Heuwell. "A Contemporary 'Voice' Is Soloists' Highlight," *San Francisco Chronicle*, December 6, 1983.

Webster, Daniel. "Ensembles Featured at Concert," *Philadelphia Inquirer*, November 20, 1975.

Webster, Daniel. "World of Sound Expanded in George Crumb's Work," *Philadelphia Inquirer*, January 10, 1973.

Composite Reviews:

Key: A = Apparition; **AV** = Ancient Voices of Children; **BA** = Black Angels; **CM** = Celestial Mechanics; **DS** = Dream Sequence; **llE** = Eleven Echoes of Autumn, 1965; **5P** = Five Pieces for Piano; **4N** = Four Nocturnes; **LA** = Lux Aeterna; **MBI/II/III/IV** = Madrigals, Books I/IV; **MK I/II** = Makrokosmos, Volumes I/II; **MSE** = Music for a Summer Evening; **N4M** = Night of the Four Moons; **NMI** = Night Music I; **SDR** = Songs, Drones, and Refrains of Death; **SV** = Sonata for Violoncello; **VB** = Vox Balaenae.

Ardoin, John. "SMU Performance Evidence of Personal Universe," *Dallas Morning News*, January 30, 1980. (AV, llE, MBIII, SV)

Asaf, Oded. "Guest: George Crumb," *Al Ha-Mishmar* (Tel Aviv) (Hebrew), November 20, 1980. (CM, 11E, 4N, MBII, N4M)

Bar-Am, Benjamin. "Concert Honouring George Crumb," *Jerusalem Post*, November 20, 1980. (CM, llE, 4N, MBII, N4M)

Browne, Lindsey. "Adelaide Postscript," *Sun Herald* (Australia), March 28, 1976. (AV, 4N, MBI/III)

Buell, Richard. "Overdoing the Wispy and the Fey," *Boston Globe*, October 6, 1980. (AV, llE, 4N, SDR, VB)

Carr, Jay. "Crumb's Music Evokes Metaphysical States," *Detroit News*, October 30, 1978. (DS, llE, VB)

Chism, Olin. "'Voices' Open Crumb Week," *Dallas Times Herald*, January 30, 1980. (AV, llE, MBIII, SV)

Chrisafides, Peter. *Adirondack Daily Enterprise*, July 17, 1972. (MBI, SV, VB)

Close, Roy M. "'Crumb' Trilogy Completed in Ambitious Way," *Minneapolis Star*, May 26, 1978. (AV, BA, DS)

Cole, Hugo. "American Music," *The Guardian*, June 7, 1973. (MBI, NMI)

Considine, J. D. "Highly Technical New Music Company Opens Successfully," *Baltimore News American*, December 17, 1979. (llE, 4N, N4M, VB)

Crutchfield, Will. "Operaworks Performs 3 Pieces by Crumb," *New York Times*, October 3, 1984. (AV, N4M, VB)

DeRhen, Andrew. "Philadelphia Composers Forum: Crumb," *Musical America*, February, 1971. (MBI/IV, N4M, NMI)

Dwyer, John. "Works of a 'Quiet American' Evoke the Spanish Mystique," *Buffalo Evening News*, June 19, 1976. (MBI/IV, MSE)

Ezrachi, Yariv. "Rich Imagination," *Yedioth Acharanoth* (Tel Aviv) (Hebrew), November 23, 1980. (CM, llE, 4N, MBII, N4M)

Felton, James. "Penn Players Touch Dark Moods of Lorca," *Philadelphia Evening Bulletin*, October 23, 1969. (MBI/IV, NMI, SDR)

Finn, Robert. "Crumb Enchants with His Wails," Cleveland *Plain Dealer*, July 28, 1973. (BA, llE, NMI)

Frankenstein, Alfred. "Lake Placid: The Contemporary Musical Experience," *Musical America*, December, 1972. (MBI, VB)

Giffin, Glenn. "'Ancient Voices' Sing Forth," *Denver Post*, April 6, 1979. (AV, VB)
Greiff, Otto de. "Comentarios musicales," *El Tiempo* (Bogotá), April 2, 1984. (NMI, MKI)
Griffiths, Paul. "Promise That Proved To Be Ephemeral," *The Times*, June 16, 1981. (MBI/IV, SV)
Griffiths, Paul. "Recitals," *Musical Times*, August, 1973. (MBI, NMI)
Hamilton, David. "Music," *The Nation*, January 25, 1975. (LA, MBI, MSE)
Hamilton, David. "Musical Events: The Mirror of Man," *New Yorker*, May 6, 1974. (llE, N4M)
Hecker, Zeke. "The Ethereal World of George Crumb," *Brattleboro Reformer* (VT), August 1, 1985. (A, 11E, 4N, SV, VB & Processional)
Henkel, Wayne J. "More Than Just Mere Crumbs," *Baltimore City Paper*, January 18, 1980. (llE, 4N, N4M, VB)
Horowitz, Joseph. "Chamber Ensemble Plays 'Newer' Music," *New York Times*, February 26, 1977. (BA, MBI)
Kerner, Leighton. "Five Uneasy Pieces," *Village Voice*, January 20, 1975. (LA, MBI, MSE)
Kerner, Leighton. "One's Company," *Village Voice*, October 23, 1984. (AV, N4M, VB)
Kraglund, John. "Much to Cheer About at Concert Featuring Crumb," Toronto *Globe and Mail*, April 1, 1974. (AV, BA, LA, VB)
Liebowitz, Michael. "Mozart and George Crumb Work for Operaworks," *Columbia Daily Spectator* (New York City), October 12, 1984. (AV, N4M, VB)
Loft, Kurt. "Crumb Concert a Rarity Among the Typical," *Tampa Tribune*, January 19, 1985. (5P, MBII, SV, VB)
Malitz, Nancy. "Crumb's Music Weaves Spell," *Cincinnati Enquirer*, March 6, 1980. (DS, VB)
Maylan, Richard. "Imaginative New American Music," *The Times* (London), June 7, 1973. (MBI, NMI)
Moore, Kevin. "Crowd Small, But Concert of Pulitzer Prize Winner's Music Superb," Syracuse *Herald-Journal*, March 8, 1984. (A, SV)
Morgan, Derek Moore. "Sound Experimental," *West Australian* (Perth), July 24, 1984. (BA, llE, MKII)
Patrick, Cas. "Music in Chapel," Hamilton College (NY) *Spectator*, March 9, 1984. (A, 5P, MBI, SV)
Porter, Andrew. "Notes on Notes on Notes," *New Yorker*, January 20, 1975. (LA, MBI,MSE)
Porter, Andrew. "Potpourri," *New Yorker*, April 28, 1973. (SDR, VB)
Potter, Keith. "George Crumb Becomes the Centre of Attraction in 'Dedicated' Festival," *Classical Music* (England), November 25, 1978. (DS, 4N, SV, VB)
Potter, Keith. "Contemporary," *Music & Musicians* (England), August, 1973. (MBI, NMI)
Price, Anne. "George Crumb Is Guest Lecturer at Festival of Contemporary Music," *Baton Rouge Morning Advocate*, February 8, 1979. (MBII, MKI, SV)
Price, Theodore. "Crumb at Shaw Festival," *Rochester Democrat & Chronicle*, August 7, 1972. (BA, LA, NMI, VB)
Putnam, Thomas. "Crumb's Sounds Beguiling," *Buffalo Courier-Express*, June 13, 1980. (MKI/II, MSE, CM)
Putnam, Thomas. "George Crumb Tops Off June Festival at UB," *Buffalo Courier-Express*, June 19, 1976. (MBI/IV, MSE)
Renfrey, James. "A Stimulating Night of Musical Madness," *The News* (Adelaide, Australia), March 19, 1976. (AV, 4N, MBI/III)
Restivo, Valerie. "Jane Bucci Assembles Fine Array of 'Adventurers'," *Albany Times-Union*, February 10, 1976. (AV, 5P, SV, VB)
Rhein, John von. "Festival Ensemble Rivals Storm at Kent," *Akron Beacon Journal*, July 27, 1973. (BA, llE, NMI)
Rice, Bill. "Masked Concert Called Fascinating," *Schenectady Gazette*, February 9, 1976. (AV, 5P, SV, VB)
Rich, Alan. "Innovations & Ovations," *New York Magazine*, April 18, 1977. (llE, N4M, VB)
Rockwell, John. "Music: George Crumb," *New York Times*, June 30, 1983. (N4M, MSE)
Rothstein, Edward. "Music: George Crumb," *New York Times*, February 6, 1984. (A, CM, llE, LA)
Schulman, Michael. "Music: New and Good," *Toronto Citizen*, April 12–25, 1974. (AV, BA, LA, VB)
Schwartz, Lloyd. "Boston Plays America. Crumb Picks Up the Pieces," *Boston Phoenix*, October 14, 1980. (AV, llE, 4N, SDR, VB)
Silsbury, Elizabeth. "Crumb Works a Revelation," *The Advertiser* (Adelaide, Australia), March 19, 1976. (AV, 4N, MBI/III)
Singer, Samuel L. "Concert Marks Composer's Birthday," *Philadelphia Inquirer*, October 19, 1969. (MBI/IV, NMI, SDR)
Smith, Patrick J. "New York," *Musical Times*, April, 1975. (MKII/MSE)
Srodoski, Joseph. "Whitney: Composers' Showcase Evening," *Music Journal*, March, 1975. (LA, MBI, MSE)
Steele, Mike. "Houlton Hurls Cosmic Pictures in Dance Set to Musical Trilogy," *Minneapolis Tribune*, May 27, 1978. (AV, BA, DS)
Strongin, Theodore. "Crumb's Selections Played at Concert," *New York Times*, November 11, 1970. (MBI/IV, N4M, NMI)
Terry, Ken. "American Composers Forum Brings Crumb's Works to Life," Schenectady *Kite*, February 18, 1976. (AV, 5P, SV, VB)
Uttley, Lois. "A Whale of a Performance of Crumb's Compositions," *Albany Knickerbocker News*, February 9, 1976. (AV, 5P, SV, VB)
Webster, Daniel. "Concert Honors Crumb," *Philadelphia Inquirer*, October 23, 1969. (MBI/IV, NMI, SDR) (Reprinted in *American Musical Digest*, December, 1969)
Webster, Daniel. "A Decade of Crumb's Exploration," *Philadelphia Inquirer*, February 27, 1979. (MBIII/IV, 5P, VB)
Webster, Daniel. "George Crumb Cited at Birthday Concert," *Philadelphia Inquirer,* October 23, 1969. (MBI/IV, 4N, SDR)
Webster, Daniel. "Museum Showcases Crumb's Virtuosity," *Philadelphia Inquirer*, April 1, 1977. (llE, N4M, VB)
Wright, Roger. "George Crumb 50th Birthday Concert," *Tempo*, June, 1979. (DS, 4N, SV, VB)
Zapolski, Milton. "Crumb's Music Proves Excitingly Different," Schenectady *Kite*, February 11, 1976. (AV, 5P, SV, VB)

Selected Choreography to Crumb's Music

Ancient Voices of Children

The Alvin Ailey Dance Theater, New York ("According to Eve")
Choreography: John Butler
Also staged by The Bat-Dor Company, Israel
The Australian Ballet ("Night Encounter")
Choreography: John Butler
The Ballet du Rhin ("La Voix")
Choreography: John Butler
The Ballet Rambert, London ("Ancient Voices of Children")
Choreography: Christopher Bruce
The Contemporary Ballet Company, New York ("Yerma")
Choreography: Domy Reiter-Soffer
Also staged by The Pittsburgh Ballet Theatre
The Dance Theater of Harlem ("Ancient Voices of Children")
Choreography: Milko Sparemblek
The Eleo Pomare Dance Company, New York ("De la tierra")
Choreography: Eleo Pomare
The Gloria Newman Dance Theater, Orange, California ("Other Voices")
Choreography: Gloria Newman
The Gudde Dancers, New York ("Ancient Voices of Children")
Choreography: Lynda Gudde
The Hamburg Ballet ("Der Schrei")
Choreography: Fred Howald
Marleen Pennison and Dancers, New York ("The Mute")
Choreography: Marleen Pennison
The Maryland Dance Theater ("Another Voice")
Choreography: Larry Warren
The Minnesota Dance Theatre ("Ancient Air")
Choreography: Loyce Houlton
The Nevada Dance Theatre ("Los Niños")
Choreography: Vassili Sulich
The North Carolina School of the Arts ("Ancient Voices of Children")
Choreography: Richard Kuch
The Noverre-Ballet, Stuttgart ("Stimmen aus der Vergangenheit")
Choreography: Jan Stripling
The Osnabrück Ballet ("Die Zǒfen")
Choreography: Wolfgang Bielefeld
The Pittsburgh Ballet Theatre ("Othello")
Choreography: John Butler
The Wiesbaden Ballet ("Hör mich, Federico . . .")
Choreography: Roberto Trinchero

Black Angels

The American Theater Laboratory, New York ("Black Angels")
Choreography: Jude Bartlett
The Ballet Rambert, London ("Black Angels")
Choreography: Christopher Bruce
The Greater Houston Ballet ("Of No Mind")
Choreography: Gilbert Rome
The Kazuko Hirabayashi Dance Theatre, New York ("Black Angels")
Choreography: Kazuko Hirabayashi
The Maryland Dance Theater ("Groundplan")
Choreography: Larry Warren
The Minnesota Dance Theatre ("Diabolus")
Choreography: Loyce Houlton
The National Ballet of Canada ("Black Angels")
Choreography: Constantin Patsalas
The New Danish Ballet Group ("Tretten Landskaber")
Choreography: Eske Holm
The Pennsylvania Ballet ("Black Angel")
Choreography: John Butler

Dream Sequence

Crowsnest, Connecticut ("Haiku")
Choreography: Martha Clarke, Felix Blaska, Robert Barnett
The Minnesota Dance Theatre ("Contemporary Aire—Discontinued Spaces")
Choreography: Loyce Houlton

Eleven Echoes of Autumn, 1965

The Kazuko Hirabayashi Dance Theater, New York ("Echoes")
Choreography: Kazuko Hirabayashi
The Repertory Dance Theatre of Utah ("Stationary Flying")
Choreography: Glen Tetley

Four Nocturnes

The Mid America Dance Company, St. Louis ("Nocturne")
Choreography: Alcine Wiltz

Lux Aeterna

The Martha Graham Dance Company ("Phaedra's Dream")
Choreography: Martha Graham

Madrigals I/IV

The Pauline Koner Dance Consort, New York ("Cantigas")
Choreography: Pauline Koner

Makrokosmos I

The Hamburg Ballet ("Die Stille")
Choreography: John Neumeier
The Juilliard Dance Ensemble, New York ("The Darkening Green")
Choreography: Kazuko Hirabayashi

Music for a Summer Evening

The Ballet Rambert, London ("Echoes of a Night Sky")
Choreography: Christopher Bruce
Also staged by The Danish Royal Ballet
The Don Redlich Dance Company, New York ("Rota")
Choreography: Hanya Holm
The Jeff Duncan Dance Repertory Company, New York ("Music for a Summer Evening")
Choreography: Jeff Duncan
The Kazuko Hirabayashi Dance Theatre, New York ("Mask of Night")
Choreography: Kazuko Hirabayashi

The London Contemporary Dance Theatre Company ("Moon Sisters")
Choreography: Celia Hulton
The Lovice Weller Dance Company, Minneapolis ("Cycle")
Choreography: Lovice Weller
The Murray Louis Dance Company, New York ("Fantasy")
Choreography: Dianne Markham

Night of the Four Moons
The Ballet Gulbenkian, Lisbon ("Night of the 4 Moons")
Choreography: Vasco Wellenkamp
The Ballet Rambert, London ("Night with Waning Moon")
Choreography: Christopher Bruce
The 5 by 2 Dance Company, New York ("Celestial Circus")
Choreography: Norman Walker
The Juilliard Dance Ensemble, New York ("Night of the 4 Moons with Lone Shadow")
Choreography: Kazuko Hirabayashi
The Nevada Dance Theatre ("La luna")
Choreography: Vassili Sulich

Songs, Drones, and Refrains of Death
The Don Redlich Dance Company, New York ("Threnody")
Choreography: Don Redlich

Vox Balaenae
The Ballet Gulbenkian, Lisbon ("Before Dawn")
Choreography: Vasco Wellenkamp
The Hamburg Ballet ("Das Echo")
Choreography: Sergej Handzic
The Minnesota Dance Theatre ("Seedless Stonemoons")
Choreography: Loyce Houlton
The Nevada Dance Theatre ("Annabel Lee")
Choreography: Vassili Sulich
The Pacific Ballet Company, Seattle ("Voice of the Whale")
Choreography: John Pasqualetti

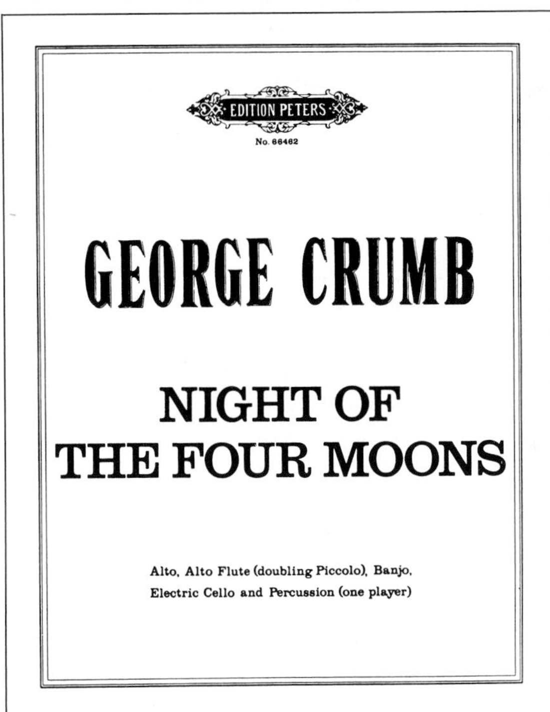

Annotated Chronological List of Works

Prefatory Remarks

George Crumb's compositional activity before the *Five Pieces for Piano* of 1962 (which he regards as his first "representative" work) falls into two categories:

1. ***Juvenilia*** — Crumb estimates that he had composed 40–50 pieces from (roughly) 1939 to 1948. These would include numerous pieces for solo piano, a large number of chamber works (many of which were written for family readings), songs and choral pieces, and pieces for string orchestra and full orchestra (most of the foregoing composed after Classical and Romantic models). Some of the more substantial pieces include: *Two Duos* for flute and clarinet (1944?), *Four Pieces* for violin and piano (1945), *Four Songs* for voice, clarinet and piano (on various English texts) (1945?), *Sonata* for piano (1945), *Poem* for orchestra (1946), *Seven Songs* for voice and piano (on various English texts) (1946), *Trio* for violin, cello and piano (1946), *Prelude and Toccata* for piano (1947), *Gethsemane* for small orchestra (1947), and *Alleluja* for a cappella chorus (1948).

2. **Student works** — Works composed during Crumb's years at Mason College, the University of Illinois, and the University of Michigan include: *Sonata* for violin and piano (1949), *A Cycle of Greek Lyrics* (5 songs) for voice and piano (1950?), *Three Pieces* for piano (1951), *Prelude and Toccata* for orchestra (1951), *Three Pastoral Pieces* for oboe and piano (1952), *String Trio* (1952), *Sonata* for viola and piano (1953), *String Quartet* (1954), *Diptych* for orchestra (1955), and two works listed below — *Sonata* for solo violoncello and *Variazioni* for orchestra.

SONATA (1955) (10 minutes) (P6056)

Solo Violoncello

Completed in Berlin in October, 1955, the Cello Sonata dates from Crumb's student days and reflects well-established traditions of composition for solo cello. The opening Fantasia is based upon the interval of a descending minor third, first heard after a series of plucked chords. The middle movement consists of a theme in binary form, three variations, and a coda in which the theme is repeated on muted strings. The final Toccata is again dominated by thirds which are played in both rising and falling patterns. (Christopher Wilkinson).

Premiere: Camilla Doppmann, cello; March 15, 1957; Ann Arbor, Michigan.

VARIAZIONI (1959) (25 minutes) (P66524)

3343 4331 Perc(5), Hp, Cel, Mand, Str

Variazioni comes at the beginning of a period that represents Crumb's decisive turn toward his mature style. It still carries over the strong influence of Bartók from the composer's youth, in addition to "a touch of Schoenberg and Berg, and a pinch of Dallapiccola."

The work is scored for large orchestra with harp, mandolin, and a considerably enlarged percussion section. The composer has exploited the possibilities of using smaller orchestras within the larger framework in order to achieve maximum contrast in color and texture. The full weight of the orchestra is felt in only three of the eight movements which constitute *Variazioni*.

In formal structure, as Crumb explains, *Variazioni* does not strictly follow the conventional pattern of theme, variations, and coda. It adds another dimension in the form of "fantasy-pieces," which serve as digressions. All the variations are derived from the original theme but the "Fantasia" sections are independent of any formal association with it. The eight parts are performed without pause.

After a short introduction of five bars, the theme (based on a twelve-tone series) is presented in a very delicate scoring. Variation I, a *pezzo antifonale* (antiphonal piece), is scored for strings alone. Variation 2 is a toccata of great intensity, which is followed by the first *Fantasia*, entitled *notturno* (nocturne). The next section, Variation 3, is a scherzo. Then comes the *Trio estatico*, Variation 4, which is the centerpiece of the entire structure and quotes the original theme in full. Variation 5, *Da capo: Burlesca*, is followed by a second *Fantasia*, a *Cadenza*, in which percussion is prominent, and which features mandolin and harp in soloistic passages. The seventh section, Variation 6, is an *Ostinato*. The eighth and final part, *Fantasia–Variazione: Elegia e coda: Tema*, rounds out the work by combining all the entities — theme, variation and fantasy — and employing all the instruments of the orchestra.

Premiere: Cincinnati Symphony Orchestra, Max Rudolf, conductor; May 8, 1965; Cincinnati.

FIVE PIECES FOR PIANO (1962) (8 minutes) (P66464)

The *Five Pieces for Piano* count among the first works in which Crumb found his individual style, a principal feature of which is an extreme sensitivity to the beauty and expressive power of small units of sound, including those produced by unconventional means. Crumb writes: "The *Five Pieces for Piano* were composed in 1962 at the request of David Burge. The work requires a considerably enlarged technique of tone production, for in addition to conventional keyboard sounds, the composer has exploited various sounds produced immediately by contact with the strings — *e.g.*, pizzicato, martellato, glissando, etc. The integration of all these resources points toward a broader concept of piano idiom. Structurally speaking, the *Five Pieces for Piano* derive from a single three note cell, first presented as a chord: B-flat, G-sharp, A. Rhythm, dynamics, and timbre are all freely organized. The work as a whole is in the form of an arch, of which the third piece (Notturno) forms the centerpiece."

Premiere: David Burge, piano; February 12, 1963; Boulder, Colorado.

NIGHT MUSIC I (1963, rev. 1976) (18½ minutes)

Soprano, Piano (Celesta), Percussion (2 players)

Notturno I:	Giocoso, estatico
Notturno II:	"Piccola Serenata"
Notturno III:	*La Luna Asoma*
Notturno IV:	Vivace; molto ritmico
Notturno V:	*Gacela de la Terrible Presencia*
Notturno VI:	"Barcarola"
Notturno VII:	Giocoso, estatico

Crumb recalls that he started *Night Music I* as a purely instrumental composition, but that it only came into focus when he decided to include two verses by the modern Spanish poet, Federico García Lorca. The composer writes: "The work as a whole is a projection of the violently contrasting moods of the two poems: La Luna Asoma (The Moon Rises), with its aura of almost ecstatic lyricism, and the intense, sardonic Gacela de la Terrible Presencia (Gacela of the Terrible Presence). The conflict of mood remains unresolved at the conclusion of the work. Structurally speaking, the seven movements (Notturni) of the composition form a readily perceptible arch design in which the Lorca poems stand as buttress points. Sections of quasi-improvisatory music are integrated into a context of precisely notated music. I have endeavored to enhance Lorca's surrealistic images by means of a highly colored chromaticism and unusual juxtapositions of timbre, register and rhythmic forms."

Premiere: Le Centre du Musique, Barbara Blanchard, soprano; January 30, 1964; Paris.

Text: Federico García Lorca
Published by Belwin-Mills Publishing Corporation

FOUR NOCTURNES (Night Music II) (1964) (9 minutes) (P66465)

Violin and Piano

Four Nocturnes is a further essay in the quiet nocturnal mood of my *Night Music I* for soprano, keyboard, and percussion (composed in 1963); hence the subtitle 'Night Music II.' The four pieces constituting the work are prefaced with the following indications:

Notturno I:	Serenamente
Notturno II:	Scorrevole; allegro possibile
Notturno III:	Contemplativo
Notturno IV:	Con un sentimento di nostalgia

The music is of the utmost delicacy and the prevailing sense of 'suspension in time' is only briefly interrupted by the animated and rhythmically more forceful second piece. The sustained lyric idea presented at the beginning of the work, the nervous tremolo effects, and the stylized bird songs are all recurrent elements.

In composing the *Four Nocturnes* I had attempted a modification of the traditional treatment of the violin-piano combination by exploiting various timbral resources of the instruments. Thus a certain integration in sound is achieved by requiring both instruments to produce harmonics, pizzicato effects, rapping sounds (on the wood of the violin; on the metal beams of the piano). The gentle rustling sounds which conclude the work are produced by the application of a percussionist's wire brush to the strings of the piano. (George Crumb).

Premiere: Paul Zukofsky, violin; George Crumb, piano; February 3, 1965; Buffalo, N.Y.

MADRIGALS, Books I/IV (1965–69)

General Notes:

The four books of *Madrigals* were composed in pairs—Books I and II in 1965 (for Jan DeGaetani, on commission from the Koussevitzky Foundation) and Books III and IV in 1969 (for Elizabeth Suderburg). Like *Night Music I*, they are based upon the beautiful poetry of Federico García Lorca. Each book is scored for mezzo-soprano and two or more instruments, and the texts consist of from one to three short sentences which dwell upon the themes of life, death, love, earth, water, and rain. The settings of the texts are subtle, atmospheric, and intimate. Crumb does not strive for any large concerted *tutti* effects, but rather for a relatively large number of sonorous gradations within a small frame of reference. The choice of just a few accompanimental instruments, each with its own unique timbral and idiomatic characteristics, permits the composer to explore their interaction and contrapuntal combination with a meticulousness and refinement that is disarming in its simplicity.

The *Madrigals* are devoid of any esoteric constructive devices except in two notable instances: the first madrigal of Book III contains isorhythm, and the first madrigal of Book IV contains strict retrogrades. In both cases, however, the use of these devices is not arbitrary, but rather suggested in the text itself. (Donald Chittum).

MADRIGALS, Book I (1965) (9 minutes) (P66458)

Soprano, Contrabass, Vibraphone

In addition to the soprano soloist, the madrigals of Book I are scored for vibraphone and contrabass (with low E tuned down to E-flat). In the first madrigal Crumb sets the single line "Verte desnuda es recordar la tierra" (To see you naked is to remember the earth) in two statements in freely measured time, which are separated by opening, middle, and closing passages based on the syllables "tai-o-tik." The second madrigal, "No piénsan en la lluvia, y se han dormido" (They do not think of the rain, and they've fallen asleep), is divided into two main sections (Rain-Death Music I and II) by three bell-like punctuating chords. And in the third madrigal, "Los muertos llevan alas de musgo" (The dead wear mossy wings), he creates a clear formal design through the internal repetition of words, syllables, and phonemes rooted in discrete motivic structures. (Donald Chittum).

Premiere: Contemporary Chamber Ensemble, Arthur Weisberg, conductor; Jan DeGaetani, mezzo-soprano; March 11, 1966; The Library of Congress, Washington, D.C.

Text: Federico García Lorca

MADRIGALS, Book II (1965) (6½ minutes) (P66459)

Soprano, Flute (also Piccolo and Alto Flute), Percussion (1 Player)

The three madrigals of Book II are set for voice, percussion and one flutist, who successively plays alto-flute, flute in C, and piccolo. The first song, the joyous and exotic "Bebe el agua tranquila de la canción añeja" (Drink the tranquil water of the antique song), consists of two statements of the text separated by short melismas on vocalic syllables, both of which are accompanied by alto-flute, antique cymbals, and glockenspiel struck with hard sticks and wire brushes. The second madrigal is a dark, slow, lamentful setting of the text "La muerte entra y sale de la taberna" (Death goes in and out of the tavern), while the last madrigal of this set is an animated response to the text "Caballito negro, ¿Dónde llevas tu jinete muerto?" (Little black horse, where are you taking your dead rider?). (Donald Chittum).

Premiere: Contemporary Chamber Ensemble, Arthur Weisberg, conductor; Jan DeGaetani, mezzo-soprano; March 11, 1966; The Library of Congress, Washington, D.C.

Text: Federico García Lorca

ELEVEN ECHOES OF AUTUMN, 1965 (Echoes I) (1966) (18 minutes) (P66457)

Violin, Alto Flute, Clarinet, Piano

Eleven Echoes of Autumn, 1965 was composed during the spring of 1966 for the Aeolian Chamber Players (on commission from Bowdoin College). The eleven pieces constituting the work are performed without interruption:

Eco 1. Fantastico
Eco 2. Languidamente, quasi lontano ("hauntingly")
Eco 3. Prestissimo
Eco 4. Con bravura
Eco 5. Cadenza I (for Alto Flute)
Eco 6. Cadenza II (for Violin)
Eco 7. Cadenza III (for Clarinet)
Eco 8. Feroce, violento
Eco 9. Serenamente, quasi lontano ("hauntingly")
Eco 10. Senza misura ("gently undulating")
Eco 11. Adagio ("like a prayer")

Each of the *echi* exploits certain timbral possibilities of the instruments. For example, *eco* 1 (for piano alone) is based entirely on the 5th partial harmonic, *eco* 2 on violin harmonics in combination with 7th partial harmonics produced on the piano (by drawing a piece of hard rubber along the strings). A delicate aura of sympathetic vibrations emerges in *echi* 3 and 4, produced in the latter case by alto flute and clarinet playing into the piano (close to the strings). At the conclusion of the work the violinist achieves a mournful, fragile timbre by playing with the bow hair completely slack.

The most important generative element of *Eleven Echoes* is the "bell motif"—a quintuplet figure based on the whole-tone interval—which is heard at the beginning of the work. This diatonic figure appears in a variety of rhythmic guises, and frequently in a highly chromatic context.

Each of the eleven pieces has its own expressive character, at times overlaid by quasi-obbligato music of contrasting character, e.g., the "wind music" of the alto flute and clarinet in *eco* 2 or the "distant mandolin music" of the violin in *eco* 3. The larger expressive curve of the work is arch-like: a gradual growth of intensity to a climactic point (*eco* 8), followed by a gradual collapse.

Although *Eleven Echoes* has certain programmatic implications for the composer, it is enough for the listener to infer the significance of the motto-quote from Federico García Lorca: ". . . y los arcos rotos donde sufre el tiempo" (". . . and the broken arches where time suffers"). These words are softly intoned as a preface to each of the three cadenzas (*echi* 5–7) and the image "broken arches" is represented visually in the notation of the music which underlies the cadenzas. (George Crumb).

Premiere: Aeolian Chamber Players; August 10, 1966; Brunswick, Maine.

ECHOES OF TIME AND THE RIVER (Four Processionals for Orchestra) (Echoes II) (1967) (20 minutes)

3(Picc)030 3330 Perc(6), 2 Pfs, Hp, Mand, Str

Crumb's preoccupation with time dates from his earlier "Autumn" Echoes, but in *Echoes of Time and the River*, this central unifying theme includes a treatment of psychological and philosophical time as well. The spatial projection of the time continuum takes the form of various "processionals"; the four movements of the suite may be realized with the players actually marching about the stage in steps of various length synchronized with the music they are performing. Many of the string and wind players are given extra antique cymbals and glockenspiel plates, and the bell sounds resonating throughout the orchestra also create a dimension of vast sonic space.

The first movement is called *Frozen Time* and features a collage of mysterious and muted textures in overlapping 7/8 metric patterns. After a time, three percussionists make their way ritualistically across the stage intoning the motto of the state of West Virginia: *"Montani semper liberi?"* (Mountaineers are always free); the "ironic" question mark has been added by the composer. The music swells to an intense *ffff* in the middle section with glissandos in all the string parts. As if in answer, the mandolinist exits playing and whispering the same motto darkly as he disappears off stage. The second movement, *Remembrance of Time*, begins with the most distant and delicate sounds imaginable (piano, percussion, harp), echoed by a phrase from García Lorca ("the broken arches where time suffers"). Fragments of joyful music erupt from various wind and brass players on stage and off, and the commotion eventually gives way to a kind of Ivesian reminiscence, evoked by serene string harmonics: "Were You There When They Crucified the Lord?"

The most free and fantastic movement is the portentous *Collapse of Time*. Like the celebrated amphibians of Aristophanes, the string players croak out the nonsense syllables *"Krek-tu-dai! Krek-tu-dai!"* while the xylophone taps out the name of the composer in Morse code. As the movement proceeds and the underlying pulse falls away, the music heads off into a wide range of special effects—bizarre, quasi-improvised fragments passed around among the various soloists (notated in circular patterns in the score!). The descent into the solitude of the finale, *Last Echoes of Time*, comes at first as a relief and relaxation from all the foregoing; once the listener is convinced of the retrospective nature of these last pages, he can begin to explore more securely the implications in these echoes of all that has gone before.

Premiere: Chicago Symphony Orchestra, Irwin Hoffman, conductor; May 26, 1967; Chicago.

Published by Belwin-Mills Publishing Corporation

SONGS, DRONES, AND REFRAINS OF DEATH (1968) (30 minutes) (P66463)

Baritone, Electric Guitar, Electric Contrabass, Amplified Piano (& Amplified Harpsichord), Two Percussionists

From 1962 until 1970 much of my creative activity was focused on the composition of an extended cycle of vocal works based on the poetry of Federico García Lorca. The cycle includes *Night Music I* (1963) for soprano, keyboard, and percussion; four books of *Madrigals* (1965–69) for soprano and a varying instrumental combination; *Songs, Drones, and Refrains of Death* (1968) for baritone, electric instruments, and percussion; *Night of the Four Moons* (1969) for alto, banjo, alto flute, amplified cello, and percussion; and *Ancient Voices of Children* (1970) for soprano, boy soprano, and seven instrumentalists.

Of the eight works constituting the cycle, *Songs, Drones, and Refrains of Death* is the largest in conception and the most intensely dramatic in its projection of Lorca's dark imagery. Although the first sketches for the work date from 1962, it was only in 1968 that I felt I had evolved a definitive form for my musical ideas. *Songs, Drones, and Refrains* was commissioned by the University of Iowa and first performed in the spring of 1969.

The important formal elements of the work are identified in the title. These are, firstly, the settings of four of Lorca's most beautiful death-poems: *The Guitar, Casida of the Dark Doves, Song of the Rider, 1860*, and *Casida of the Boy Wounded by the Water*. Each of these settings is preceded by an instrumental "refrain" (also containing vocal elements projected by the instrumentalists, in most cases purely phonetic sounds) which presents, in various guises, the rhythmic, fateful *motif* heard at the beginning of the work. And finally, three long "Death-Drones" (based on the interval of the fourth, and played by the amplified contrabass) dominate the musical texture in the first and last songs, and in Refrain 3.

García Lorca's poetry, with its fantastically rich expression and evocative power, provides an admirable vehicle for musical re-creation. *The Guitar*, starkly fatalistic, portrays a mood of utter desolation; and yet, there is also a sense of wonder, of profound mystery. The opening lines of the poem—"The lament of the guitar begins. The wine cups of daybreak are broken. The lament of the guitar begins. It is useless to hush it. It is impossible to hush it."—contain one of Lorca's oft recurrent images: the guitar as the primitive voice of the world's darkness and evil (in another poem, *Malagueña*: "Black horses and villainous people move along the deep paths of the guitar"). My setting of this poem includes cadenzas in quasi-Flamenco style for the more surreal electric guitar.

The *Casida of the Dark Doves*, with its undercurrent of irony (indicated in the score: "gently sardonic; in a bizarre, fantastic style"), provides a necessary moment of relief from the prevailing darkness and intensity of the work. I have sought to enhance the eerie whimsy of the poem by directing the baritone to sing in variously stylized manners ("mock-lyric," "mock-menacing," or "in mock-chant style"). The instrumental parts in the score are laid out in circular notations, which represent, symbolically, "el Sol" and "la Luna" (Sun and Moon).

The *Song of the Rider, 1860* is a poem of violence and terror. In my earlier *Madrigals, Book II*, I had set only the refrain lines ("Little black horse. Whither with your dead rider? Little cold horse. What a scent of the flower of a knife!"), but in this complete setting of the poem I feel that I have more faithfully conveyed the demonic power of Lorca's imagination. The song is headed with the direction: "breathlessly, with relentlessly driving rhythm!" and the image of the galloping little horse is projected by the wild, hammered rhythms of lujon, crotales, drums, mallet instruments, and electric harpsichord. The climax of the song is marked by a thundering passage entitled "Cadenza appassionata for two drummers." The prototype of the genre represented by *Song of the Rider, 1860* is obviously Schubert's *Erlkönig*.

The final *Casida of the Boy Wounded by the Water* is my favorite of the various Lorca poems I have set over the years. The dream-like beginning of this song, with its gentle oscillation between the pitches B/G-sharp and the tender lyricism of the baritone melody, is consciously reminiscent of Mahler. The third and final "Death-drone" announces the dark, impassioned central stanza of the poem. The drone takes the form of a huge, sustained crescendo; at the point of maximum intensity ("What a fury of love, what a wounding edge, such nocturnal murmurs, such a white death!") the screaming voice of a flexitone is heard; the drone seems to "explode," and as the intensity subsides the music takes on an aura of transfiguration. The opening music is heard once again, this time punctuated by the deep bourdon sounds of piano and contrabass. Two gently flowing phrases played on water-tuned crystal glasses conclude the work.

Lorca's haunting, even mystical vision of death—which embodies, and yet transcends, the ancient Spanish tradition—is the seminal force of his dark genius. In composing *Songs, Drones, and Refrains of Death* I wanted to find a musical language which might complement this very beautiful poetry. (George Crumb).

Premiere: Center for New Music, University of Iowa; Harold Heap, baritone; William Hibbard, conductor; March 29, 1969; Iowa City.

Text: Federico García Lorca

MADRIGALS, Book III (1969) (7½ minutes) (P66460)

Soprano, Harp, Percussion (1 Player)

The first madrigal of Book III contains an isorhythmic setting of "La noche canta desnuda sobre los puentes de marzo" (Night sings naked above the bridges of March). Crumb uses two different isorhythmic patterns with *talea* of ten measures and seven measures, respectively, for the harp and the percussion. The vocal part, however, does not participate in the isorhythmic organization. The second song of this book is one of the shortest of all the madrigals and is a slow, calm setting of the line "Quiero dormir el sueño de las manzanas para aprender un llanto que me limpie de tierra" (I want to sleep the sleep of apples, to learn a lament that will cleanse me of earth). The last, and longest, song of Book III is a lullaby that is again scored for voice, harp, and vibraphone, based on the text: "Nana, niño, nana del caballo grande que no quiso el agua" (Lullaby, child, lullaby of the proud horse who would not drink water). (Donald Chittum).

Premiere: University of Washington Contemporary Group, Elizabeth Suderburg, soprano; March 6, 1970; Seattle.

Text: Federico García Lorca

MADRIGALS, Book IV (1969) (9 minutes) (P66461)

Soprano, Flute (also Piccolo and Alto Flute), Harp, Contrabass, Percussion (1 Player)

The first madrigal of Book IV, "¿Por qué nací entre espejos?" (Why was I born surrounded by mirrors?) contains retrograded passages between sections, within sections, and as part of the motivic ideas themselves. Thus the retrogrades exist on the macrostructural, sectional, and microstructural levels, simultaneously. When using these retrogrades, however, Crumb is careful to exchange material between the voice and the instruments in order to give the madrigal both a sense of growth and unity. The following "Tu cuerpo, con la sombra violeta de mis manos, era un arcangel de frío" (Through my hands' violet shadow, your body was an archangel, cold) is a freely set lament, with its single line of text not uttered until near the end of the piece; the soprano is instructed to sing on a glissando, and not to dwell on given pitches. The last song is a relentless and implacable setting of "¡La muerte me está mirando desde las torres de Córdoba!" (Death is watching me from the towers of Córdoba!). (Donald Chittum).

Premiere: University of Washington Contemporary Group, Elizabeth Suderburg, soprano; March 6, 1970; Seattle.

Text: Federico García Lorca

NIGHT OF THE FOUR MOONS (1969) (16 minutes) (P66462)

Alto, Alto Flute (also Piccolo), Banjo, Electric Cello, Percussion (1 Player)

Night of the Four Moons, commissioned by the Philadelphia Chamber Players, was composed in 1969 during the Apollo 11 flight (July 16–24). The work is scored for alto (or mezzo-soprano), alto flute (doubling piccolo), banjo, electric cello, and percussion. The percussion includes Tibetan prayer stones, Japanese Kabuki blocks, alto African thumb piano (mbira), and Chinese temple gong in addition to the more usual vibraphone, crotales, tambourine, bongo drums, suspended cymbal and tamtam. The singer is also required to play finger cymbals, castanets, glockenspiel and tamtam.

I suppose that *Night of the Four Moons* is really an "occasional" work, since its inception was an artistic response to an external event. The texts—extracts drawn from the poems of Federico García Lorca—symbolize my own rather ambivalent feelings *vis-à-vis* Apollo 11. The texts of the third and fourth songs seemed strikingly prophetic!

The first three songs, with their very brief texts, are, in a sense, merely introductory to the dramatically sustained final song. *The moon is dead, dead*... is primarily an instrumental piece in a primitive rhythmical style, with the Spanish words stated almost parenthetically by the singer. The conclusion of the text is whispered by the flutist over the mouthpiece of his instrument. *When the moon rises* . . . (marked in the score: "languidly, with a sense of loneliness") contains delicate passages for the prayer stones and the banjo (played "in bottleneck style," i.e., with a glass rod). The vocal phrases are quoted literally from my earlier (1963) *Night Music I* (which contains a complete setting of this poem). *Another obscure Adam dreams* . . . ("hesitantly, with a sense of mystery") is a fabric of fragile instrumental timbre, with the text set like an incantation.

The concluding poem (inspired by an ancient Gypsy legend)—*Run away moon, moon, moon!* . . .—provides the climactic moment of the cycle. The opening stanza of the poem requires the singer to differentiate between the "shrill, metallic" voice of the Child and the "coquettish, sensual" voice of the Moon. At a point marked by a sustained cello harmonic and the clattering of Kabuki blocks (*Drumming the plain,/the horseman was coming near* . . .), the performers (excepting the cellist) slowly walk off stage while singing or playing their "farewell" phrases. As they exit, they strike an antique cymbal, which reverberates in unison with the cello harmonic. The epilogue of the song (*Through the sky goes the moon/holding a child by the hand*) was conceived as a simultaneity of two musics: "Musica Mundana" ("Music of the Spheres"), played by the onstage cellist; and "Musica Humana" ("Music of Mankind"), performed offstage by singer, alto flute, banjo, and vibraphone. The offstage music ("Berceuse, in stile Mahleriano") is to emerge and fade like a distant radio signal. The F-sharp Major tonality of the "Musica Humana" and the theatrical gesture of the preceding processionals recall the concluding pages of Haydn's "Farewell" Symphony. (George Crumb).

Premiere: Philadelphia Chamber Players; Anna May Courtney, Mezzo-soprano; March 3, 1970; Springfield, Pennsylvania.

Text: Federico García Lorca

BLACK ANGELS (Thirteen Images from the Dark Land) (Images I) (1970) (25 minutes) (P66304)

Electric String Quartet

I. DEPARTURE
1. Threnody I: Night of the Electric Insects [Tutti]
2. Sounds of Bones and Flutes [Trio]
3. Lost Bells [Duo]
4. Devil-music [Solo: Cadenza accompagnata]
5. Danse Macabre [Duo]
   (Duo alternativo: Dies Irae)

II. ABSENCE
6. Pavana Lachrymae (Der Tod und das Mädchen) [Trio]
   (Solo obbligato: Insect Sounds)
7. Threnody II: Black Angels! [Tutti]
8. Sarabanda de la Muerte Oscura [Trio]
   (Solo obbligato: Insect Sounds)
9. Lost Bells (Echo) [Duo]
   (Duo alternativo: Sounds of Bones and Flutes)

III. RETURN
10. God-music [Solo: Aria accompagnata]
11. Ancient Voices [Duo]
12. Ancient Voices (Echo) [Trio]
13. Threnody III: Night of the Electric Insects [Tutti]

Black Angels (Thirteen Images from the Dark Land) was conceived as a kind of parable on our troubled contemporary world. The numerous quasi-programmatic allusions in the work are therefore symbolic, although the essential polarity—God versus Devil—implies more than a purely metaphysical reality. The image of the "black angel" was a conventional device used by early painters to symbolize the fallen angel.

The underlying structure of *Black Angels* is a huge arch-like design which is suspended from the three "Threnody" pieces. The work portrays a voyage of the soul. The three stages of this voyage are Departure (fall from grace), Absence (spiritual annihilation) and Return (redemption).

The numerological symbolism of *Black Angels*, while perhaps not immediately perceptible to the ear, is nonetheless quite faithfully reflected in the musical structure. These "magical" relationships are variously expressed; *e.g.*, in terms of phrase-length, groupings of single tones, durations, patterns of repetition, etc. An important pitch element in the work—descending E, A, and D-sharp—also symbolizes the fateful numbers 7-13. At certain points in the score there occurs a kind of ritualistic counting in various languages, including German, French, Russian, Hungarian, Japanese and Swahili.

There are several allusions to tonal music in *Black Angels*: a quotation from Schubert's "Death and the Maiden" quartet (in the *Pavana Lachrymae* and also faintly echoed on the last page of the work); an original *Sarabanda*, which is stylistically synthetic; the sustained B-major tonality of *God-Music*; and several references to the Latin sequence *Dies Irae* ("Day of Wrath"). The work abounds in conventional musical symbolisms such as the *Diabolus in Musica* (the interval of the tritone) and the *Trillo Di Diavolo* (the "Devil's trill," after Tartini).

The amplification of the stringed instruments in *Black Angels* is intended to produce a highly surrealistic effect. This surrealism is heightened by the use of certain unusual string effects; *e.g.*, pedal tones (the intensely obscene sounds of the *Devil-Music*); bowing on the "wrong" side of the strings (to produce the viol-consort effect); trilling on the strings with thimble-capped fingers. The performers also play maracas, tam-tams and water-tuned crystal goblets, the latter played with the bow for the "glass-harmonica" effect in *God-Music*.

Black Angels was commissioned by the University of Michigan and first performed by the Stanley Quartet. The score is inscribed: "finished on Friday the Thirteenth, March, 1970 (in tempore belli)." (George Crumb).

Premiere: The Stanley Quartet; October 23, 1970; Ann Arbor, Michigan.

ANCIENT VOICES OF CHILDREN (1970) (25 minutes) (P66303)

Soprano, Boy Soprano, Oboe, Mandolin, Harp, Electric Piano (& Toy Piano), Percussion (3 Players)

I. El niño busca su voz
   (The little boy was looking for his voice)
   "Dances of the Ancient Earth" [Interlude]
II. Me he perdido muchas veces por el mar
   (I have lost myself in the sea many times)
III. ¿De dónde vienes, amor, mi niño?
   (From where do you come, my love, my child?)
IV. Todas las tardes en Granada, todas las tardes se muere un niño
   (Each afternoon in Granada, a child dies each afternoon)
   "Ghost Dance" [Interlude]
V. Se ha llenado de luces mi corazón de seda
   (My heart of silk is filled with lights)

Ancient Voices of Children was composed during the summer of 1970 on commission from the Elizabeth Sprague Coolidge Foundation, while I was in residence at Tanglewood, Massachusetts. This work forms part of an extended cycle of vocal compositions based on the poetry of Federico García Lorca which has absorbed much of my compositional energy over the past eight years.

In *Ancient Voices of Children*, as in my earlier Lorca settings, I have sought musical images that enhance and reinforce the powerful yet strangely haunting imagery of Lorca's poetry. I feel that the essential meaning of this poetry is concerned with the most primary things: life, death, love, the smell of the earth, the sounds of the wind and the sea. These "*ur*-concepts" are embodied in a language which is primitive and stark, but which is capable of infinitely subtle nuance.

The texts of *Ancient Voices* are fragments of longer poems which I have grouped into a sequence that seemed to suggest a "larger rhythm" in terms of musical continuity. The two purely instrumental movements—"Dances of the Ancient Earth" and "Ghost Dance"—are dance-interludes rather than commentaries on the texts. These two pieces, together with the 3rd song, subtitled "Dance of the Sacred Life-Cycle" (which contains a rising-falling *ostinato* bolero rhythm in the drums), can be performed by a solo dancer.

The vocal style in the cycle ranges from the virtuosic to the intimately lyrical, and in my conception of the work I very much had in mind Jan DeGaetani's enormous technical and timbral flexibility. Perhaps the most characteristic vocal effect in *Ancient Voices* is produced by the mezzo-soprano singing a kind of fantastic vocalise (based on purely phonetic sounds) into an amplified piano, thereby producing a shimmering aura of echoes. The inclusion of a part for boy soprano seemed the best solution for those passages in the text where Lorca clearly implies a child's voice. The boy soprano is heard offstage until the very last page of the work, at which point he joins the mezzo-soprano onstage for the closing vocalise.

The instruments employed in *Ancient Voices* were chosen for their particular timbral potentialities. The pianist also plays toy piano (in the 4th song), the mandolinist musical saw (2nd song)—although a separate player can be used for the saw—and the oboist harmonica (4th song). Certain special instrumental effects are used to heighten the "expressive intensity"—*e.g.*, "bending" the pitch of the piano by application of a chisel to the strings (2nd song); use of a paper-threaded harp (in "Dances of the Ancient Earth"); the frequent "pitch-bending" of the oboe, harp and mandolin. The mandolin has one set of strings tuned a quarter-tone low in order to give a special pungency to its tone. The three percussionists command a wide range of instruments, including Tibetan prayer stones, Japanese temple bells and tuned tom-toms. The instrumentalists are frequently called upon to sing, shout and whisper.

In composing *Ancient Voices of Children* I was conscious of an urge to fuse various unrelated stylistic elements. I was intrigued with the idea of juxtaposing the seemingly incongruous: a suggestion of Flamenco with a Baroque quotation ("Bist du bei mir," from the Notebook of Anna Magdalena Bach), or a reminiscence of Mahler with a breath of the Orient. It later occurred to me that both Bach and Mahler drew upon many disparate sources in their own music without sacrificing "stylistic purity."

It is sometimes of interest to a composer to recall the original impulse—the "creative germ"—of a compositional project. In the case of *Ancient Voices* I felt this impulse to be the climactic final words of the last song: ". . . and I will go very far . . . to ask Christ the Lord to give me back my ancient soul of a child." (George Crumb).

Premiere: The Contemporary Chamber Ensemble, Arthur Weisberg, conductor; Jan DeGaetani, mezzo-soprano; Michael Dash, boy soprano; October 31, 1970; The Library of Congress, Washington, D.C.

Premiere of complete Lorca Cycle: New Directions Ensemble, Kenneth Moore, conductor; Neva Pilgrim and Darleen Kliewer, sopranos; Carol Brunk, alto; Frederick Gersten, baritone; February 26, 1972; Oberlin Conservatory.

Text: Federico García Lorca

VOX BALAENAE ("VOICE OF THE WHALE") for Three Masked Players (1971) (18 minutes) (P66466)

Electric Flute, Electric Cello, Amplified Piano

Vocalise (. . . for the beginning of time)
Variations on Sea-Time
  Sea Theme
  Archeozoic [Var. I]
  Proterozoic [Var. II]
  Paleozoic [Var. III]
  Mesozoic [Var. IV]
  Cenozoic [Var. V]
Sea-Nocturne (. . . for the end of time)

Voice of the Whale (Vox Balaenae), composed in 1971 for the New York Camerata, is scored for flute, cello and piano (all amplified in concert performance). The work was inspired by the singing of the humpback whale, a tape recording of which I had heard two or three years previously. Each of the three performers is required to wear a black half-mask (or visor-mask). The masks, by effacing the sense of human projection, are intended to represent, symbolically, the powerful impersonal forces of nature (i.e. nature dehumanized). I have also suggested that the work be performed under a deep-blue stage lighting.

The form of *Voice of the Whale* is a simple three-part design, consisting of a prologue, a set of variations named after the geological eras, and an epilogue.

The opening *Vocalise* (marked in the score: "wildly fantastic, grotesque") is a kind of cadenza for the flutist, who simultaneously plays his instrument and sings into it. This combination of instrumental and vocal sound produces an eerie, surreal timbre, not unlike the sounds of the humpback whale. The conclusion of the cadenza is announced by a parody of the opening measures of Strauss' *Also sprach Zarathustra*.

The *Sea-Theme* ("solemn, with calm majesty") is presented by the cello (in harmonics), accompanied by dark, fateful chords of strummed piano strings. The following sequence of variations begins with the haunting sea-gull cries of the *Archeozoic* ("timeless, inchoate") and, gradually increasing in intensity, reaches a strident climax in the *Cenozoic* ("dramatic, with a feeling of destiny"). The emergence of man in the Cenozoic era is symbolized by a partial restatement of the *Zarathustra* reference.

The concluding *Sea-Nocturne* ("serene, pure, transfigured") is an elaboration of the *Sea-Theme*. The piece is couched in the "luminous" tonality of B Major and there are shimmering sounds of antique cymbals (played alternately by the cellist and flutist). In composing the *Sea-Nocturne* I wanted to suggest "a larger rhythm of nature" and a sense of suspension in time. The concluding gesture of the work is a gradually dying series of repetitions of a 10-note figure. In concert performance, the last figure is to be played "in pantomime" (to suggest a *diminuendo* beyond the threshold of hearing!); for recorded performances, the figure is played as a "fade-out." (George Crumb).

Premiere: The New York Camerata; March 17, 1972; The Library of Congress, Washington, D.C.

LUX AETERNA for Five Masked Musicians (1971) (15 minutes) (P66495)

Soprano, Bass Flute (& Soprano Recorder), Sitar, Percussion (2 Players)

Lux Aeterna (1971) is scored for soprano, bass flute (doubling the soprano recorder), sitar, and two percussionists. The familiar Latin text utilized is: Lux aeterna luceat eis, Domine. Requiem aeternam dona eis, Domine, et lux perpetua luceat eis. (May eternal light shine on them, O Lord. Grant them everlasting rest, O Lord, and let perpetual light shine upon them.)

The work is in one movement, most of which is to be played "very slowly, with a sense of meditative time; pregnant with mystery." The opening sound, while related rhythmically to the opening of the *Four Nocturnes*, gives clear indication of how incredibly far Crumb's sense of sonorous invention has evolved in the intervening years. A crotale (antique cymbal) is placed near the center of a timpano membrane; after striking the crotale sharply ("with a very hard beater"), the percussionist moves the timpano pedal up and down in a specified rhythm, thereby "bending" the pitch of the crotale in that same rhythm. Crumb adds, in the score, that the sound should be "shimmering, iridescent!" This is only one of the several luminous percussion effects (many of which are not the least bit "percussive") in this score.

Interrupting this slow music on four occasions is a Refrain entitled "Masked Dance: Elegy for a Dead Prince." These four Refrains will be recognized instantly by the entrance of the sitar, which plays throughout each (and nowhere else). Listeners who know the score of *Black Angels* are aware that numerology is one of Crumb's pet fascinations and will not be surprised that the four Refrains contain, successively, 77, 55, 33, and 11 beats.

The vocal writing consists primarily of melismas on the Latin text or, as at the first entrance, on vowels derived from the text. The composer provides the following performance instructions:

The performance of *Lux Aeterna* requires certain theater effects. All performers (including the conductor) should wear black masks (masks of the visor or domino types) and, if possible, black robes. The flutist and sitar player should sit in the lotus position. The stage should be totally dark before the performance begins, with the instrumentalists and the conductor in position onstage. A deep red lighting gradually comes up, at which point the soprano slowly walks on stage. She lights the candle (positioned at the stage center), and the performance begins. At the conclusion of the work, the soprano slowly walks over to the burning candle and extinguishes it. Then the deep red lighting fades to total darkness.

A solo dancer (also masked) can be included in *Lux Aeterna*, if desired. The dancer should perform only in the refrain sections (Masked Dance: "Elegy for a Dead Prince"), and should remain frozen in position during the other music. The dance should be symbolic and ritualistic; the lighted candle might serve as a focal point for the dancer, like a moth attracted to a flame. (David Burge).

Premiere: Philadelphia Composers' Forum, Jenneke Barton, mezzo-soprano; January 16, 1972; Richmond, Virginia.

Text: from the Requiem Mass (Latin)

MAKROKOSMOS, Volume I (Twelve Fantasy-Pieces after the Zodiac for Amplified Piano) (1972) (33 minutes) (P66539a)

Part One

1. Primeval Sounds (Genesis I) *Cancer* [G.R.]
2. Proteus *Pisces* [W.R.C.]
3. Pastorale (from the Kingdom of Atlantis, ca. 10,000 B.C.) *Taurus* [J.B.]
4. Crucifixus [SYMBOL] *Capricorn* [R.L.F.]

Part Two

5. The Phantom Gondolier *Scorpio* [G.H.C.]
6. Night-Spell I *Sagittarius* [A.W.]
7. Music of Shadows (for Aeolian Harp) *Libra* [P.Z.]
8. The Magic Circle of Infinity (Moto perpetuo) [SYMBOL] *Leo* [C.D.]

Part Three

9. The Abyss of Time *Virgo* [A.S.]
10. Spring-Fire *Aries* [D.R.B.]
11. Dream Images (Love-Death Music) *Gemini* [F.G.L.]
12. Spiral Galaxy [SYMBOL] *Aquarius* [B.W.]

Makrokosmos, Volume I was composed in 1972 for my friend David Burge. Ten years previously, in 1962 (we were then colleagues at the University of Colorado), he had commissioned and premiered my *Five Pieces for Piano*. I was very much excited about the expanding possibilities of piano idiom—it seemed as if a whole new world were opening up to composers; and I was especially impressed by Burge's immediate and total mastery of this new idiom, which implied an organic synthesis of conventional (keyboard) and unconventional (inside the piano) techniques. I wanted to do a sequel to the *Five Pieces*, but, alas, several attempts proved abortive. One set of sketches was assimilated into my *Songs, Drones, and Refrains of Death*; other ideas wandered homelessly through the years; and two or three germinal ideas finally evolved into *Makrokosmos*.

The title and format of my *Makrokosmos* reflect my admiration for two great 20th-century composers of piano music—Béla Bartók and Claude Debussy. I was thinking, of course, of Bartók's *Mikrokosmos* and Debussy's *24 Preludes* (a second zodiacal set, *Makrokosmos, Volume II*, was completed in 1973, thus forming a sequence of 24 "fantasy-pieces"). However, these are purely external associations, and I suspect that the "spiritual impulse" of my music is more akin to the darker side of Chopin, and even to the child-like fantasy of early Schumann.

And then there is always the question of the "larger world" of concepts and ideas which influence the evolution of a composer's language. While composing *Makrokosmos*, I was aware of certain recurrent haunting images. At times quite vivid, at times vague and almost subliminal, these images seemed to coalesce around the following several ideas (given in no logical sequence, since there is none): the "magical properties" of music; the problem of the origin of evil; the "timelessness" of time; a sense of the profound ironies of life (so beautifully expressed in the music of Mozart and Mahler); the haunting words of Pascal: *"Le silence éternel des espaces infinis m'effraie"* ("The eternal silence of infinite space terrifies me"); and these few lines of Rilke: *"Und in den Nächten fällt die schwere Erde aus allen Sternen in die Einsamkeit. Wir alle fallen. Und doch ist Einer, welcher dieses Fallen unendlich sanft in seinen Händen hält"* ("And in the nights the heavy earth is falling from all the stars down into loneliness. We are all falling. And yet there is One who holds this falling endlessly gently in his hands").

Each of the twelve "fantasy-pieces" is associated with a different sign of the zodiac and with the initials of a person born under that sign. I had whimsically wanted to pose an "enigma" with these subscript initials; however, my perspicacious friends quickly identified the Aries of *Spring-Fire* as David Burge, and the Scorpio of *The Phantom Gondolier* as myself. (George Crumb).

Premiere: David Burge, piano; February 8, 1973; Colorado Springs, Colorado.

MAKROKOSMOS, Volume II (Twelve Fantasy-Pieces after the Zodiac for Amplified Piano) (1973) (33 minutes) (P66539b)

Part One

1. Morning Music (Genesis II) *Cancer* [J. DeG. W.]
2. The Mystic Chord *Sagittarius* [R.M.]
3. Rain-Death Variations *Pisces* [F.C.]
4. Twin Suns (Doppelgänger aus der Ewigkeit) [SYMBOL] *Gemini* [E.A.C.]

Part Two

5. Ghost-Nocturne: for the Druids of Stonehenge (Night-Spell II) *Virgo* [A.B.]
6. Gargoyles *Taurus* [P.P.]
7. Tora! Tora! Tora! (Cadenza Apocalittica) *Scorpio* [L.K.]
8. A Prophecy of Nostradamus [SYMBOL] *Aries* [H.W.]

Part Three

9. Cosmic Wind *Libra* [S.B.]
10. Voices from "Corona Borealis" *Aquarius* [E.M.C.]
11. Litany of the Galactic Bells *Leo* [R.V.]
12. Agnus Dei [SYMBOL] *Capricorn* [R.W.]

Makrokosmos (Volume II), like its predecessor Volume I, is comprised of 12 pieces laid out in three groups of four each. I conceive of the whole work as a very gradual intensification in tempo and dynamics up to the climactic eighth piece ("A Prophecy of Nostradamus") and a subsequent spinning out to the beautifully sustained and almost hypnotic *Dona Nobis Pacem* conclusion. Of course each piece has its own very characteristic sound and mood, and its duration is nicely calculated, psychologically speaking, so that both performer and listener become totally involved and absorbed in its expressive import. Nonetheless, I strongly sense the broad architecture and ongoing development of the work as a whole and want to project this in my performance.

The composer's descriptive markings are precise and very helpful to the performer, since such terminology suggests and "evokes" the quality of sound that the composer had in mind. Each piece provides a fine example, but I will mention only three. In the first piece ("Morning Music"), the markings "exuberantly" and "primitive" suggest to me those particular qualities of rhythm and timbre that are essential to the effective projection of the music. The eighth piece ("A Prophecy of Nostradamus") carries the inscription "Stark, powerful; molto pesante!" These words particularly describe the ponderous quality of the Lisztian minor triads, which, sustained and repeated, suggest the inexorable rhythm of a slow, majestic march. The twelfth piece ("Agnus Dei") bears the poetic phrase "as if suspended in endless time." For the performer, these words provide the precise key to the interpretation of a problematic passage consisting of a four-fold repetition of a single, long phrase. Would the composer prefer that the listener ignore these verbal descriptions while hearing the music? I would hope not, since the descriptions are intimately connected with the musical conception itself and would, therefore, enhance the listener's appreciation.

Makrokosmos (Volume II) sounds as though the piano has become an orchestra unto itself. There is, in fact, an enormously wide range of sound, timbre, touch, dynamics, etc. A variety of factors—amplification, various vocal effects, the imaginative exploitation of the three pedals, effects produced by the fingers in contact with the strings, and the use of external devices—contribute to this. The amplification of the piano by a conventional microphone suspended over the strings gives the instrument a greater presence than normal; however, the amplification must not result in any distortion of the sound. The amplification enhances many of the very delicate effects, such as pizzicato playing and muting of the piano strings. The above-mentioned external devices are three in number: a sheet of paper resting on the strings (in the first piece), two glass tumblers (in the fifth piece), and a percussionist's wire brush (in the ninth piece).

Other than the sustained whistling throughout the tenth piece, the vocal effects are sparse but especially effective. I would mention the singing in the fifth and twelfth pieces, the unvoiced singing ("wind sound") in the ninth piece, the shouting at the end of the seventh piece, and the whispering in the twelfth piece. The use of "inside-the-piano" effects is quite extensive and includes plucking the strings (pizzicato) with either the fingernail or the fingertip, muting the strings to alter the tone quality or touching the nodes to produce harmonics, and glissando over the strings with either fingernail or fingertip. A particularly characteristic percussive effect is obtained by striking the metal structural beams of the piano with the knuckles. I hope that the above description will not appear unduly detailed, but I do feel that the listener is entitled to know why the piano sounds the way it does.

The one use of quotation in *Makrokosmos (Volume II)* is beautifully subtle. In the eleventh piece ("Litany of the Galactic Bells"), the opening music—a shimmering bell effect which obviously recalls the Coronation Scene from Mussorgsky's *Boris Godunov*—gradually subsides and moves almost imperceptibly into a short excerpt from Beethoven's *Hammerklavier* Sonata. The effect is somewhat like the changing colors of a prism.

Makrokosmos (Volume II) is written out in a very precise notation, but the music will at times sound quite free and flexible, almost improvisatory. The last piece of each of the three parts (i.e., the fourth, eighth and twelfth pieces) are printed in a geometric design or "symbolic" notation. I feel that the composer was thereby subconsciously compelling the performer to play the work from memory. And so I have. I feel that this definitely helps the performer to mesmerize his audience for an enriching, half-hour musical experience.

As in *Makrokosmos (Volume I)* each piece is associated with a different sign of the Zodiac and with the initials of a person born under the sign. However, I feel that these inscriptions are more or less symbolic in character and therefore do not affect the performance of the music. Otherwise I would be letting the stars, or character of the person, guide my interpretation. An interesting thought, but heavens, how would I approach "The Mystic Chord," which bears the initials R.M.?! (*Robert Miller*).

Premiere: Robert Miller, piano; November 12, 1974; Alice Tully Hall, New York City.

Premiere of *Makrokosmos*, Volumes I & II together: David Burge, piano; February 4, 1975; Wichita, Kansas.

Annotated Chronological List of Works (Continued)

MUSIC FOR A SUMMER EVENING (MAKROKOSMOS III) (1974) (40 minutes) (P66590)

Two Amplified Pianos and Percussion (2 Players)

I. Nocturnal Sounds (The Awakening)
II. Wanderer-Fantasy
III. The Advent
IV. Myth
V. Music of the Starry Night

Music for a Summer Evening (Makrokosmos III), for two amplified pianos and percussion, was completed in February, 1974. The work was commissioned by the Fromm Foundation and was written specifically for (and is dedicated to) Gilbert Kalish, James Freeman, Raymond DesRoches, and Richard Fitz.

I feel that *Summer Evening* projects a clearly articulated large expressive curve over its approximately 40-minute duration. The first, third, and fifth movements, which are scored for the full ensemble of instruments and laid out on a large scale, would seem to define the primary import of the work (which might be interpreted as a kind of "cosmic drama"). On the other hand, the wistfully evocative "Wanderer-Fantasy" (mostly for the two pianos alone) and the somewhat atavistic "Myth" (for percussion instruments) were conceived of as dream-like pieces functioning as intermezzos within the overall sequence of movements.

The three larger movements carry poetic quotations which were very much in my thoughts during the sketching-out process, and which, I believe, find their symbolic resonance in the sounds of *Summer Evening*. "Nocturnal Sounds" is inscribed with an excerpt from Quasimodo: *"Odo risonanze effimere, oblío di piena notte nell'acqua stellata"* ("I hear ephemeral echoes, oblivion of full night in the starred water"); "The Advent" is associated with a passage from Pascal: *"Le silence éternel des espaces infinis m'effraie"* ("The eternal silence of infinite space terrifies me"); and the last movement, "Music of the Starry Night," cites these transcendentally beautiful images of Rilke: *"Und in den Nächten fällt die schwere Erde aus allen Sternen in die Einsamkeit. Wir alle fallen. Und doch ist Einer, welcher dieses Fallen unendlich sanft in seinen Händen hält."* ("And in the nights the heavy earth is falling from all the stars down into loneliness. We are all falling. And yet there is One who holds this falling endlessly gently in His hands.")

Music for a Summer Evening, in respect to style and compositional technique, is very much related to my *Makrokosmos, Volumes I* and *II*, for solo amplified piano (composed in 1972 and 1973, respectively). I think of the three works as forming a trilogy, especially in view of the fact that they share several important thematic elements. The most egregious example of self-plagiarism would be "The Advent" of *Summer Evening*, which is simply an elaboration of the *Twin Suns* piece of *Makrokosmos, Volume II*. I might mention, too, that "Music of the Starry Night" was originally sketched out for solo piano for inclusion in *Makrokosmos, Volume II*; however, as the sketch evolved, it readily became apparent that my "cosmic" conception was quite beyond the capabilities of ten fingers!

The combination of two pianos and percussion instruments was, of course, first formulated by Béla Bartók in his *Sonata* of 1937, and it is curious that other composers did not subsequently contribute to the genre. Bartók was one of the very first composers to write truly expressive passages for the percussion instruments; since those days there has been a veritable revolution in percussion technique and idiom and new music has inevitably assimilated these developments. The battery of percussion instruments required for *Summer Evening* is extensive and includes vibraphone, xylophone, glockenspiel, tubular bells, crotales (antique cymbals), bell tree, claves, maracas, sleighbells, wood blocks and temple blocks, triangles, and several varieties of drums, tam-tams, and cymbals. Certain rather exotic (and in some cases, quite ancient) instruments are occasionally employed for their special timbral characteristics, for example: two slide-whistles (in "Wanderer-Fantasy"); a metal thunder-sheet (in "The Advent"); African log drum, quijada del asino (jawbone of an ass), sistrum, Tibetan prayer stones, musical jug, alto recorder, and, in "Myth," African thumb piano and guiro (played by the pianists). Some of the more ethereal sounds of *Summer Evening* are produced by drawing a contrabass bow over tam-tams, crotales, and vibraphone plates. This kaleidoscopic range of percussion timbre is integrated with a great variety of special sounds produced by the pianists. In "Music of the Starry Night," for example, the piano strings are covered with sheets of paper, thereby producing a rather surrealistic distortion of the piano tone when the keys are struck.

As in several of my other works, the musical fabric of *Summer Evening* results largely from the elaboration of tiny cells into a sort of mosaic design. This time-hallowed technique seems to function in much new music, irrespective of style, as a primary structural *modus*. In its overall style, *Summer Evening* might be described as either more or less atonal, or more or less tonal. The more overtly tonal passages can be defined in terms of the basic polarity F-sharp/d-sharp minor (or, enharmonically, G-flat/e-flat minor). This (most traditional) polarity is twice stated in "The Advent"—in the opening crescendo passages ("majestic, like a larger rhythm of nature"), and in the concluding "Hymn for the Nativity of the Star-Child." It is stated once again in "Music of the Starry Night," with the quotation of passages from Bach's d-sharp minor fugue (*Well-tempered Clavier*, Book II) and a concluding "Song of Reconciliation" in G-flat (overlaid by an intermittently resounding "Five-fold Galactic Bells" in F-sharp). One other structural device which the astute listener may perceive is the isorhythmic construction of "Myth," which consists of simultaneously performed taleas of 13, 7, and 11 bars. (George Crumb).

Premiere: Gilbert Kalish, James Freeman, pianists, and Raymond DesRoches, Richard Fitz, percussionists; March 30, 1974; Swarthmore, Pennsylvania.

DREAM SEQUENCE (Images II) (1976) (15 minutes) (P66690)

Violin, Cello, Piano, Percussion (1 Player), offstage "Glass Harmonica" (2 Players)

Dream Sequence is scored for violin, cello, piano, and percussion plus an offstage "glass harmonica" that requires two players. The percussion instruments consist of five Japanese temple bells, four crotales, sleighbells, one maraca, two suspended cymbals, and a Thai wooden buffalo bell. The pianist has three tuned crystal goblets and the offstage players have four.

The "glass harmonica" chord, while quiet ("quasi subliminal!"), is present, nevertheless, throughout the entire work. The makeup of this chord—C-sharp, E, A, D—is a first inversion major triad with an added fourth above.

The meditative nature of *Dream Sequence* is apparent in the first words of the score: "Poised, timeless, breathing, as an afternoon in late summer." To otherwise describe this score, *all of which is contained on two pages*, would be fruitless.

Those listening without score in hand should be advised that the piano in most of its midrange has sheets of paper lying on the strings, causing what the composer describes as "delicate vibrations." The percussionist provides pulsating bell sounds and eerie drone effects (*pppp sempre*); these delicate shadings of color magically complement the sounds of the other instruments. However, it is the violin and cello that eventually dominate *Dream Sequence*, playing *concertino* to the *ripieno* of the piano, percussion and glass harmonica. Playing brief, antiphonal, ever-varied phrases, always closely responding to one another, they create the rich, colorful embroidery of the sound tapestry that constitutes the work.

Dream Sequence evokes in its psychological effect something akin to an actual dream. Fugitive, wispy images seem to drift in and out of the consciousness, assuming subtly varied shapes with each recurrence. At one, and only one moment in the "sequence" of images does the sleeper seem roused to semi-wakefulness (announced by sudden, sharp *forte* passages in the piano); the music then relapses gradually to deep somnolence with the concluding "cicada-drone" music. (David Burge).

Premiere: Aeolian Chamber Players; October 17, 1976; Brunswick, Maine.

STAR-CHILD—A Parable for Soprano, Antiphonal Children's Voices, Male Speaking Choir and Bell Ringers, and Large Orchestra (1977) (33 minutes) (P66711)

4444 6731 Perc(8), Organ, Str

Star-Child, completed in March, 1977, was commissioned by the Ford Foundation and written for Irene Gubrud, soprano, and Pierre Boulez and the New York Philharmonic. The score bears a dedication to my two sons, David and Peter.

Star-Child represents my largest work in terms of the performing forces required (most of my writing has been concentrated in the chamber dimension, and even my earlier orchestral music is fairly modest in its instrumentation). It seems to me that when a Latin text is involved, a large, monolithic quality is suggested. Also, I was interested in constructing a work with the maximum contrasts of textures and timbres. However, the full weight of the orchestra is employed only in the *Apocalyptica* section, with its driving rhythms and sustained *fortissimo*.

The title was suggested by another of my works, *Music for a Summer Evening (Makrokosmos III)*, in which there is a section called "Hymn for the Advent of the Star-Child." In addition, there are certain pertinent references in *Star-Child*'s Latin texts to "children of light" in the Biblical quote (in "Hymn for the New Age") and to finding the light in a world of darkness (in "Advent of the Children of Light"). Binding the work together is a sense of progression from darkness (or despair) to light (or joy and spiritual realization) as expressed by both music and text—a conception that is at the same time medieval and romantic. For instance, the idea of dark and light is reflected in the orchestration, for the earlier sections of *Star-Child* favor the darker instruments (the lower brass, bassoons, contrabassoon), while near the end the effect is quite different when the children sing amidst the luminous sounds of handbells, antique cymbals, glockenspiel, and tubular bells. However, there is no esoteric philosophical basis to *Star-Child*. It is simply a work within the tradition of music having a finale which expresses the hope that, after a struggle or after dark implications, there is something beyond. I feel, too, that the Latin texts transcend doctrine and convey universal meaning.

Four conductors are required for *Star-Child*, two primary and two secondary. Conductor I conducts all of the vocal passages and also all of the winds and six of the percussionists until the concluding portion of the work. Conductor II conducts all the strings and two of the percussionists throughout. During the "Hymn for the New Age" the winds divide into smaller groupings, and at this point Conductor III directs the brass instruments and three percussionists while Conductor IV leads the clarinets, flutes and vibraphone.

Star-Child is continuous, despite sectional divisions. The germinal idea, "Music of the Spheres" (strings, *pianississimo*), moves throughout the work in a circular and therefore static manner, a kind of background music over which the human drama is enacted. This idea consists of a continuum of chords built upon the interval of a perfect fifth. Over these slow-moving strains of "suspended" music I have superimposed (in the manner of Charles Ives!) a sequence of boldly contrasting musics. The necessity for four conductors arose from the fact that each music has its own tempo and metrics (metrics tend to be odd-numbered: the opening string music is in 11/4 time, the entire *Apocalyptica* in 5/16, and there are other sections based on sevens and threes). The four conductors do *not* synchronize and therefore all sense of vertical alignment is erased. I had even imagined that the "visual counterpoint" of the four-fold conducting would produce a choreography of its own!

Star-Child contains a number of programmatic or pictorial allusions. The seven trumpets of the apocalypse are represented, quite literally, by seven trumpets—two in the orchestra and five positioned around the auditorium. This extended passage of trumpet cadenzas climaxes with a heroic high F on the fateful seventh trumpet. Also, the four horsemen of the apocalypse are represented, not quite so literally, by four drummers playing sixteen tom-toms. "Dies Irae" is quoted at several points in a rather surreal whole-tone transformation: the first phrase of it is extensively used in the *Apocalyptica*, while its three phrases comprise the soft brass music that accompanies the children's chorus at the end. "Voice Crying in the Wilderness," with a text consisting of extracts from the "Dies Irae," is a long duet for solo soprano and solo trombonist (the trombonist is in front of the orchestra for this section). The "Voice" is therefore a composite voice, with the trombone functioning as a kind of *doppelgänger*.

Star-Child's eight percussionists play a wide range of instruments. Some of the more characteristic are: iron chains, flexatones, pot lids (struck with metal beaters), sizzle cymbals, a metal thunder sheet, log drums and a wind machine. Some of the more usual instruments are required in pairs, *e.g.* vibraphones, sets of timpani, bass drums, and tubular bells. Since the percussion instruments are arranged in a semicircular fashion around the orchestra, their multicolored timbres and textures totally impregnate the orchestral fabric. (George Crumb).

Premiere: New York Philharmonic, Pierre Boulez, conductor; David Gilbert, James Chambers, Larry Newland, assistant conductors; Irene Gubrud, soprano; the Boys' Choirs of the Little Church Around The Corner and Trinity School; the Bell Ringers of Trinity School; May 5, 1977; New York City.

Texts: freely adapted from *Dies Irae* and *Massacre of the Innocents* (13th century); John, XII-36 (Latin)

CELESTIAL MECHANICS (MAKROKOSMOS IV) (1979) (25 minutes) (P66788)

Cosmic Dances for Amplified Piano—4 Hands

I. Alpha Centauri
II. Beta Cygni
III. Gamma Draconis
IV. Delta Orionis

Celestial Mechanics, completed in April, 1979, is the fourth in a series of works entitled (or subtitled) *Makrokosmos*. The first two works were scored for solo piano and the third (*Music for a Summer Evening*) for two pianos and percussion.

I had long been tempted to try my hand at the four-hand medium, perhaps because I myself have been a passionate four-hand player over the years. The best of the original four-hand music—which includes, of course, those many superb works by Mozart, Schubert, and Brahms—occupies a very special niche in the literature of music. The idiom, a strange hybrid of the pianistic and the orchestral, lends itself readily to a very free and spontaneous kind of music—one thinks of the many collections of dances of various types and of the predilection for the "fantasy" genre. The present work, therefore, comprising a suite of "cosmic" dances composed in a rather "fantastic" style, falls squarely within the tradition.

My sole departure from tradition occurs at two points in the score where I have enlarged the medium to six-hands; and so, in the whimsical manner of Ives, the page turner must contribute more substantively to the performance than is his wont.

The title *Celestial Mechanics* was borrowed from the French mathematician Laplace. The titles for the four movements (added after the music was completed!) are the beautiful names of stars of the first through the fourth magnitude. The majestic movement of the stars does indeed suggest the image of a "cosmic choreography" and, in fact, I briefly considered opting for an alternate title (proposed by my brother, punster that he is)—*The Celestial Ballroom*. (George Crumb).

Premiere: Gilbert Kalish, Paul Jacobs, pianists; November 18, 1979; Alice Tully Hall, New York City.

Premiere of complete *Makrokosmos* Cycle: Ivar Mikhashoff, Aki Takahashi, Stephen and Frieda Manes, pianists; Jan Williams and Lynn Harbold, percussionists; June 12, 1980; Buffalo, New York.

APPARITION (22 minutes) (1979) (P66832)

Elegiac Songs and Vocalises for Soprano and Amplified Piano

Written in 1979 for Jan DeGaetani and Gilbert Kalish, *Apparition* is George Crumb's first work for solo voice and piano, and his first setting in English (apart from a number of songs composed in his early years). The text of *Apparition* is extracted from Walt Whitman's "When Lilacs Last in the Dooryard Bloom'd," part of a set of poems grouped under the title *Memories of President Lincoln*. Whitman wrote "When Lilacs. . ." during the weeks following the assassination of Abraham Lincoln, April 14, 1865. Although Whitman's poem is specifically an elegy to Lincoln, Crumb has chosen most of his text from a section sub-titled "Death Carol." This is a pause in the direct reference to Lincoln, and contains some of Whitman's most imaginative writing on the experience of death.

In *Apparition*, each song and vocalise form a piece of a larger vision, eventually coalescing as a tableau. The literary and musical materials focus on concise, highly contrasting metaphors for existence and death. Yet Crumb's cycle offers the listener reassurance. For just as in Whitman's verse, death is never depicted as an ending of life. Instead, it is circular, always a beginning or an enriched return to a universal life-force.

I. The Night in Silence under Many a Star

The piano opens the cycle with a pulsating evocation of Nature, accompanying the soprano who sings of symbols of eternity: "the night," symbolic of the physical universe; "The ocean shore," symbolic of motion and time; "the soul," representative of consciousness; and "the body turning to thee," illustrative of the cycle of life and death. With the presentation of this symbology a stage is set, upon which more personal visions of death will appear.

Vocalise 1: Summer Sounds

Vocalise 1 sharpens the focus from the vastness of the first song to a more specific time and location—further preparation for the more personal elegies which follow.

II. When Lilacs Last in the Dooryard Bloom'd

This brief, delicate song contains the only text not from the "Death Carol." Whitman's memory of the fragrance of blooming lilacs became his symbol for the time-period following Lincoln's assassination. Crumb's setting conjures an elusive scent—gently drifting, intermixing, and separating . . . an expression of an ineffably sad memory.

III. Dark Mother Always Gliding Near with Soft Feet

This reverential elegy combines an intense personal plea with an instinctively religious hope for death as release. Crumb's religiously allusive use of chant and imitative counterpoint further define this song as a prayer.

Vocalise 2: Invocation

Crumb has often balanced his quiet and ecstatic visions with representations of the evil aspects of nature. This vocalise is a harsh, primal invocation. It leads without pause into the fourth song.

IV. Approach Strong Deliveress!

Death as emancipation is one of the most ancient human desires. In Whitman's metaphor of death as feminine and life-resurrecting, the concept of a deliveress is forceful and redemptive. Crumb reflects this in a relentlessly driving march. Propelled by implacable energy, this song is joyous in its hope for and embracement of death.

Vocalise 3: Death Carol ("Song of the Nightbird")

The singer of Whitman's "Death Carol" was a solitary hermit thrush:

'the grey-brown bird I know receiv'd us
And he sang the carol of death . . .

From deep secluded recesses,
Came the carol of the bird.'

V. Come Lovely and Soothing Death

Constructed as the culminant song of the cycle, this intensely personal summoning and welcoming of death transforms and extends the musical imagery of the preceding songs and vocalises into a final transcendent statement of the inevitability of death's arrival, "to all, to each."

VI. The Night in Silence under Many a Star

After death, the forces of Nature remain: physicality, motion, consciousness, and life. Recapitulating the opening of the cycle, with no textual changes and only minor musical adjustments, Crumb re-affirms Whitman's view of the circularity of life and death. (William Bland).

Premiere: Jan DeGaetani, mezzo-soprano; Gilbert Kalish, piano; January 13, 1981; New York City.

Text: from Walt Whitman's "When Lilacs Last in the Dooryard Bloom'd"

A LITTLE SUITE FOR CHRISTMAS, A.D. 1979 (1980) (15 minutes) (P66833)

Piano Solo

1. The Visitation
2. Berceuse for the Infant Jesu
3. The Shepherds' Noël
4. Adoration of the Magi
5. Nativity Dance
6. Canticle of the Holy Night
7. Carol of the Bells

A Little Suite for Christmas, A.D. 1979 was composed for pianist Lambert Orkis.

The idea of a set of piano pieces reflecting on different aspects of the Christmas event may remind the reader of the *Vingt Regards sur l'Enfant-Jésus* (1944) of Olivier Messiaen, and one can point to certain general stylistic traits shared by Messiaen and Crumb. But Crumb's work is on a much more modest scale than the French composer's massive pianistic compendium. In fact, it is a "little" suite by comparison with several earlier piano works by Crumb. It does not call for the piano to be amplified to create the "larger-than-life" sound quality desired in the four volumes of *Makrokosmos* (1972, 1973, 1974, 1979). Nor does the piece involve "symbolic" notations (where the staves are arranged in shapes of a cross or circle), vocal effects from the performer, or the use of additional objects to modify the piano sound, all of which appear in the *Makrokosmos* series. However, in the *Little Suite*, Crumb does continue in his refined use of harmonics, muted tones, and pizzicati, using these in combination with material performed on the keyboard in the conventional fashion.

The music created with these means is sometimes contemplative in mood, as in the hushed reverence of the second movement, or the surreal setting of the 16th century "Coventry Carol" in the sixth; sometimes visionary, as in the solemn repeated chords and melodic patterns of the first movement or the exuberant cosmic dance of the fifth.

Crumb uses a curious example of self-reference in the fourth piece, "Adoration of the Magi." In this movement, there appears twice, in pizzicati, a melodic fragment from the "Wanderer-Fantasy" movement of *Music for a Summer Evening*. A connection is thus made with the Magi who have "wandered" from afar to Bethlehem. Although this is a particularly private example of musical symbolism, it is consistent with Crumb's use of quotation to add an additional level of musical expressiveness. (James Primosch).

Premiere: Lambert Orkis, piano; December 14, 1980; The Smithsonian Institution, Washington, D.C.

GNOMIC VARIATIONS (1981) (25 minutes) (P66905)

Piano Solo

Gnomic Variations was commissioned and first performed by pianist Jeffrey Jacob.

"The title *Gnomic Variations* refers to the terseness and compression of the work's construction. A gnome symbolizes the maxim or aphorism, the pithy statement that in a few words encompasses a large idea.

The theme and each of the 18 variations which follow establish their own highly individualistic and autonomous character. Although the variations proceed without interruption, the work is cast into three large sections which are clearly marked by silences. Both the internal structure of the theme, its AA'BA'' form, and its melodic development and harmonic implications are subjected to the technique of variation.

The pianist plays a good deal of *Gnomic Variations* inside the piano. The strings are plucked, struck, strummed, scraped, and muted at various places. The piano, however, is not "prepared" (i.e., no objects are placed inside the piano in advance). The rapid shifting from keyboard to strings is, at times, fiendishly difficult.

The terse, aphoristic character of *Gnomic Variations* is defined at the outset: the composition begins with a brief unaccompanied melodic line of interlocking tritones. The low and middle register pitches are alternately muted and plucked, and the resulting sense of primal power prepares the listener for the outbursts of rhythmic energy which occur sporadically throughout the work. The first three propulsive and turbulent variations precede a mesmerizing passage (Variation 4) of cross-rhythms and undisturbed placidity. Variation 5 introduces the technique of scraping the metal windings of low register strings with the fingernails of the left hand. This quiet rasping sound is combined with upper register major seconds played *pianissimo* on the keys with the right hand. The resulting effect is at once haunting and entrancing. The final variation of the section uses a variety of muting techniques to produce an extended passage of vibrant intensity.

The second of *Gnomic Variations'* three sections contains a diversity of musical materials. The stern, repeated sonorities of Variation 7 (the first variation of this section) are followed by violent outbursts of percussive low register sounds and brilliant upper register runs. The next three variations, quiet and filled with atmospheric sonorities and effects, evoke a sense of wonder and awe, the suspension of time and implied motion.

The third section opens with the ominously mysterious variation 13 and builds in intensity through the next three variations to a profoundly moving climax in the penultimate variation of the work. Thunderous sounds from the lowest register of the piano (produced by striking the strings with the hands) support brilliant upper register chords. *Gnomic Variations* closes with a restatement of the opening theme, incorporating bell-like harmonics into the sonority.

The brevity and forcefulness of its musical material make *Gnomic Variations* one of Crumb's most concentrated and powerful works." (Jeffrey Jacob).

Premiere: Jeffrey Jacob, piano; December 12, 1982; The National Gallery of Art, Washington, D.C.

PASTORAL DRONE (1982) (8 minutes) (P66965)

Organ Solo

Pastoral Drone, commissioned by the American Guild of Organists and composed in the summer of 1982, represents my first essay in the solo organ genre (my *Star-Child* of 1977 included organ as an addition to the orchestral resources).

Pastoral Drone, cast in one continuous movement, was conceived as an evocation of an ancient "open-air" music. The underpinning of the work is provided by relentless drones executed on the organ pedals. The periodical "bending" of the basic drone sound (a lower D-sharp and a higher G-sharp, spaced as an interval of the 11th) announces the principal structural articulations of the work. The drone is overlaid by strident, sharply-etched rhythms in the manual parts and the dynamic throughout is *sempre fortissimo* ("boldly resounding"). The characteristic sound of *Pastoral Drone* will suggest a kind of colossal musette. (George Crumb).

Premiere: David Craighead, organ; June 27, 1984; San Francisco.

PROCESSIONAL (1983) (12 minutes) (P66991)

Piano Solo

Processional was composed in 1983 for Gilbert Kalish.

Like much of my music, this work is strongly tonal, but integrates chromatic, modal, and whole-tone elements. The descending 6 tones stated at the beginning present the basic harmonic cell, subsequently elaborated by varied cluster combinations and permutations. Although *Processional* is basically a continuum of sustained legato playing, the tiny melodic fragments (which intermittently emerge and recede) provide contrast in articulation. The formal design of the work is closely linked to its dynamic curve.

I think of *Processional* as an "experiment in harmonic chemistry" (Debussy's description of his *Images* for piano)—the music is concerned with the prismatic effect of subtle changes of harmonic color and frequent modulation. I felt no need for the resources of the "extended piano" and limited myself to the contrasts of color and texture available through the conventional mode of playing on the keys.

The title was suggested by the music's obsessive reiteration of pulse ("sempre pulsando, estaticamente") and broad "unfolding" gestures. Perhaps the music suggests more a "processional of nature" rather than any sort of festive or sombre "human" processional? (George Crumb).

Premiere: Gilbert Kalish, piano; July 26, 1984; Tanglewood, Lenox, Massachusetts.

A HAUNTED LANDSCAPE (1984) (18 minutes) (P67003)

3(Picc)3(EH)3(E♭Cl)3(Cbsn) 4331 Perc(4), T, 2 Hps, Pf, Str

A Haunted Landscape was commissioned by the New York Philharmonic.

The work is scored for rather conventional forces: woodwinds in threes (with the usual doublings of piccolo, English horn, E-flat clarinet and contrabassoon), "Tchaikovsky" brass plus a third trumpet, two harps and piano, percussion, and strings. The piano is amplified and functions pretty much as an extension of the percussion section. The role of the percussion (a timpanist and four other players) is very important, as is usually the case in contemporary orchestral works. In addition to the more common percussion instruments, I have included parts for certain "exotic" instruments—Caribbean steel drums, Cambodian angklungs, Japanese Kabuki blocks, the Brazilian cuica, and the Appalachian hammered dulcimer.

A Haunted Landscape is not programmatic in any sense. The title reflects my feeling that certain places on the planet Earth are imbued with an aura of mystery. I can vividly recall the "shock of recognition" I felt on seeing Andalusia for the first time after having been involved with the poetry of García Lorca for so many years. I felt a similar sense of *déjà vu* on visits to Jerusalem and to Delphos in Greece. Even in the West Virginia woods one senses the ghosts of the vanished Indians. Places can inspire feelings of reverence or of brooding menace (like the deserted battlefields of ancient wars). Sometimes one feels an idyllic sense of time suspended. The contemplation of a landscape can induce complex psychological states and perhaps music is an ideal medium for delineating the tiny, subtle nuances of emotion and sensibility which hover between the subliminal and the conscious.

A Haunted Landscape is cast in a single, continuous movement. A unifying factor is provided by a very low B-flat, sustained throughout by two solo contrabassists. I had imagined that this low B-flat (60 cycles—the frequency of alternating current) was an immutable law of nature and represented a kind of "cosmic drone." But, alas, science defeats art—a chemist friend informed me that alternating current is arbitrarily determined by man and that B-flat is not even international, much less intergalactic! (George Crumb).

Premiere: The New York Philharmonic, Arthur Weisberg, conductor; June 7, 1984; Avery Fisher Hall, New York City.

THE SLEEPER (1984) (3 minutes) (P67015)

Soprano and Piano

For the text of this little song I have excerpted only a very few lines from Edgar Allan Poe's poem. Admittedly the sense is thereby considerably altered (Poe's poem is somewhat lugubrious in its total effect), but I do feel that there is such a thing as "composer's license." Besides, I was specifically asked for a *short* song!

The sparse, tenuous textures and extremely soft dynamic of *The Sleeper* will project a kind of "minimalissimo" character. I have used a range of timbral devices in the piano part to suggest that transcendental feeling which Poe's eerie images of nature invoke—rustling glissandos on the strings of the instrument, delicate muted effects, and bell-like harmonics (which ring in the midnight hour in the first bars of the song).

The vocal part, which is quite simple in style and based entirely on a few tiny melodic cells, requires great sensitivity to nuances of pitch and timbre. I have endeavored to compress an intense and even expansive expressivity into a very small frame, which is, I suppose, what writing a little song is all about. (George Crumb).

Premiere: Jan DeGaetani, mezzo-soprano; Gilbert Kalish, piano; December 4, 1984; Carnegie Hall, New York City.

Text: from Edgar Allan Poe's "The Sleeper"